SUSE OpenStack Cloud 6 - End User Guide

A catalogue record for this book is available from the Hong Kong Public Libraries.

Published in Hong Kong by Samurai Media Limited.

Email: info@samuraimedia.org

ISBN 978-988-8406-47-0

Contents

1 Documentation Conventions

The following notices and typographical conventions are used in this documentation:

Warning

Vital information you must be aware of before proceeding. Warns you about security issues, potential loss of data, damage to hardware, or physical hazards.

Important

Important information you should be aware of before proceeding.

Note

Additional information, for example about differences in software versions.

Tip

Helpful information, like a guideline or a piece of practical advice.

```
tux > command
```

Commands than can be run by any user, including the root user.

```
root # command
```

Commands that must be run with root privileges. In many cases you can also prefix these commands with the **sudo** command to run them.

2 How can I use an OpenStack cloud?

As an OpenStack cloud end user, you can provision your own resources within the limits set by cloud administrators.

The examples in this guide show you how to perform tasks by using the following methods:

- OpenStack dashboard. Use this web-based graphical interface, code named horizon (https://git.openstack.org/cgit/openstack/horizon) ↗, to view, create, and manage resources.

- OpenStack command-line clients. Each core OpenStack project has a command-line client that you can use to run simple commands to view, create, and manage resources in a cloud and automate tasks by using scripts.

You can modify these examples for your specific use cases.

In addition to these ways of interacting with a cloud, you can access the OpenStack APIs directly or indirectly through cURL (http://curl.haxx.se) ↗ commands or open SDKs. You can automate access or build tools to manage resources and services by using the native OpenStack APIs or the EC2 compatibility API.

To use the OpenStack APIs, it helps to be familiar with HTTP/1.1, RESTful web services, the OpenStack services, and JSON or XML data serialization formats.

2.1 Who should read this book?

This book is written for anyone who uses virtual machines and cloud resources to develop software or perform research. You should have years of experience with Linux-based tool sets and be comfortable using both GUI and CLI based tools. While this book includes some information about using Python to create and manage cloud resources, Python knowledge is not a pre-requisite for reading this book.

3 OpenStack dashboard

As a cloud end user, you can use the OpenStack dashboard to provision your own resources within the limits set by administrators. You can modify the examples provided in this section to create other types and sizes of server instances.

3.1 Log in to the dashboard

The dashboard is generally installed on the controller node.

1. Ask the cloud operator for the host name or public IP address from which you can access the dashboard, and for your user name and password.

2. Open a web browser that has JavaScript and cookies enabled.

    Note

   To use the Virtual Network Computing (VNC) client for the dashboard, your browser must support HTML5 Canvas and HTML5 WebSockets. The VNC client is based on noVNC. For details, see noVNC: HTML5 VNC Client (https://github.com/kanaka/noVNC/blob/master/README.md) ↗. For a list of supported browsers, see Browser support (https://github.com/kanaka/noVNC/wiki/Browser-support) ↗.

3. In the address bar, enter the host name or IP address for the dashboard, for example `https://ipAddressOrHostName/`.

    Note

   If a certificate warning appears when you try to access the URL for the first time, a self-signed certificate is in use, which is not considered trustworthy by default. Verify the certificate or add an exception in the browser to bypass the warning.

4. On the Log In page, enter your user name and password, and click *Sign In*.
   The top of the window displays your user name. You can also access the *Settings* tab (*Section 3.1.4, "OpenStack dashboard — Settings tab"*) or sign out of the dashboard.
   The visible tabs and functions in the dashboard depend on the access permissions, or roles, of the user you are logged in as.

- If you are logged in as an end user, the *Project* tab (*Section 3.1.1, "OpenStack dashboard — Project tab"*) and *Identity* tab (*Section 3.1.3, "OpenStack dashboard — Identity tab"*) are displayed.

- If you are logged in as an administrator, the *Project* tab (*Section 3.1.1, "OpenStack dashboard — Project tab"*) and *Admin* tab (*Section 3.1.2, "OpenStack dashboard — Admin tab"*) and *Identity* tab (*Section 3.1.3, "OpenStack dashboard — Identity tab"*) are displayed.

3.1.1   OpenStack dashboard — *Project* tab

Projects are organizational units in the cloud, and are also known as tenants or accounts. Each user is a member of one or more projects. Within a project, a user creates and manages instances.

From the *Project* tab, you can view and manage the resources in a selected project, including instances and images. You can select the project from the drop down menu at the top left.

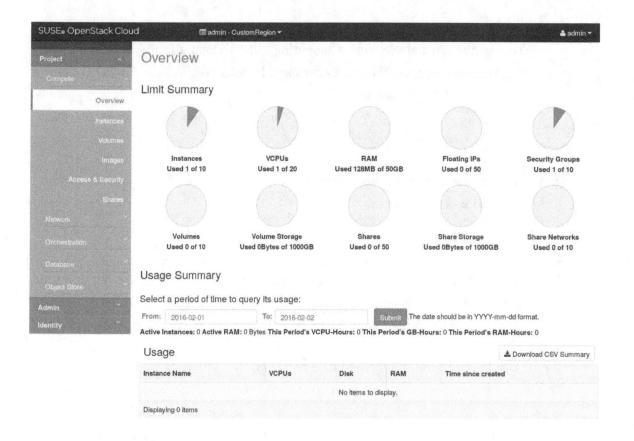

FIGURE 3.1: PROJECT TAB

From the *Project* tab, you can access the following categories:

3.1.1.1 *Compute* tab

- *Overview*: View reports for the project.

- *Instances*: View, launch, create a snapshot from, stop, pause, or reboot instances, or connect to them through VNC.

- *Volumes*: Use the following tabs to complete these tasks:

    - *Volumes*: View, create, edit, and delete volumes.

    - *Volume Snapshots*: View, create, edit, and delete volume snapshots.

- *Images*: View images and instance snapshots created by project users, plus any images that are publicly available. Create, edit, and delete images, and launch instances from images and snapshots.

- *Access & Security*: Use the following tabs to complete these tasks:

    - *Security Groups*: View, create, edit, and delete security groups and security group rules.

    - *Key Pairs*: View, create, edit, import, and delete key pairs.

    - *Floating IPs*: Allocate an IP address to or release it from a project.

    - *API Access*: View API endpoints.

3.1.1.2 *Network* tab

- *Network Topology*: View the network topology.

- *Networks*: Create and manage public and private networks.

- *Routers*: Create and manage routers.

3.1.1.3 *Orchestration* tab

- *Stacks*: Use the REST API to orchestrate multiple composite cloud applications.

- *Resource Types*: Show a list of all the supported resource types for HOT templates.

3.1.1.4 *Object Store* tab

- *Containers*: Create and manage containers and objects.

3.1.2 OpenStack dashboard — *Admin* tab

Administrative users can use the *Admin* tab to view usage and to manage instances, volumes, flavors, images, networks and so on.

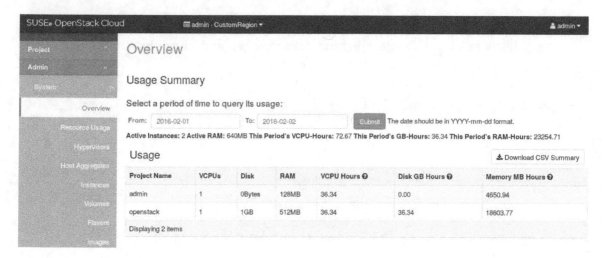

FIGURE 3.2: ADMIN TAB

From the *Admin* tab, you can access the following category to complete these tasks:

3.1.2.1 *System* tab

- *Overview*: View basic reports.

- *Resource Usage*: Use the following tabs to view the following usages:

  - *Usage Report*: View the usage report.

  - *Stats*: View the statistics of all resources.

- *Hypervisors*: View the hypervisor summary.

- *Host Aggregates*: View, create, and edit host aggregates. View the list of availability zones.

- *Instances*: View, pause, resume, suspend, migrate, soft or hard reboot, and delete running instances that belong to users of some, but not all, projects. Also, view the log for an instance or access an instance through VNC.

- *Volumes*: Use the following tabs to complete these tasks:

    - *Volumes*: View, create, manage, and delete volumes.

    - *Volume Types*: View, create, manage, and delete volume types.

    - *Volume Snapshots*: View, manage, and delete volume snapshots.

- *Flavors*: View, create, edit, view extra specifications for, and delete flavors. A flavor is size of an instance.

- *Images*: View, create, edit properties for, and delete custom images.

- *Networks*: View, create, edit properties for, and delete networks.

- *Routers*: View, create, edit properties for, and delete routers.

- *Defaults*: View default quota values. Quotas are hard-coded in OpenStack Compute and define the maximum allowable size and number of resources.

- *Metadata Definitions*: Import namespace and view the metadata information.

- *System Information*: Use the following tabs to view the service information:

    - *Services*: View a list of the services.

    - *Compute Services*: View a list of all Compute services.

    - *Block Storage Services*: View a list of all Block Storage services.

    - *Network Agents*: View the network agents.

    - *Orchestration Services*: View a list of all Orchestration services.

3.1.3 OpenStack dashboard — *Identity* tab

FIGURE 3.3: IDENTITY TAB

- *Projects*: View, create, assign users to, remove users from, and delete projects.

- *Users*: View, create, enable, disable, and delete users.

3.1.4 OpenStack dashboard — *Settings* tab

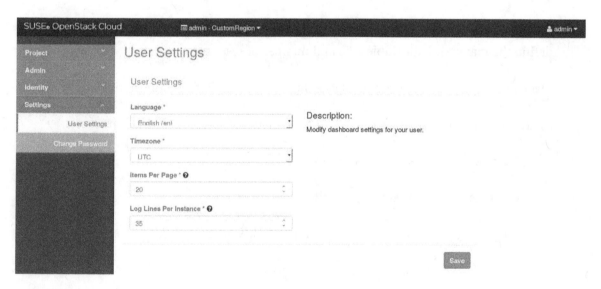

FIGURE 3.4: SETTINGS TAB

Click the *Settings* button from the user drop down menu at the top right of any page, you will see the *Settings* tab.

- *User Settings*: View and manage dashboard settings.

- *Change Password*: Change the password of the user.

3.2 Upload and manage images

A virtual machine image, referred to in this document simply as an image, is a single file that contains a virtual disk that has a bootable operating system installed on it. Images are used to create virtual machine instances within the cloud. For information about creating image files, see the OpenStack Virtual Machine Image Guide (http://docs.openstack.org/image-guide/) ↗.

Depending on your role, you may have permission to upload and manage virtual machine images. Operators might restrict the upload and management of images to cloud administrators or operators only. If you have the appropriate privileges, you can use the dashboard to upload and manage images in the admin project.

 Note

You can also use the **openstack**, **glance** and **nova** command-line clients or the Image service and Compute APIs to manage images.

3.2.1 Upload an image

Follow this procedure to upload an image to a project:

1. Log in to the dashboard.

2. Select the appropriate project from the drop down menu at the top left.

3. On the *Project* tab, open the *Compute* tab and click *Images* category.

4. Click *Create Image*.
   The *Create An Image* dialog box appears.

5. Enter the following values:

Name	Enter a name for the image.

Description	Enter a brief description of the image.
Image Source	Choose the image source from the drop-down list. Your choices are *Image Location* and *Image File.*
Image File or *Image Location*	Based on your selection for *Image Source,* you either enter the location URL of the image in the *Image Location* field, or browse for the image file on your file system and add it.
Format	Select the image format (for example, QCOW2) for the image.
Architecture	Specify the architecture. For example, `i386` for a 32-bit architecture or `x86_64` for a 64-bit architecture.
Minimum Disk (GB)	Leave this field empty.
Minimum RAM (MB)	Leave this field empty.
Copy Data	Specify this option to copy image data to the Image service.
Public	Select this check box to make the image public to all users with access to the current project.
Protected	Select this check box to ensure that only users with permissions can delete the image.

6. Click *Create Image.*

The image is queued to be uploaded. It might take some time before the status changes from Queued to Active.

3.2.2 Update an image

Follow this procedure to update an existing image.

1. Log in to the dashboard.

2. Select the appropriate project from the drop down menu at the top left.

3. Select the image that you want to edit.

4. In the *Actions* column, click the menu button and then select *Edit Image* from the list.

5. In the *Update Image* dialog box, you can perform various actions. For example:

   - Change the name of the image.

   - Select the *Public* check box to make the image public.

   - Clear the *Public* check box to make the image private.

6. Click *Update Image*.

3.2.3 Delete an image

Deletion of images is permanent and **cannot** be reversed. Only users with the appropriate permissions can delete images.

1. Log in to the dashboard.

2. Select the appropriate project from the drop down menu at the top left.

3. On the *Project* tab, open the *Compute* tab and click *Images* category.

4. Select the images that you want to delete.

5. Click *Delete Images*.

6. In the *Confirm Delete Images* dialog box, click *Delete Images* to confirm the deletion.

3.3 Configure access and security for instances

Before you launch an instance, you should add security group rules to enable users to ping and use SSH to connect to the instance. Security groups are sets of IP filter rules that define networking access and are applied to all instances within a project. To do so, you either add rules to the default security group *Section 3.3.1, "Add a rule to the default security group"* or add a new security group with rules.

Key pairs are SSH credentials that are injected into an instance when it is launched. To use key pair injection, the image that the instance is based on must contain the `cloud-init` package. Each project should have at least one key pair. For more information, see the section *Section 3.3.2, "Add a key pair"*.

If you have generated a key pair with an external tool, you can import it into OpenStack. The key pair can be used for multiple instances that belong to a project. For more information, see the section *Section 3.3.3, "Import a key pair"*.

 Note

A key pair belongs to an individual user, not to a project. To share a key pair across multiple users, each user needs to import that key pair.

When an instance is created in OpenStack, it is automatically assigned a fixed IP address in the network to which the instance is assigned. This IP address is permanently associated with the instance until the instance is terminated. However, in addition to the fixed IP address, a floating IP address can also be attached to an instance. Unlike fixed IP addresses, floating IP addresses are able to have their associations modified at any time, regardless of the state of the instances involved.

3.3.1 Add a rule to the default security group

This procedure enables SSH and ICMP (ping) access to instances. The rules apply to all instances within a given project, and should be set for every project unless there is a reason to prohibit SSH or ICMP access to the instances.

This procedure can be adjusted as necessary to add additional security group rules to a project, if your cloud requires them.

Note

When adding a rule, you must specify the protocol used with the destination port or source port.

1. Log in to the dashboard.

2. Select the appropriate project from the drop down menu at the top left.

3. On the *Project* tab, open the *Compute* tab and click *Access & Security* category. The *Security Groups* tab shows the security groups that are available for this project.

4. Select the default security group and click *Manage Rules*.

5. To allow SSH access, click *Add Rule*.

6. In the *Add Rule* dialog box, enter the following values:

   - **Rule**: SSH

   - **Remote**: CIDR

   - **CIDR**: 0.0.0.0/0

    Note

   To accept requests from a particular range of IP addresses, specify the IP address block in the *CIDR* box.

7. Click *Add*.
   Instances will now have SSH port 22 open for requests from any IP address.

8. To add an ICMP rule, click *Add Rule*.

9. In the *Add Rule* dialog box, enter the following values:

   - **Rule**: All ICMP

   - **Direction**: Ingress

   - **Remote**: CIDR

   - **CIDR**: 0.0.0.0/0

10. Click *Add*.

    Instances will now accept all incoming ICMP packets.

3.3.2   Add a key pair

Create at least one key pair for each project.

1. Log in to the dashboard.

2. Select the appropriate project from the drop down menu at the top left.

3. On the *Project* tab, open the *Compute* tab and click *Access & Security* category.

4. Click the *Key Pairs* tab, which shows the key pairs that are available for this project.

5. Click *Create Key Pair*.

6. In the *Create Key Pair* dialog box, enter a name for your key pair, and click *Create Key Pair*.

7. Respond to the prompt to download the key pair.

3.3.3   Import a key pair

1. Log in to the dashboard.

2. Select the appropriate project from the drop down menu at the top left.

3. On the *Project* tab, open the *Compute* tab and click *Access & Security* category.

4. Click the *Key Pairs* tab, which shows the key pairs that are available for this project.

5. Click *Import Key Pair*.

6. In the *Import Key Pair* dialog box, enter the name of your key pair, copy the public key into the *Public Key* box, and then click *Import Key Pair*.

7. Save the `*.pem` file locally.

8. To change its permissions so that only you can read and write to the file, run the following command:

```
$ chmod 0600 yourPrivateKey.pem
```

Note

If you are using the Dashboard from a Windows computer, use PuTTYgen to load the `*.pem` file and convert and save it as `*.ppk`. For more information see the WinSCP web page for PuTTYgen (http://winscp.net/eng/docs/ui_puttygen) ↗.

9. To make the key pair known to SSH, run the **ssh-add** command.

```
$ ssh-add yourPrivateKey.pem
```

The Compute database registers the public key of the key pair.

The Dashboard lists the key pair on the *Access & Security* tab.

3.3.4 Allocate a floating IP address to an instance

When an instance is created in OpenStack, it is automatically assigned a fixed IP address in the network to which the instance is assigned. This IP address is permanently associated with the instance until the instance is terminated.

However, in addition to the fixed IP address, a floating IP address can also be attached to an instance. Unlike fixed IP addresses, floating IP addresses can have their associations modified at any time, regardless of the state of the instances involved. This procedure details the reservation of a floating IP address from an existing pool of addresses and the association of that address with a specific instance.

1. Log in to the dashboard.

2. Select the appropriate project from the drop down menu at the top left.

3. On the *Project* tab, open the *Compute* tab and click *Access & Security* category.

4. Click the *Floating IPs* tab, which shows the floating IP addresses allocated to instances.

5. Click *Allocate IP To Project*.

6. Choose the pool from which to pick the IP address.

7. Click *Allocate IP*.

8. In the *Floating IPs* list, click *Associate*.

9. In the *Manage Floating IP Associations* dialog box, choose the following options:

    - The *IP Address* field is filled automatically, but you can add a new IP address by clicking the + button.

    - In the *Port to be associated* field, select a port from the list.
      The list shows all the instances with their fixed IP addresses.

10. Click *Associate*.

 Note

> To disassociate an IP address from an instance, click the *Disassociate* button.

To release the floating IP address back into the pool of addresses, the *Release Floating IP* option at the *Actions* column.

3.4   Launch and manage instances

Instances are virtual machines that run inside the cloud. You can launch an instance from the following sources:

- Images uploaded to the Image service.

- Image that you have copied to a persistent volume. The instance launches from the volume, which is provided by the `cinder-volume` API through iSCSI.

- Instance snapshot that you took.

3.4.1   Launch an instance

1. Log in to the dashboard.

2. Select the appropriate project from the drop down menu at the top left.

3. On the *Project* tab, open the *Compute* tab and click *Instances* category.

The dashboard shows the instances with its name, its private and floating IP addresses, size, status, task, power state, and so on.

4. Click *Launch Instance*.

5. In the *Launch Instance* dialog box, specify the following values:
Details tab

Availability Zone

By default, this value is set to the availability zone given by the cloud provider (for example, `us-west` or `apac-south`). For some cases, it could be `nova`.

Instance Name

Assign a name to the virtual machine.

 Note

The name you assign here becomes the initial host name of the server.

After the server is built, if you change the server name in the API or change the host name directly, the names are not updated in the dashboard.

Server names are not guaranteed to be unique when created so you could have two instances with the same host name.

Flavor

Specify the size of the instance to launch.

 Note

The flavor is selected based on the size of the image selected for launching an instance. For example, while creating an image, if you have entered the value in the *Minimum RAM (MB)* field as 2048, then on selecting the image, the default flavor is `m1.small`.

Instance Count

To launch multiple instances, enter a value greater than `1`. The default is `1`.

Instance Boot Source

Your options are:

Boot from image

If you choose this option, a new field for *Image Name* displays. You can select the image from the list.

Boot from snapshot

If you choose this option, a new field for *Instance Snapshot* displays. You can select the snapshot from the list.

Boot from volume

If you choose this option, a new field for *Volume* displays. You can select the volume from the list.

Boot from image (creates a new volume)

With this option, you can boot from an image and create a volume by entering the *Device Size* and *Device Name* for your volume. Click the *Delete on Terminate* option to delete the volume on terminating the instance.

Boot from volume snapshot (creates a new volume)

Using this option, you can boot from a volume snapshot and create a new volume by choosing *Volume Snapshot* from a list and adding a *Device Name* for your volume. Click the *Delete on Terminate* option to delete the volume on terminating the instance.

Image Name

This field changes based on your previous selection. If you have chosen to launch an instance using an image, the *Image Name* field displays. Select the image name from the dropdown list.

Instance Snapshot

This field changes based on your previous selection. If you have chosen to launch an instance using a snapshot, the *Instance Snapshot* field displays. Select the snapshot name from the dropdown list.

Volume

> This field changes based on your previous selection. If you have chosen to launch an instance using a volume, the *Volume* field displays. Select the volume name from the dropdown list. If you want to delete the volume on instance terminate, check the *Delete on Terminate* option.

Access & Security tab

Key Pair

> Specify a key pair.
>
> If the image uses a static root password or a static key set (neither is recommended), you do not need to provide a key pair to launch the instance.

Security Groups

> Activate the security groups that you want to assign to the instance.
>
> Security groups are a kind of cloud firewall that define which incoming network traffic is forwarded to instances.
>
> If you have not created any security groups, you can assign only the default security group to the instance.

Networking tab

Selected Networks

> To add a network to the instance, click the + in the *Available Networks* field.

Post-Creation tab

Customization Script Source

> Specify a customization script that runs after your instance launches.

Advanced Options tab

Disk Partition

> Select the type of disk partition from the dropdown list:

Automatic

> Entire disk is single partition and automatically resizes.

Manual

> Faster build times but requires manual partitioning.

6. Click *Launch*.

   The instance starts on a compute node in the cloud.

 Note

   If you did not provide a key pair, security groups, or rules, users can access the instance only from inside the cloud through VNC. Even pinging the instance is not possible without an ICMP rule configured.

You can also launch an instance from the *Images* or *Volumes* category when you launch an instance from an image or a volume respectively.

When you launch an instance from an image, OpenStack creates a local copy of the image on the compute node where the instance starts.

For details on creating images, see Creating images manually (http://docs.openstack.org/image-guide/create-images-manually.html) ↗ in the *OpenStack Virtual Machine Image Guide.*

When you launch an instance from a volume, note the following steps:

* To select the volume from which to launch, launch an instance from an arbitrary image on the volume. The arbitrary image that you select does not boot. Instead, it is replaced by the image on the volume that you choose in the next steps.
  To boot a Xen image from a volume, the image you launch in must be the same type, fully virtualized or paravirtualized, as the one on the volume.

* Select the volume or volume snapshot from which to boot. Enter a device name. Enter `vda` for KVM images or `xvda` for Xen images.

3.4.2   Connect to your instance by using SSH

To use SSH to connect to your instance, you use the downloaded keypair file.

 Note

   The user name is `ubuntu` for the Ubuntu cloud images on TryStack.

1. Copy the IP address for your instance.

2. Use the **ssh** command to make a secure connection to the instance. For example:

```
$ ssh -i MyKey.pem ubuntu@10.0.0.2
```

3. At the prompt, type yes.

3.4.3   Track usage for instances

You can track usage for instances for each project. You can track costs per month by showing meters like number of vCPUs, disks, RAM, and uptime for all your instances.

1. Log in to the dashboard.

2. Select the appropriate project from the drop down menu at the top left.

3. On the *Project* tab, open the *Compute* tab and click *Overview* category.

4. To query the instance usage for a month, select a month and click *Submit*.

5. To download a summary, click *Download CSV Summary*.

3.4.4   Create an instance snapshot

1. Log in to the dashboard.

2. Select the appropriate project from the drop down menu at the top left.

3. On the *Project* tab, open the *Compute* tab and click the *Instances* category.

4. Select the instance from which to create a snapshot.

5. In the *Actions* column, click *Create Snapshot*.

6. In the *Create Snapshot* dialog box, enter a name for the snapshot, and click *Create Snapshot*. The Images category shows the instance snapshot.

To launch an instance from the snapshot, select the snapshot and click *Launch*. Proceed with launching an instance.

3.4.5 Manage an instance

1. Log in to the dashboard.

2. Select the appropriate project from the drop down menu at the top left.

3. On the *Project* tab, open the *Compute* tab and click *Instances* category.

4. Select an instance.

5. In the menu list in the *Actions* column, select the state.
   You can resize or rebuild an instance. You can also choose to view the instance console log, edit instance or the security groups. Depending on the current state of the instance, you can pause, resume, suspend, soft or hard reboot, or terminate it.

3.5 Create and manage networks

The OpenStack Networking service provides a scalable system for managing the network connectivity within an OpenStack cloud deployment. It can easily and quickly react to changing network needs (for example, creating and assigning new IP addresses).

Networking in OpenStack is complex. This section provides the basic instructions for creating a network and a router. For detailed information about managing networks, refer to the OpenStack Cloud Administrator Guide (http://docs.openstack.org/admin-guide-cloud/networking.html) ↗.

3.5.1 Create a network

1. Log in to the dashboard.

2. Select the appropriate project from the drop down menu at the top left.

3. On the *Project* tab, open the *Network* tab and click *Networks* category.

4. Click *Create Network*.

5. In the *Create Network* dialog box, specify the following values.
   Network tab
   Network Name: Specify a name to identify the network.

Admin State: The state to start the network in.

Create Subnet: Select this check box to create a subnet

You do not have to specify a subnet when you create a network, but if you do not specify a subnet, any attached instance receives an Error status.

Subnet tab

Subnet Name: Specify a name for the subnet.

Network Address: Specify the IP address for the subnet.

IP Version: Select IPv4 or IPv6.

Gateway IP: Specify an IP address for a specific gateway. This parameter is optional.

Disable Gateway: Select this check box to disable a gateway IP address.

Subnet Details tab

Enable DHCP: Select this check box to enable DHCP.

Allocation Pools: Specify IP address pools.

DNS Name Servers: Specify a name for the DNS server.

Host Routes: Specify the IP address of host routes.

6. Click *Create*.

   The dashboard shows the network on the *Networks* tab.

3.5.2   Create a router

1. Log in to the dashboard.

2. Select the appropriate project from the drop down menu at the top left.

3. On the *Project* tab, open the *Network* tab and click *Routers* category.

4. Click *Create Router*.

5. In the *Create Router* dialog box, specify a name for the router and *External Network*, and click *Create Router*.

   The new router is now displayed in the *Routers* tab.

6. To connect a private network to the newly created router, perform the following steps:

   1. On the *Routers* tab, click the name of the router.

   2. On the *Router Details* page, click the *Interfaces* tab, then click *Add Interface*.

3. In the *Add Interface* dialog box, select a *Subnet*.

Optionally, in the *Add Interface* dialog box, set an *IP Address* for the router interface for the selected subnet.

If you choose not to set the *IP Address* value, then by default OpenStack Networking uses the first host IP address in the subnet.

The *Router Name* and *Router ID* fields are automatically updated.

7. Click *Add Interface*.

You have successfully created the router. You can view the new topology from the *Network Topology* tab.

3.6 Create and manage object containers

OpenStack Object Storage provides a distributed, API-accessible storage platform that can be integrated directly into an application or used to store any type of file, including VM images, backups, archives, or media files. In the OpenStack dashboard, you can only manage containers and objects.

In OpenStack Object Storage, containers provide storage for objects in a manner similar to a Windows folder or Linux file directory, though they cannot be nested. An object in OpenStack consists of the file to be stored in the container and any accompanying metadata.

3.6.1 Create a container

1. Log in to the dashboard.

2. Select the appropriate project from the drop down menu at the top left.

3. On the *Project* tab, open the *Object Store* tab and click *Containers* category.

4. Click *Create Container*.

5. In the *Create Container* dialog box, enter a name for the container, and then click *Create Container*.

You have successfully created a container.

Note

To delete a container, click the *More* button and select *Delete Container*.

3.6.2   Upload an object

1. Log in to the dashboard.

2. Select the appropriate project from the drop down menu at the top left.

3. On the *Project* tab, open the *Object Store* tab and click *Containers* category.

4. Select the container in which you want to store your object.

5. Click *Upload Object*.
   The *Upload Object To Container: <name>* dialog box appears. <name> is the name of the container to which you are uploading the object.

6. Enter a name for the object.

7. Browse to and select the file that you want to upload.

8. Click *Upload Object*.

You have successfully uploaded an object to the container.

 Note

To delete an object, click the *More button* and select *Delete Object*.

3.6.3   Manage an object

To edit an object

1. Log in to the dashboard.

2. Select the appropriate project from the drop down menu at the top left.

3. On the *Project* tab, open the *Object Store* tab and click *Containers* category.

4. Select the container in which you want to store your object.

5. Click the menu button and choose *Edit* from the dropdown list. The *Edit Object* dialog box is displayed.

6. Browse to and select the file that you want to upload.

7. Click *Update Object*.

 Note

To delete an object, click the menu button and select *Delete Object*.

To copy an object from one container to another

1. Log in to the dashboard.

2. Select the appropriate project from the drop down menu at the top left.

3. On the *Project* tab, open the *Object Store* tab and click *Containers* category.

4. Select the container in which you want to store your object.

5. Click the menu button and choose *Copy* from the dropdown list.

6. In the *Copy Object* launch dialog box, enter the following values:

   • *Destination Container*: Choose the destination container from the list.

   • *Path*: Specify a path in which the new copy should be stored inside of the selected container.

   • *Destination object name*: Enter a name for the object in the new container.

7. Click *Copy Object*.

To create a metadata-only object without a file

You can create a new object in container without a file available and can upload the file later when it is ready. This temporary object acts a place-holder for a new object, and enables the user to share object metadata and URL info in advance.

1. Log in to the dashboard.

2. Select the appropriate project from the drop down menu at the top left.

3. On the *Project* tab, open the *Object Store* tab and click *Containers* category.

4. Select the container in which you want to store your object.

5. Click *Upload Object.*

   The *Upload Object To Container:* <name> dialog box is displayed.

   <name> is the name of the container to which you are uploading the object.

6. Enter a name for the object.

7. Click *Update Object.*

To create a pseudo-folder

Pseudo-folders are similar to folders in your desktop operating system. They are virtual collections defined by a common prefix on the object's name.

1. Log in to the dashboard.

2. Select the appropriate project from the drop down menu at the top left.

3. On the *Project* tab, open the *Object Store* tab and click *Containers* category.

4. Select the container in which you want to store your object.

5. Click *Create Pseudo-folder.*

   The *Create Pseudo-Folder in Container* <name> dialog box is displayed. <name> is the name of the container to which you are uploading the object.

6. Enter a name for the pseudo-folder.

   A slash (/) character is used as the delimiter for pseudo-folders in Object Storage.

7. Click *Create.*

3.7   Create and manage volumes

Volumes are block storage devices that you attach to instances to enable persistent storage. You can attach a volume to a running instance or detach a volume and attach it to another instance at any time. You can also create a snapshot from or delete a volume. Only administrative users can create volume types.

3.7.1 Create a volume

1. Log in to the dashboard.

2. Select the appropriate project from the drop down menu at the top left.

3. On the *Project* tab, open the *Compute* tab and click *Volumes* category.

4. Click *Create Volume*.
   In the dialog box that opens, enter or select the following values.
   Volume Name: Specify a name for the volume.
   Description: Optionally, provide a brief description for the volume.
   Volume Source: Select one of the following options:

   - No source, empty volume: Creates an empty volume. An empty volume does not contain a file system or a partition table.

   - Image: If you choose this option, a new field for *Use image as a source* displays. You can select the image from the list.

   - Volume: If you choose this option, a new field for *Use volume as a source* displays. You can select the volume from the list. Options to use a snapshot or a volume as the source for a volume are displayed only if there are existing snapshots or volumes.

   Type: Leave this field blank.
   Size (GB): The size of the volume in gibibytes (GiB).
   Availability Zone: Select the Availability Zone from the list. By default, this value is set to the availability zone given by the cloud provider (for example, `us-west` or `apac-south`). For some cases, it could be `nova`.

5. Click *Create Volume*.

The dashboard shows the volume on the *Volumes* tab.

3.7.2 Attach a volume to an instance

After you create one or more volumes, you can attach them to instances. You can attach a volume to one instance at a time.

1. Log in to the dashboard.

2. Select the appropriate project from the drop down menu at the top left.

3. On the *Project* tab, open the *Compute* tab and click *Volumes* category.

4. Select the volume to add to an instance and click *Edit Attachments*.

5. In the *Manage Volume Attachments* dialog box, select an instance.

6. Enter the name of the device from which the volume is accessible by the instance.

 Note

The actual device name might differ from the volume name because of hypervisor settings.

7. Click *Attach Volume*.

The dashboard shows the instance to which the volume is now attached and the device name.

You can view the status of a volume in the Volumes tab of the dashboard. The volume is either Available or In-Use.

Now you can log in to the instance and mount, format, and use the disk.

3.7.3 Detach a volume from an instance

1. Log in to the dashboard.

2. Select the appropriate project from the drop down menu at the top left.

3. On the *Project* tab, open the *Compute* tab and click the *Volumes* category.

4. Select the volume and click *Edit Attachments*.

5. Click *Detach Volume* and confirm your changes.

A message indicates whether the action was successful.

3.7.4 Create a snapshot from a volume

1. Log in to the dashboard.

2. Select the appropriate project from the drop down menu at the top left.

3. On the *Project* tab, open the *Compute* tab and click *Volumes* category.

4. Select a volume from which to create a snapshot.

5. In the *Actions* column, click *Create Snapshot*.

6. In the dialog box that opens, enter a snapshot name and a brief description.

7. Confirm your changes.
   The dashboard shows the new volume snapshot in Volume Snapshots tab.

3.7.5 Edit a volume

1. Log in to the dashboard.

2. Select the appropriate project from the drop down menu at the top left.

3. On the *Project* tab, open the *Compute* tab and click *Volumes* category.

4. Select the volume that you want to edit.

5. In the *Actions* column, click *Edit Volume*.

6. In the *Edit Volume* dialog box, update the name and description of the volume.

7. Click *Edit Volume*.

 Note

You can extend a volume by using the *Extend Volume* option available in the *More* dropdown list and entering the new value for volume size.

3.7.6 Delete a volume

When you delete an instance, the data in its attached volumes is not deleted.

1. Log in to the dashboard.

2. Select the appropriate project from the drop down menu at the top left.

3. On the *Project* tab, open the *Compute* tab and click *Volumes* category.

4. Select the check boxes for the volumes that you want to delete.

5. Click *Delete Volumes* and confirm your choice.
   A message indicates whether the action was successful.

3.8   Create and manage shares

Shares are file storage that you provide access to instances. You can allow access to a share to a running instance or deny access to a share and allow access to it to another instance at any time. You can also delete a share. You can create snapshot from a share if the driver supports it. Only administrative users can create share types.

3.8.1   Create a share

1. Log in to the dashboard, choose a project, and click *Shares*.

2. Click *Create Share*.
   In the dialog box that opens, enter or select the following values.
   Share Name: Specify a name for the share.
   Description: Optionally, provide a brief description for the share.
   Share Type: Choose a share type.
   Size (GB): The size of the share in gibibytes (GiB).
   Share Protocol: Select NFS, CIFS, GlusterFS, or HDFS.
   Share Network: Choose a share network.
   Metadata: Enter metadata for the share creation if needed.

3. Click *Create Share*.

The dashboard shows the share on the *Shares* tab.

3.8.2   Delete a share

1. Log in to the dashboard, choose a project, and click *Shares*.

2. Select the check boxes for the shares that you want to delete.

3. Click *Delete Shares* and confirm your choice.
   A message indicates whether the action was successful.

3.8.3 Allow access

1. Log in to the dashboard, choose a project, and click *Shares*.

2. Go to the share that you want to allow access and choose *Manage Rules* from Actions.

3. Click *Add rule*.
   Access Type: Choose ip, user, or cert.
   Access Level: Choose read-write or read-only.
   Access To: Fill in Access To field.

4. Click *Add Rule*.
   A message indicates whether the action was successful.

3.8.4 Deny access

1. Log in to the dashboard, choose a project, and click *Shares*.

2. Go to the share that you want to deny access and choose *Manage Rules* from Actions.

3. Choose the rule you want to delete.

4. Click *Delete rule* and confirm your choice.
   A message indicates whether the action was successful.

3.8.5 Edit share metadata

1. Log in to the dashboard, choose a project, and click *Shares*.

2. Go to the share that you want to edit and choose *Edit Share Metadata* from Actions.

3. *Metadata*: To add share metadata, use key = value. To unset metadata, use key.

4. Click *Edit Share Metadata.*

   A message indicates whether the action was successful.

3.8.6   Edit share

1. Log in to the dashboard, choose a project, and click *Shares.*

2. Go to the share that you want to edit and choose *Edit Share* from Actions.

3. *Share Name*: Enter a new share name.

4. *Description*: Enter a new description.

5. Click *Edit Share.*

   A message indicates whether the action was successful.

3.8.7   Extend share

1. Log in to the dashboard, choose a project, and click *Shares.*

2. Go to the share that you want to edit and choose *Extend Share* from Actions.

3. *New Size (GB)*: Enter new size.

4. Click *Extend Share.*

   A message indicates whether the action was successful.

3.8.8   Create share network

1. Log in to the dashboard, choose a project, click *Shares*, and click *Share Networks.*

2. Click *Create Share Network.*

   In the dialog box that opens, enter or select the following values.

   Name: Specify a name for the share network.

   Description: Optionally, provide a brief description for the share network.

   Neutron Net: Choose a neutron network.

   Neutron Subnet: Choose a neutron subnet.

3. Click *Create Share Network*.

The dashboard shows the share network on the *Share Networks* tab.

3.8.9   Delete a share network

1. Log in to the dashboard, choose a project, click *Shares*, and click *Share Networks*.

2. Select the check boxes for the share networks that you want to delete.

3. Click *Delete Share Networks* and confirm your choice.
   A message indicates whether the action was successful.

3.8.10   Edit share network

1. Log in to the dashboard, choose a project, click *Shares*, and click *Share Networks*.

2. Go to the share network that you want to edit and choose *Edit Share Network* from Actions.

3. *Name*: Enter a new share network name.

4. *Description*: Enter a new description.

5. Click *Edit Share Network*.
   A message indicates whether the action was successful.

3.8.11   Create security service

1. Log in to the dashboard, choose a project, click *Shares*, and click *Security Services*.

2. Click *Create Security Service*.
   In the dialog box that opens, enter or select the following values.
   Name: Specify a name for the security service.
   DNS IP: Enter the DNS IP address.
   Server: Enter the server name.
   Domain: Enter the domain name.
   User: Enter the user name.

Password: Enter the password.

Confirm Password: Enter the password again to confirm.

Type: Choose the type from Active Directory, LDAP, or Kerberos.

Description: Optionally, provide a brief description for the security service.

3. Click *Create Security Service*.

The dashboard shows the security service on the *Security Services* tab.

3.8.12 Delete a security service

1. Log in to the dashboard, choose a project, click *Shares*, and click *Security Services*.

2. Select the check boxes for the security services that you want to delete.

3. Click *Delete Security Services* and confirm your choice.
   A message indicates whether the action was successful.

3.8.13 Edit security service

1. Log in to the dashboard, choose a project, click *Shares*, and click *Security Services*.

2. Go to the security service that you want to edit and choose *Edit Security Service* from Actions.

3. *Name*: Enter a new security service name.

4. *Description*: Enter a new description.

5. Click *Edit Security Service*.
   A message indicates whether the action was successful.

3.9 Launch and manage stacks

OpenStack Orchestration is a service that you can use to orchestrate multiple composite cloud applications. This service supports the use of both the Amazon Web Services (AWS) CloudFormation template format through both a Query API that is compatible with CloudFormation and the native OpenStack *Heat Orchestration Template (HOT)* format through a REST API.

These flexible template languages enable application developers to describe and automate the deployment of infrastructure, services, and applications. The templates enable creation of most OpenStack resource types, such as instances, floating IP addresses, volumes, security groups, and users. Once created, the resources are referred to as stacks.

The template languages are described in the Template Guide (http://docs.openstack.org/developer/heat/template_guide/index.html) ↗ in the Heat developer documentation (http://docs.openstack.org/developer/heat/) ↗.

3.9.1   Launch a stack

1. Log in to the dashboard.

2. Select the appropriate project from the drop down menu at the top left.

3. On the *Project* tab, open the *Orchestration* tab and click *Stacks* category.

4. Click *Launch Stack*.

5. In the *Select Template* dialog box, specify the following values:

Template Source	Choose the source of the template from the list.
Template URL/File/Data	Depending on the source that you select, enter the URL, browse to the file location, or directly include the template.
Environment Source	Choose the source of the environment from the list. The environment files contain additional settings for the stack.
Environment File/Data	Depending on the source that you select, browse to the file location, directly include the environment

6. Click *Next*.

7. In the *Launch Stack* dialog box, specify the following values:

Stack Name	Enter a name to identify the stack.
Creation Timeout (minutes)	Specify the number of minutes that can elapse before the launch of the stack times out.
Rollback On Failure	Select this check box if you want the service to roll back changes if the stack fails to launch.
Password for user "demo"	Specify the password that the default user uses when the stack is created.
DBUsername	Specify the name of the database user.
LinuxDistribution	Specify the Linux distribution that is used in the stack.
DBRootPassword	Specify the root password for the database.
KeyName	Specify the name of the key pair to use to log in to the stack.
DBName	Specify the name of the database.
DBPassword	Specify the password of the database.
InstanceType	Specify the flavor for the instance.

8. Click *Launch* to create a stack. The *Stacks* tab shows the stack.

After the stack is created, click on the stack name to see the following details:

Topology

The topology of the stack.

Overview

The parameters and details of the stack.

Resources

The resources used by the stack.

Events

The events related to the stack.

3.9.2 Manage a stack

1. Log in to the dashboard.

2. Select the appropriate project from the drop down menu at the top left.

3. On the *Project* tab, open the *Orchestration* tab and click *Stacks* category.

4. Select the stack that you want to update.

5. Click *Change Stack Template*.

6. In the *Select Template* dialog box, select the new template source or environment source.

7. Click *Next*.
   The *Update Stack Parameters* window appears.

8. Enter new values for any parameters that you want to update.

9. Click *Update*.

3.9.3 Delete a stack

When you delete a stack, you cannot undo this action.

1. Log in to the dashboard.

2. Select the appropriate project from the drop down menu at the top left.

3. On the *Project* tab, open the *Orchestration* tab and click *Stacks* category.

4. Select the stack that you want to delete.

5. Click *Delete Stack*.

6. In the confirmation dialog box, click *Delete Stack* to confirm the deletion.

3.10 Create and manage databases

The Database service provides scalable and reliable cloud provisioning functionality for both relational and non-relational database engines. Users can quickly and easily use database features without the burden of handling complex administrative tasks.

3.10.1 Create a database instance

Prerequisites. Before you create a database instance, you need to configure a default datastore and make sure you have an appropriate flavor for the type of database instance you want.

1. **Configure a default datastore.**

   Because the dashboard does not let you choose a specific datastore to use with an instance, you need to configure a default datastore. The dashboard then uses the default datastore to create the instance.

   1. Add the following line to `/etc/trove/trove.conf`:

      ```
      default_datastore = DATASTORE_NAME
      ```

      Replace `DATASTORE_NAME` with the name that the administrative user set when issuing the **trove-manage** command to create the datastore. You can use the trove **datastore-list** command to display the datastores that are available in your environment.

      For example, if your MySQL data store name is set to `mysql`, your entry would look like this:

      ```
      default_datastore = mysql
      ```

   2. Restart Database services on the controller node:

      ```
      # service trove-api restart
      # service trove-taskmanager restart
      ```

```
# service trove-conductor restart
```

2. **Verify flavor.**

   Make sure an appropriate flavor exists for the type of database instance you want.

Create database instance. Once you have configured a default datastore and verified that you have an appropriate flavor, you can create a database instance.

1. Log in to the dashboard.

2. From the CURRENT PROJECT on the *Project* tab, select the appropriate project.

3. On the *Project* tab, open the *Database* tab and click *Instances* category. This lists the instances that already exist in your environment.

4. Click *Launch Instance*.

5. In the *Launch Database* dialog box, specify the following values.
   Details
   Database Name: Specify a name for the database instance.
   Flavor: Select an appropriate flavor for the instance.
   Volume Size: Select a volume size. Volume size is expressed in GB.
   Initialize Databases: Initial Database
   Optionally provide a comma separated list of databases to create, for example:
   `database1`, `database2`, `database3`
   Initial Admin User: Create an initial admin user. This user will have access to all the databases you create.
   Password: Specify a password associated with the initial admin user you just named.
   Host: Optionally, allow the user to connect only from this host. If you do not specify a host, this user will be allowed to connect from anywhere.

6. Click the *Launch* button. The new database instance appears in the databases list.

3.10.2 Backup and restore a database

You can use Database services to backup a database and store the backup artifact in the Object Storage service. Later on, if the original database is damaged, you can use the backup artifact to restore the database. The restore process creates a database instance.

This example shows you how to back up and restore a MySQL database.

3.10.2.1 To backup the database instance

1. Log in to the dashboard.

2. From the CURRENT PROJECT on the *Project* tab, select the appropriate project.

3. On the *Project* tab, open the *Database* tab and click *Instances* category. This displays the existing instances in your system.

4. Click *Create Backup*.

5. In the *Backup Database* dialog box, specify the following values:
   Name
   Specify a name for the backup.
   Database Instance
   Select the instance you want to back up.

6. Click *Backup*. The new backup appears in the backup list.

3.10.2.2 To restore a database instance

Now assume that your original database instance is damaged and you need to restore it. You do the restore by using your backup to create a new database instance.

1. Log in to the dashboard.

2. From the CURRENT PROJECT on the *Project* tab, select the appropriate project.

3. On the *Project* tab, open the *Database* tab and click *Backups* category. This lists the available backups.

4. Check the backup you want to use and click *Restore Backup*.

5. In the *Launch Database* dialog box, specify the values you want for the new database instance.

6. Click the *Restore From Database* tab and make sure that this new instance is based on the correct backup.

7. Click *Launch*.

   The new instance appears in the database instances list.

3.10.3   Update a database instance

You can change various characteristics of a database instance, such as its volume size and flavor.

3.10.3.1   To change the volume size of an instance

1. Log in to the dashboard.

2. From the CURRENT PROJECT on the *Project* tab, select the appropriate project.

3. On the *Project* tab, open the *Database* tab and click *Instances* category. This displays the existing instances in your system.

4. Check the instance you want to work with. In the *Actions* column, expand the drop down menu and select *Resize Volume*.

5. In the *Resize Database Volume* dialog box, fill in the *New Size* field with an integer indicating the new size you want for the instance. Express the size in GB, and note that the new size must be larger than the current size.

6. Click *Resize Database Volume*.

3.10.3.2   To change the flavor of an instance

1. Log in to the dashboard.

2. From the CURRENT PROJECT on the *Project* tab, select the appropriate project.

3. On the *Project* tab, open the *Database* tab and click *Instances* category. This displays the existing instances in your system.

4. Check the instance you want to work with. In the *Actions* column, expand the drop down menu and select *Resize Instance*.

5. In the *Resize Database Instance* dialog box, expand the drop down menu in the *New Flavor* field. Select the new flavor you want for the instance.

6. Click *Resize Database Instance*.

4 OpenStack command-line clients

4.1 Overview

Each OpenStack project provides a command-line client, which enables you to access the project API through easy-to-use commands. For example, the Compute service provides a nova command-line client.

You can run the commands from the command line, or include the commands within scripts to automate tasks. If you provide OpenStack credentials, such as your user name and password, you can run these commands on any computer.

Internally, each command uses cURL command-line tools, which embed API requests. OpenStack APIs are RESTful APIs, and use the HTTP protocol. They include methods, URIs, media types, and response codes.

OpenStack APIs are open-source Python clients, and can run on Linux or Mac OS X systems. On some client commands, you can specify a debug parameter to show the underlying API request for the command. This is a good way to become familiar with the OpenStack API calls.

As a cloud end user, you can use the OpenStack dashboard to provision your own resources within the limits set by administrators. You can modify the examples provided in this section to create other types and sizes of server instances.

The following table lists the command-line client for each OpenStack service with its package name and description.

OpenStack services and clients

TABLE 4.1: OPENSTACK SERVICES AND CLIENTS

Service	Client	Package	Description
Application catalog	murano	python-muranoclient	Creates and manages applications.
Block Storage	cinder	python-cinderclient	Creates and manages volumes.
Clustering service	senlin	python-senlinclient	Creates and manages clustering services.

Service	Client	Package	Description
Compute	nova	python-novaclient	Creates and manages images, instances, and flavors.
Containers service	magnum	python-magnumclient	Creates and manages containers.
Database service	trove	python-troveclient	Creates and manages databases.
Data processing	sahara	python-saharaclient	Creates and manages Hadoop clusters on OpenStack.
Deployment service	fuel	python-fuelclient	Plans deployments.
Identity	keystone	python-keystoneclient	Creates and manages users, tenants, roles, endpoints, and credentials.
Image service	glance	python-glanceclient	Creates and manages images.
Key Manager service	barbican	python-barbicanclient	Creates and manages keys.
Monitoring	monasca	python-monascaclient	Monitoring solution.
Networking	neutron	python-neutronclient	Configures networks for guest servers.
Object Storage	swift	python-swiftclient	Gathers statistics, lists items, updates metadata, and uploads, downloads, and deletes files stored by the Object Storage service. Gains

Service	Client	Package	Description
			access to an Object Storage installation for ad hoc processing.
Orchestration	heat	python-heatclient	Launches stacks from templates, views details of running stacks including events and resources, and updates and deletes stacks.
Rating service	cloudkitty	python-cloudkittyclient	Rating service.
Shared file systems	manila	python-manilaclient	Creates and manages shared file systems.
Telemetry	ceilometer	python-ceilometerclient	Creates and collects measurements across OpenStack.
Telemetry v3	gnocchi	python-gnocchiclient	Creates and collects measurements across OpenStack.
Workflow service	mistral	python-mistralclient	Workflow service for OpenStack cloud.
Common client	openstack	python-openstackclient	Common client for the OpenStack project.

4.2   Install the OpenStack command-line clients

Install the prerequisite software and the Python package for each OpenStack client.

4.2.1   Install the prerequisite software

Most Linux distributions include packaged versions of the command-line clients that you can install directly, see *Section 4.2.2.2, "Installing from packages"*.

If you need to install the source package for the command-line package, the following table lists the software needed to run the command-line clients, and provides installation instructions as needed.

Prerequisite	Description
Python 2.7 or later	Currently, the clients do not support Python 3.
setuptools package	Installed by default on Mac OS X. Many Linux distributions provide packages to make setuptools easy to install. Search your package manager for setuptools to find an installation package. If you cannot find one, download the setuptools package directly from https://pypi.python.org/pypi/setuptools ↗. The recommended way to install setuptools on Microsoft Windows is to follow the documentation provided on the setuptools website (https://pypi.python.org/pypi/setuptools ↗). Another option is to use the unofficial binary installer maintained by Christoph Gohlke (http://www.lfd.uci.edu/~gohlke/pythonlibs/#setuptools (http://www.lfd.uci.edu/~gohlke/pythonlibs/#setuptools) ↗).
pip package	To install the clients on a Linux, Mac OS X, or Microsoft Windows system, use pip. It is easy to use, ensures that you get the latest version of the clients from the Python Package Index (https://pypi.python.org/) ↗, and lets you update or remove the packages later on. Since the installation process compiles source files, this requires the related Python development package for your operating system and distribution. Install pip through the package manager for your system: **MacOS** ```# easy_install pip``` **Microsoft Windows**

Prerequisite	Description

	Ensure that the `C:\Python27\Scripts` directory is defined in the `PATH` environment variable, and use the `easy_install` command from the setuptools package:
	
	```\nC:\>easy_install pip\n```
	
	Another option is to use the unofficial binary installer provided by Christoph Gohlke (http://www.lfd.uci.edu/~gohlke/python-libs/#pip ↗).
	
	Ubuntu and Debian
	
	```\n# apt-get install python-dev python-pip\n```
	
	Note that extra dependencies may be required, per operating system, depending on the package being installed, such as is the case with Tempest.
	
	Red Hat Enterprise Linux, CentOS, or Fedora.
	
	A packaged version enables you to use yum to install the package:
	
	```\n# yum install python-devel python-pip\n```
	
	There are also packaged versions of the clients available in RDO (https://www.rdoproject.org/) ↗ that enable yum to install the clients as described in *Section 4.2.2.2, "Installing from packages"*.
	
	SUSE Linux Enterprise Server
	
	A packaged version available in the Open Build Service (https://build.opensuse.org/package/show?package=python-pip&project=Cloud:OpenStack:Master (https://build.opensuse.org/package/show?package=python-pip&project=Cloud:OpenStack:Master) ↗) enables you to use YaST or zypper to install the package.

Prerequisite	Description
	First, add the Open Build Service repository:
| | ```
# zypper addrepo -f obs://Cloud:OpenStack: \
Liberty/SLE_12 Liberty
``` |
| | Then install pip and use it to manage client installation: |
| | ```
# zypper install python-devel python-pip
``` |
	There are also packaged versions of the clients available that enable zypper to install the clients as described in *Section 4.2.2.2, "Installing from packages"*.
	openSUSE
	You can install pip and use it to manage client installation:
| | ```
# zypper install python-devel python-pip
``` |
| | There are also packaged versions of the clients available that enable zypper to install the clients as described in *Section 4.2.2.2, "Installing from packages"*. |

4.2.2 Install the OpenStack client

The following example shows the command for installing the OpenStack client with `pip`, which supports multiple services.

```
# pip install python-openstackclient
```

The following clients, while valid, are de-emphasized in favor of a common client. Instead of installing and learning all these clients, we recommend installing and using the OpenStack client. You may need to install an individual project's client because coverage is not yet sufficient in the OpenStack client. If you need to install an individual client's project, replace the `<project>` name in this `pip install` command using the list below.

```
# pip install python-<project>client
```
```

- `barbican` - Key Manager Service API

- `ceilometer` - Telemetry API

- `cinder` - Block Storage API and extensions

- `cloudkitty` - Rating service API

- `designate` - DNS service API

- `fuel` - Deployment service API

- `glance` - Image service API

- `gnocchi` - Telemetry API v3

- `heat` - Orchestration API

- `magnum` - Containers service API

- `manila` - Shared file systems API

- `mistral` - Workflow service API

- `monasca` - Monitoring API

- `murano` - Application catalog API

- `neutron` - Networking API

- `nova` - Compute API and extensions

- `sahara` - Data Processing API

- `senlin` - Clustering service API

- `swift` - Object Storage API

- `trove` - Database service API

- `openstack` - Common OpenStack client supporting multiple services

The following CLIs are deprecated in favor of `openstack`, the Common OpenStack client supporting multiple services:

- `keystone` - Identity service API and extensions

While you can install the `keystone` client for interacting with version 2.0 of the service's API, you should use the `openstack` client for all Identity interactions.

4.2.2.1 Installing with pip

Use pip to install the OpenStack clients on a Linux, Mac OS X, or Microsoft Windows system. It is easy to use and ensures that you get the latest version of the client from the Python Package Index (https://pypi.python.org/pypi) ↗. Also, pip enables you to update or remove a package. Install each client separately by using the following command:

- For Mac OS X or Linux:

```
# pip install python-PROJECTclient
```

- For Microsoft Windows:

```
C:\>pip install python-PROJECTclient
```

4.2.2.2 Installing from packages

RDO, openSUSE, SUSE Linux Enterprise, Debian, and Ubuntu have client packages that can be installed without `pip`.

- On Red Hat Enterprise Linux, CentOS, or Fedora, use `yum` to install the clients from the packaged versions available in RDO (https://www.rdoproject.org/) ↗:

```
# yum install python-PROJECTclient
```

- For Ubuntu or Debian, use `apt-get` to install the clients from the packaged versions:

```
# apt-get install python-PROJECTclient
```

- For openSUSE, use `zypper` to install the clients from the distribution packages service:

```
# zypper install python-PROJECTclient
```

- For SUSE Linux Enterprise Server, use `zypper` to install the clients from the distribution packages in the Open Build Service. First, add the Open Build Service repository:

```
# zypper addrepo -f obs://Cloud:OpenStack:Liberty/SLE_12 Liberty
```

Then you can install the packages:

```
# zypper install python-PROJECTclient
```

4.2.3 Upgrade or remove clients

To upgrade a client, add the `--upgrade` option to the **pip install** command:

```
# pip install --upgrade python-PROJECTclient
```

To remove the client, run the **pip uninstall** command:

```
# pip uninstall python-PROJECTclient
```

4.2.4 What's next

Before you can run client commands, you must create and source the `PROJECT-openrc.sh` file to set environment variables. See .

4.3 Discover the version number for a client

Run the following command to discover the version number for a client:

```
$ PROJECT --version
```

For example, to see the version number for the `nova` client, run the following command:

```
$ nova --version
2.31.0
```

4.4   Set environment variables using the OpenStack RC file

To set the required environment variables for the OpenStack command-line clients, you must create an environment file called an OpenStack rc file, or `openrc.sh` file. If your OpenStack installation provides it, you can download the file from the OpenStack dashboard as an administrative user or any other user. This project-specific environment file contains the credentials that all OpenStack services use.

When you source the file, environment variables are set for your current shell. The variables enable the OpenStack client commands to communicate with the OpenStack services that run in the cloud.

 Note

> Defining environment variables using an environment file is not a common practice on Microsoft Windows. Environment variables are usually defined in the *Advanced* › *System Properties* dialog box.

4.4.1   Download and source the OpenStack RC file

1. Log in to the OpenStack dashboard, choose the project for which you want to download the OpenStack RC file, on the *Project* tab, open the *Compute* tab and click *Access & Security*.

2. On the *API Access* tab, click *Download OpenStack RC File* and save the file. The filename will be of the form `PROJECT-openrc.sh` where `PROJECT` is the name of the project for which you downloaded the file.

3. Copy the `PROJECT-openrc.sh` file to the computer from which you want to run OpenStack commands.
   For example, copy the file to the computer from which you want to upload an image with a `glance` client command.

4. On any shell from which you want to run OpenStack commands, source the `PROJECT-openrc.sh` file for the respective project.

In the following example, the `demo-openrc.sh` file is sourced for the demo project:

```
$ source demo-openrc.sh
```

5. When you are prompted for an OpenStack password, enter the password for the user who downloaded the `PROJECT-openrc.sh` file.

4.4.2   Create and source the OpenStack RC file

Alternatively, you can create the `PROJECT-openrc.sh` file from scratch, if you cannot download the file from the dashboard.

1. In a text editor, create a file named `PROJECT-openrc.sh` and add the following authentication information:

```
export OS_USERNAME=username
export OS_PASSWORD=password
export OS_TENANT_NAME=projectName
export OS_AUTH_URL=https://identityHost:portNumber/v2.0
# The following lines can be omitted
export OS_TENANT_ID=tenantIDString
export OS_REGION_NAME=regionName
export OS_CACERT=/path/to/cacertFile
```

2. On any shell from which you want to run OpenStack commands, source the `PROJECT-openrc.sh` file for the respective project. In this example, you source the `admin-openrc.sh` file for the admin project:

```
$ source admin-openrc.sh
```

 Note

You are not prompted for the password with this method. The password lives in clear text format in the `PROJECT-openrc.sh` file. Restrict the permissions on this file to avoid security problems. You can also remove the `OS_PASSWORD` variable from the file, and use the `--password` parameter with OpenStack client commands instead.

Note

You must set the `OS_CACERT` environment variable when using the https protocol in the `OS_AUTH_URL` environment setting because the verification process for the TLS (HTTPS) server certificate uses the one indicated in the environment. This certificate will be used when verifying the TLS (HTTPS) server certificate.

4.4.3   Override environment variable values

When you run OpenStack client commands, you can override some environment variable settings by using the options that are listed at the end of the `help` output of the various client commands. For example, you can override the `OS_PASSWORD` setting in the `PROJECT-openrc.sh` file by specifying a password on a **openstack** command, as follows:

```
$ openstack --os-password PASSWORD service list
```

Where `PASSWORD` is your password.

A user specifies their username and password credentials to interact with OpenStack, using any client command. These credentials can be specified using various mechanisms, namely, the environment variable or command-line argument. It is not safe to specify the password using either of these methods.

For example, when you specify your password using the command-line client with the `--os-password` argument, anyone with access to your computer can view it in plain text with the `ps` field.

To avoid storing the password in plain text, you can prompt for the OpenStack password interactively.

4.5   Manage images

The cloud operator assigns roles to users. Roles determine who can upload and manage images. The operator might restrict image upload and management to only cloud administrators or operators.

You can upload images through the `glance` client or the Image service API. You can use the `nova` client for the image management. The latter provides mechanisms to list and delete images, set and delete image metadata, and create images of a running instance or snapshot and backup types.

After you upload an image, you cannot change it.

For details about image creation, see the Virtual Machine Image Guide (http://docs.openstack.org/image-guide/) ↗.

4.5.1 List or get details for images (glance)

To get a list of images and to get further details about a single image, use **glance image-list** and **glance image-show** commands.

```
$ glance image-list
+-----------+-------------------------------+-------------+------------------+----------
+---------+
| ID        | Name                          | Disk Format | Container Format | Size     |
 Status |
+-----------+-------------------------------+-------------+------------------+----------
+---------+
| 397e7...  | cirros-0.3.2-x86_64-uec       | ami         | ami              | 25165824 |
 active |
| df430...  | cirros-0.3.2-x86_64-uec-kernel | aki        | aki              | 4955792  |
 active |
| 3cf85...  | cirros-0.3.2-x86_64-uec-ramdisk | ari       | ari              | 3714968  |
 active |
| 7e514...  | myCirrosImage                 | ami         | ami              | 14221312 |
 active |
+-----------+-------------------------------+-------------+------------------+----------
+---------+
```

```
$ glance image-show myCirrosImage
+-----------------------------------+----------------------------------------------------+
| Property                          | Value                                              |
+-----------------------------------+----------------------------------------------------+
```

```
| Property 'base_image_ref'            | 397e713c-b95b-4186-ad46-6126863ea0a9 |
| Property 'image_location'            | snapshot                             |
| Property 'image_state'               | available                            |
| Property 'image_type'                | snapshot                             |
| Property 'instance_type_ephemeral_gb' | 0                                   |
| Property 'instance_type_flavorid'    | 2                                    |
| Property 'instance_type_id'          | 5                                    |
| Property 'instance_type_memory_mb'   | 2048                                 |
| Property 'instance_type_name'        | m1.small                             |
| Property 'instance_type_root_gb'     | 20                                   |
| Property 'instance_type_rxtx_factor' | 1                                    |
| Property 'instance_type_swap'        | 0                                    |
| Property 'instance_type_vcpu_weight' | None                                 |
| Property 'instance_type_vcpus'       | 1                                    |
| Property 'instance_uuid'             | 84c6e57d-a6b1-44b6-81eb-fcb36afd31b5 |
| Property 'kernel_id'                 | df430cc2-3406-4061-b635-a51c16e488ac |
| Property 'owner_id'                  | 66265572db174a7aa66eba661f58eb9e     |
| Property 'ramdisk_id'                | 3cf852bd-2332-48f4-9ae4-7d926d50945e |
| Property 'user_id'                   | 376744b5910b4b4da7d8e6cb483b06a8     |
| checksum                             | 8e4838effa1969ad591655d6485c7ba8     |
| container_format                     | ami                                  |
| created_at                           | 2013-07-22T19:45:58                  |
| deleted                              | False                                |
| disk_format                          | ami                                  |
| id                                   | 7e5142af-1253-4634-bcc6-89482c5f2e8a |
| is_public                            | False                                |
| min_disk                             | 0                                    |
| min_ram                              | 0                                    |
| name                                 | myCirrosImage                        |
| owner                                | 66265572db174a7aa66eba661f58eb9e     |
| protected                            | False                                |
| size                                 | 14221312                             |
| status                               | active                               |
| updated_at                           | 2013-07-22T19:46:42                  |
+--------------------------------------+--------------------------------------+
```

When viewing a list of images, you can also use `grep` to filter the list, as follows:

```
$ glance image-list | grep 'cirros'
| 397e713c-b95b-4186-ad46-612... | cirros-0.3.2-x86_64-uec          | ami | ami | 25165824 |
 active |
| df430cc2-3406-4061-b635-a51... | cirros-0.3.2-x86_64-uec-kernel   | aki | aki | 4955792  |
 active |
| 3cf852bd-2332-48f4-9ae4-7d9... | cirros-0.3.2-x86_64-uec-ramdisk | ari | ari | 3714968  |
 active |
```

 Note

To store location metadata for images, which enables direct file access for a client, update the `/etc/glance/glance-api.conf` file with the following statements:

- `show_multiple_locations = True`

- `filesystem_store_metadata_file = filePath`, where filePath points to a JSON file that defines the mount point for OpenStack images on your system and a unique ID. For example:

```
[{
    "id": "2d9bb53f-70ea-4066-a68b-67960eaae673",
    "mountpoint": "/var/lib/glance/images/"
}]
```

After you restart the Image service, you can use the following syntax to view the image's location information:

```
$ glance --os-image-api-version 2 image-show imageID
```

For example, using the image ID shown above, you would issue the command as follows:

```
$ glance --os-image-api-version 2 image-show 2d9bb53f-70ea-4066-
a68b-67960eaae673
```

4.5.2 Create or update an image (glance)

To create an image, use **`glance image-create`**:

```
$ glance image-create imageName
```

To update an image by name or ID, use **`glance image-update`**:

```
$ glance image-update imageName
```

The following list explains the optional arguments that you can use with the `create` and `update` commands to modify image properties. For more information, refer to Image service chapter in the OpenStack Command-Line Interface Reference (http://docs.openstack.org/cli-reference/index.html) ↗.

`--name NAME`

   The name of the image.

`--disk-format DISK_FORMAT`

   The disk format of the image. Acceptable formats are ami, ari, aki, vhd, vmdk, raw, qcow2, vdi, and iso.

`--container-format CONTAINER_FORMAT`

   The container format of the image. Acceptable formats are ami, ari, aki, bare, docker, and ovf.

`--owner TENANT_ID --size SIZE`

   The tenant who should own the image. The size of image data, in bytes.

`--min-disk DISK_GB`

   The minimum size of the disk needed to boot the image, in gigabytes.

`--min-ram DISK_RAM`

   The minimum amount of RAM needed to boot the image, in megabytes.

`--location IMAGE_URL`

   The URL where the data for this image resides. For example, if the image data is stored in swift, you could specify `swift://account:key@example.com/container/obj`.

`--file FILE`

   Local file that contains the disk image to be uploaded during the update. Alternatively, you can pass images to the client through stdin.

`--checksum CHECKSUM`

> Hash of image data to use for verification.

`--copy-from IMAGE_URL`

> Similar to `--location` in usage, but indicates that the image server should immediately copy the data and store it in its configured image store.

`--is-public [True|False]`

> Makes an image accessible for all the tenants (admin-only by default).

`--is-protected [True|False]`

> Prevents an image from being deleted.

`--property KEY=VALUE`

> Arbitrary property to associate with image. This option can be used multiple times.

`--purge-props`

> Deletes all image properties that are not explicitly set in the update request. Otherwise, those properties not referenced are preserved.

`--human-readable`

> Prints the image size in a human-friendly format.

The following example shows the command that you would use to upload a CentOS 6.3 image in qcow2 format and configure it for public access:

```
$ glance image-create --name centos63-image --disk-format qcow2 \
  --container-format bare --is-public True --file ./centos63.qcow2
```

The following example shows how to update an existing image with a properties that describe the disk bus, the CD-ROM bus, and the VIF model:

 Note

> When you use OpenStack with VMware vCenter Server, you need to specify the `vmware_disktype` and `vmware_adaptertype` properties with **glance image-create**. Also, we recommend that you set the `hypervisor_type="vmware"` property. For more information, see Images with VMware vSphere (http://docs.openstack.org/liberty/config-reference/content/vmware.html#VMware_images) ↗ in the *OpenStack Configuration Reference*.

```
$ glance image-update \
    --property hw_disk_bus=scsi \
    --property hw_cdrom_bus=ide \
    --property hw_vif_model=e1000 \
    f16-x86_64-openstack-sda
```

Currently the libvirt virtualization tool determines the disk, CD-ROM, and VIF device models based on the configured hypervisor type (`libvirt_type` in `/etc/nova/nova.conf` file). For the sake of optimal performance, libvirt defaults to using virtio for both disk and VIF (NIC) models. The disadvantage of this approach is that it is not possible to run operating systems that lack virtio drivers, for example, BSD, Solaris, and older versions of Linux and Windows.

If you specify a disk or CD-ROM bus model that is not supported, see the *Table 4.2, "Disk and CD-ROM bus model values"*. If you specify a VIF model that is not supported, the instance fails to launch. See the *Table 4.3, "VIF model values"*.

The valid model values depend on the `libvirt_type` setting, as shown in the following tables.

Disk and CD-ROM bus model values

TABLE 4.2: DISK AND CD-ROM BUS MODEL VALUES

libvirt_type setting	Supported model values
qemu or kvm	• ide • scsi • virtio
xen	• ide • xen

VIF model values

TABLE 4.3: VIF MODEL VALUES

libvirt_type setting	Supported model values
qemu or kvm	• e1000 • ne2k_pci

libvirt_type setting	Supported model values
	• pcnet • rtl8139 • virtio
xen	• e1000 • netfront • ne2k_pci • pcnet • rtl8139
vmware	• VirtualE1000 • VirtualPCNet32 • VirtualVmxnet

4.5.3 Troubleshoot image creation

If you encounter problems in creating an image in the Image service or Compute, the following information may help you troubleshoot the creation process.

- Ensure that the version of qemu you are using is version 0.14 or later. Earlier versions of qemu result in an `unknown option -s` error message in the `nova-compute.log` file.

- Examine the `/var/log/nova-api.log` and `/var/log/nova-compute.log` log files for error messages.

4.6 Manage volumes

A volume is a detachable block storage device, similar to a USB hard drive. You can attach a volume to only one instance. To create and manage volumes, you use a combination of `nova` and `cinder` client commands.

4.6.1   Migrate a volume

As an administrator, you can migrate a volume with its data from one location to another in a manner that is transparent to users and workloads. You can migrate only detached volumes with no snapshots.

Possible use cases for data migration include:

- Bring down a physical storage device for maintenance without disrupting workloads.

- Modify the properties of a volume.

- Free up space in a thinly-provisioned back end.

Migrate a volume with the **cinder migrate** command, as shown in the following example:

```
$ cinder migrate volumeID destinationHost --force-host-copy True|False
```

In this example, `--force-host-copy True` forces the generic host-based migration mechanism and bypasses any driver optimizations.

 Note

>   If the volume is in use or has snapshots, the specified host destination cannot accept the volume. If the user is not an administrator, the migration fails.

4.6.2   Create a volume

This example creates a `my-new-volume` volume based on an image.

1. List images, and note the ID of the image that you want to use for your volume:

```
$ nova image-list

+------------------------+------------------------------------+--------
+------------------------+
| ID                     | Name                               | Status | Server
    |
+------------------------+------------------------------------+--------
+------------------------+
```

```
| 397e713c-b95b-4186... | cirros-0.3.2-x86_64-uec         | ACTIVE |
     |
| df430cc2-3406-4061... | cirros-0.3.2-x86_64-uec-kernel  | ACTIVE |
     |
| 3cf852bd-2332-48f4... | cirros-0.3.2-x86_64-uec-ramdisk | ACTIVE |
     |
| 7e5142af-1253-4634... | myCirrosImage                   | ACTIVE | 84c6e57d-
a6b1-44b6-81... |
| 89bcd424-9d15-4723... | mysnapshot                      | ACTIVE | f51ebd07-
c33d-4951-87... |
+----------------------+--------------------------------+--------
+-------------------------+
```

2. List the availability zones, and note the ID of the availability zone in which you want to create your volume:

```
$ cinder availability-zone-list


+------+-----------+
| Name |  Status   |
+------+-----------+
| nova | available |
+------+-----------+
```

3. Create a volume with 8 gibibytes (GiB) of space, and specify the availability zone and image:

```
$ cinder create 8 --display-name my-new-volume --image-id 397e713c-b95b-4186-
ad46-6126863ea0a9 --availability-zone nova


+--------------------+----------------------------------------+
|      Property      |                 Value                  |
+--------------------+----------------------------------------+
|    attachments     |                  []                    |
| availability_zone  |                 nova                   |
|      bootable      |                 false                  |
```

```
|      created_at      |      2013-07-25T17:02:12.472269      |
|  display_description |                 None                 |
|     display_name     |             my-new-volume            |
|          id          | 573e024d-5235-49ce-8332-be1576d323f8 |
|       image_id       | 397e713c-b95b-4186-ad46-6126863ea0a9 |
|       metadata       |                  {}                  |
|         size         |                  8                   |
|      snapshot_id     |                 None                 |
|     source_volid     |                 None                 |
|        status        |               creating               |
|      volume_type     |                 None                 |
+----------------------+--------------------------------------+
```

4. To verify that your volume was created successfully, list the available volumes:

```
$ cinder list

+------------------+-----------+------------------+------+-------------+----------
+-------------+
|        ID        |  Status   |  Display Name    | Size | Volume Type | Bootable |
 Attached to |
+------------------+-----------+------------------+------+-------------+----------
+-------------+
| 573e024d-523... | available |  my-new-volume   |  8   |     None    |   true   |
       |
| bd7cf584-45d... | available | my-bootable-vol  |  8   |     None    |   true   |
       |
+------------------+-----------+------------------+------+-------------+----------
+-------------+
```

If your volume was created successfully, its status is available. If its status is error, you might have exceeded your quota.

4.6.3   Attach a volume to an instance

1. Attach your volume to a server, specifying the server ID and the volume ID:

```
$ nova volume-attach 84c6e57d-a6b1-44b6-81eb-fcb36afd31b5 573e024d-5235-49ce-8332-
be1576d323f8 /dev/vdb


+----------+------------------------------------------+
| Property | Value                                    |
+----------+------------------------------------------+
| device   | /dev/vdb                                 |
| serverId | 84c6e57d-a6b1-44b6-81eb-fcb36afd31b5     |
| id       | 573e024d-5235-49ce-8332-be1576d323f8     |
| volumeId | 573e024d-5235-49ce-8332-be1576d323f8     |
+----------+------------------------------------------+
```

Note the ID of your volume.

2. Show information for your volume:

```
$ cinder show 573e024d-5235-49ce-8332-be1576d323f8
```

The output shows that the volume is attached to the server with ID `84c6e57d-a6b1-44b6-81eb-fcb36afd31b5`, is in the nova availability zone, and is bootable.

```
+------------------------------+-------------------------------------------+
|           Property           |                   Value                   |
+------------------------------+-------------------------------------------+
|          attachments         |         [{u'device': u'/dev/vdb',         |
|                              |         u'server_id': u'84c6e57d-a         |
|                              |            u'id': u'573e024d-...           |
|                              |         u'volume_id': u'573e024d...        |
|       availability_zone      |                    nova                   |
|           bootable           |                    true                   |
|          created_at          |         2013-07-25T17:02:12.000000        |
|      display_description     |                    None                   |
|         display_name         |                my-new-volume              |
|              id              |    573e024d-5235-49ce-8332-be1576d323f8   |
|           metadata           |                     {}                    |
|     os-vol-host-attr:host    |                  devstack                 |
```

```
| os-vol-tenant-attr:tenant_id |         66265572db174a7aa66eba661f58eb9e      |
|             size             |                      8                        |
|          snapshot_id         |                    None                       |
|          source_volid        |                    None                       |
|            status            |                   in-use                      |
|     volume_image_metadata    |           {u'kernel_id': u'df430cc2...,        |
|                              |             u'image_id': u'397e713c...,        |
|                              |             u'ramdisk_id': u'3cf852bd...,      |
|                              |  |u'image_name': u'cirros-0.3.2-x86_64-uec'}|  |
|          volume_type         |                    None                       |
+------------------------------+-----------------------------------------------+
```

4.6.4 Resize a volume

1. To resize your volume, you must first detach it from the server. To detach the volume from your server, pass the server ID and volume ID to the following command:

```
$ nova volume-detach 84c6e57d-a6b1-44b6-81eb-fcb36afd31b5   573e024d-5235-49ce-8332-
be1576d323f8
```

The **volume-detach** command does not return any output.

2. List volumes:

```
$ cinder list
+----------------+-----------+------------------+------+-------------+----------
+-------------+
|       ID       |  Status   |  Display Name    | Size | Volume Type | Bootable | Attached
to |
+----------------+-----------+------------------+------+-------------+----------
+-------------+
| 573e024d-52... | available |  my-new-volume   |  8   |    None     |   true   |
   |
| bd7cf584-45... | available | my-bootable-vol  |  8   |    None     |   true   |
   |
```

```
+-----------------+------------+-------------------+------+-------------+-----------
+-------------+
```

Note that the volume is now available.

3. Resize the volume by passing the volume ID and the new size (a value greater than the old one) as parameters:

```
$ cinder extend 573e024d-5235-49ce-8332-be1576d323f8 10
```

The **extend** command does not return any output.

4.6.5 Delete a volume

1. To delete your volume, you must first detach it from the server. To detach the volume from your server and check for the list of existing volumes, see steps 1 and 2 in *Section 4.6.4, "Resize a volume"*.
Delete the volume using either the volume name or ID:

```
$ cinder delete my-new-volume
```

The **delete** command does not return any output.

2. List the volumes again, and note that the status of your volume is `deleting`:

```
$ cinder list
+-----------------+------------+-------------------+------+-------------+-----------
+-------------+
|        ID       |   Status   |    Display Name   | Size | Volume Type | Bootable |
 Attached to |
+-----------------+------------+-------------------+------+-------------+-----------
+-------------+
| 573e024d-523... |  deleting  |   my-new-volume   |  8   |     None    |   true   |
     |
| bd7cf584-45d... |  available | my-bootable-vol   |  8   |     None    |   true   |
     |
```

```
+------------------+------------+------------------+------+-------------+----------
+-------------+
```

When the volume is fully deleted, it disappears from the list of volumes:

```
$ cinder list
+------------------+------------+------------------+------+-------------+----------
+-------------+
|       ID         |  Status    |  Display Name    | Size | Volume Type | Bootable |
 Attached to |
+------------------+------------+------------------+------+-------------+----------
+-------------+
| bd7cf584-45d... | available  | my-bootable-vol  |  8   |    None     |   true   |
      |
+------------------+------------+------------------+------+-------------+----------
+-------------+
```

4.6.6 Transfer a volume

You can transfer a volume from one owner to another by using the **cinder transfer*** commands. The volume donor, or original owner, creates a transfer request and sends the created transfer ID and authorization key to the volume recipient. The volume recipient, or new owner, accepts the transfer by using the ID and key.

 Note

The procedure for volume transfer is intended for tenants (both the volume donor and recipient) within the same cloud.

Use cases include:

- Create a custom bootable volume or a volume with a large data set and transfer it to a customer.

- For bulk import of data to the cloud, the data ingress system creates a new Block Storage volume, copies data from the physical device, and transfers device ownership to the end user.

4.6.6.1 Create a volume transfer request

1. While logged in as the volume donor, list the available volumes:

```
$ cinder list
+----------------+-----------+--------------+------+-------------+----------
+-------------+
|       ID       |   Status  | Display Name | Size | Volume Type | Bootable | Attached
 to |
+----------------+-----------+--------------+------+-------------+----------
+-------------+
| 72bfce9f-cac... |   error   |     None     |  1   |    None     |  false   |
    |
| a1cdace0-08e... | available |     None     |  1   |    None     |  false   |
    |
+----------------+-----------+--------------+------+-------------+----------
+-------------+
```

2. As the volume donor, request a volume transfer authorization code for a specific volume:

```
$ cinder transfer-create volumeID
```

The volume must be in an `available` state or the request will be denied. If the transfer request is valid in the database (that is, it has not expired or been deleted), the volume is placed in an `awaiting transfer` state. For example:

```
$ cinder transfer-create a1cdace0-08e4-4dc7-b9dc-457e9bcfe25f
```

The output shows the volume transfer ID in the `id` row and the authorization key.

```
+------------+--------------------------------------+
|  Property  |                Value                 |
+------------+--------------------------------------+
|  auth_key  |           b2c8e585cbc68a80           |
| created_at |      2013-10-14T15:20:10.121458      |
|     id     | 6e4e9aa4-bed5-4f94-8f76-df43232f44dc |
|    name    |                None                  |
```

```
| volume_id  | a1cdace0-08e4-4dc7-b9dc-457e9bcfe25f |
+------------+--------------------------------------+
```

 Note

Optionally, you can specify a name for the transfer by using the `--display-name`
`displayName` parameter.

 Note

While the `auth_key` property is visible in the output of `cinder transfer-cre-`
`ate VOLUME_ID`, it will not be available in subsequent `cinder transfer-show`
`TRANSFER_ID` commands.

3. Send the volume transfer ID and authorization key to the new owner (for example, by email).

4. View pending transfers:

```
$ cinder transfer-list
+--------------------------------------+--------------------------------------+--------+
|                 ID                   |               VolumeID               | Name |
+--------------------------------------+--------------------------------------+--------+
| 6e4e9aa4-bed5-4f94-8f76-df43232f44dc | a1cdace0-08e4-4dc7-b9dc-457e9bcfe25f | None |
+--------------------------------------+--------------------------------------+--------+
```

5. After the volume recipient, or new owner, accepts the transfer, you can see that the transfer is no longer available:

```
$ cinder transfer-list
+----+-----------+------+
| ID | Volume ID | Name |
+----+-----------+------+
+----+-----------+------+
```

4.6.6.2 Accept a volume transfer request

1. As the volume recipient, you must first obtain the transfer ID and authorization key from the original owner.

2. Accept the request:

```
$ cinder transfer-accept transferID authKey
```

For example:

```
$ cinder transfer-accept 6e4e9aa4-bed5-4f94-8f76-df43232f44dc
  b2c8e585cbc68a80
+------------+--------------------------------------+
|  Property  |                 Value                |
+------------+--------------------------------------+
|     id     | 6e4e9aa4-bed5-4f94-8f76-df43232f44dc |
|    name    |                 None                 |
| volume_id  | a1cdace0-08e4-4dc7-b9dc-457e9bcfe25f |
+------------+--------------------------------------+
```

 Note

If you do not have a sufficient quota for the transfer, the transfer is refused.

4.6.6.3   Delete a volume transfer

1. List available volumes and their statuses:

```
$ cinder list
+-------------+----------------+----------------+------+-------------+----------
+-------------+
|     ID      |    Status      | Display Name | Size | Volume Type | Bootable | Attached
  to |
+-------------+----------------+----------------+------+-------------+----------
+-------------+
| 72bfce9f... |    error       |      None    |  1   |    None     |  false   |
    |
```

```
| a1cdace0... |awaiting-transfer|      None      | 1  |     None      | false   |
    |
+-------------+-----------------+----------------+------+---------------+---------
+-------------+
```

2. Find the matching transfer ID:

```
$ cinder transfer-list
+-------------------------------------+----------------------------------------+------+
|                 ID                  |                VolumeID                | Name |
+-------------------------------------+----------------------------------------+------+
| a6da6888-7cdf-4291-9c08-8c1f22426b8a | a1cdace0-08e4-4dc7-b9dc-457e9bcfe25f | None |
+-------------------------------------+----------------------------------------+------+
```

3. Delete the volume:

```
$ cinder transfer-delete transferID
```

For example:

```
$ cinder transfer-delete a6da6888-7cdf-4291-9c08-8c1f22426b8a
```

4. Verify that transfer list is now empty and that the volume is again available for transfer:

```
$ cinder transfer-list
+----+-----------+------+
| ID | Volume ID | Name |
+----+-----------+------+
+----+-----------+------+
```

```
$ cinder list
+----------------+-----------+--------------+------+-------------+---------
+-------------+
|       ID       |  Status   | Display Name | Size | Volume Type | Bootable | Attached
  to |
+----------------+-----------+--------------+------+-------------+---------
+-------------+
```

```
| 72bfce9f-ca... |  error    |    None    | 1 |    None    | false   |
|                |
| a1cdace0-08... | available |    None    | 1 |    None    | false   |
|                |
+----------------+-----------+------------+---+-----------+---------+--------
+-------------+
```

4.7   Manage shares

A share is provided by file storage. You can give access to a share to instances. To create and
manage shares, you use `manila` client commands.

4.7.1   Create a share network

1. Create a share network.

```
$ manila share-network-create --name mysharenetwork --description "My Manila
 network" --neutron-net-id 394246ed-d3fd-4a30-a456-7042ce3429b9 --neutron-subnet-id
 8f56d97d-8495-4a5b-8544-9ae4ee9390fc
+-------------------+--------------------------------------+
| Property          | Value                                |
+-------------------+--------------------------------------+
| name              | mysharenetwork                       |
| segmentation_id   | None                                 |
| created_at        | 2015-08-17T21:13:29.607489           |
| neutron_subnet_id | 8f56d97d-8495-4a5b-8544-9ae4ee9390fc |
| updated_at        | None                                 |
| network_type      | None                                 |
| neutron_net_id    | 394246ed-d3fd-4a30-a456-7042ce3429b9 |
| ip_version        | None                                 |
| nova_net_id       | None                                 |
| cidr              | None                                 |
| project_id        | d80a6323e99f4f22a26ad2accd3ec791     |
| id                | ccd6b453-8b05-4508-bbce-93bfe660451f |
```

```
| description       | My Manila network                  |
+------------------+------------------------------------+
```

2. List share networks.

```
$ manila share-network-list
+-----------------------------------------+-----------------+
| id                                      | name            |
+-----------------------------------------+-----------------+
| ccd6b453-8b05-4508-bbce-93bfe660451f    | mysharenetwork  |
+-----------------------------------------+-----------------+
```

4.7.2   Create a share

1. Create a share.

```
$ manila create --name myshare --description "My Manila share" --share-network
 ccd6b453-8b05-4508-bbce-93bfe660451f NFS 1
+------------------+--------------------------------------+
| Property         | Value                                |
+------------------+--------------------------------------+
| status           | creating                             |
| description      | My Manila share                      |
| availability_zone | nova                                |
| share_network_id | ccd6b453-8b05-4508-bbce-93bfe660451f |
| export_locations | []                                   |
| host             | None                                 |
| snapshot_id      | None                                 |
| is_public        | False                                |
| id               | 2fe736d1-08ac-46f9-a482-8f224405f2a7 |
| size             | 1                                    |
| name             | myshare                              |
| share_type       | default                              |
| created_at       | 2015-08-17T21:17:23.777696           |
| export_location  | None                                 |
```

```
| share_proto       | NFS                              |
| project_id        | d80a6323e99f4f22a26ad2accd3ec791 |
| metadata          | {}                               |
+-------------------+----------------------------------+
```

2. Show a share.

```
$ manila show 2fe736d1-08ac-46f9-a482-8f224405f2a7
+-------------------+--------------------------------------+
| Property          | Value                                |
+-------------------+--------------------------------------+
| status            | creating                             |
| description       | My Manila share                      |
| availability_zone | nova                                 |
| share_network_id  | ccd6b453-8b05-4508-bbce-93bfe660451f |
| export_locations  | []                                   |
| host              | ubuntuManila@generic1#GENERIC1       |
| snapshot_id       | None                                 |
| is_public         | False                                |
| id                | 2fe736d1-08ac-46f9-a482-8f224405f2a7 |
| size              | 1                                    |
| name              | myshare                              |
| share_type        | default                              |
| created_at        | 2015-08-17T21:17:23.000000           |
| export_location   | None                                 |
| share_proto       | NFS                                  |
| project_id        | d80a6323e99f4f22a26ad2accd3ec791     |
| metadata          | {}                                   |
+-------------------+--------------------------------------+
```

3. List shares.

```
$ manila list
+------------------------------------+---------+------+-------------+------------
+----------+-----------+---------------------------------------------------------
+-------------------------------+
```

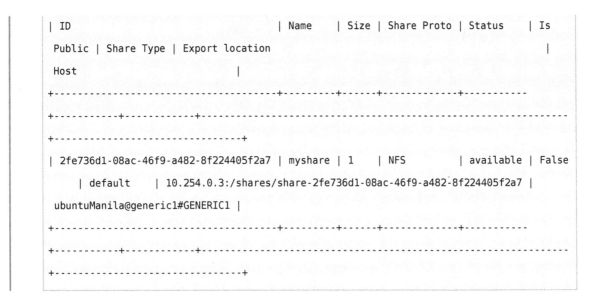

```
| ID                                   | Name     | Size | Share Proto | Status    | Is
Public | Share Type | Export location                                            |
Host                        |
+--------------------------------------+----------+------+-------------+-----------
+-----------+------------+--------------------------------------------------------
+------------------------------+
| 2fe736d1-08ac-46f9-a482-8f224405f2a7 | myshare  | 1    | NFS         | available | False
     | default    | 10.254.0.3:/shares/share-2fe736d1-08ac-46f9-a482-8f224405f2a7 |
ubuntuManila@generic1#GENERIC1 |
+--------------------------------------+----------+------+-------------+-----------
+-----------+------------+--------------------------------------------------------
+------------------------------+
```

4.7.3 Allow access

1. Allow access.

```
$ manila access-allow 2fe736d1-08ac-46f9-a482-8f224405f2a7 ip 192.100.00.168
+--------------+--------------------------------------+
| Property     | Value                                |
+--------------+--------------------------------------+
| share_id     | 2fe736d1-08ac-46f9-a482-8f224405f2a7 |
| deleted      | False                                |
| created_at   | 2015-08-17T21:36:52.025125           |
| updated_at   | None                                 |
| access_type  | ip                                   |
| access_to    | 192.100.00.168                       |
| access_level | rw                                   |
| state        | new                                  |
| deleted_at   | None                                 |
| id           | d73d04ca-a97e-42bb-94b1-e01c72c8e50e |
+--------------+--------------------------------------+
```

2. List access.

```
$ manila access-list 2fe736d1-08ac-46f9-a482-8f224405f2a7

+-------------------------------------+-------------+----------------+--------------
+--------+
| id                                  | access type | access to      | access level |
 state  |
+-------------------------------------+-------------+----------------+--------------
+--------+
| d73d04ca-a97e-42bb-94b1-e01c72c8e50e | ip         | 192.100.00.168 | rw           |
 active |
+-------------------------------------+-------------+----------------+--------------
+--------+
```

The access is created.

4.7.4   Deny access

1. Deny access.

```
$ manila access-deny 2fe736d1-08ac-46f9-a482-8f224405f2a7 d73d04ca-a97e-42bb-94b1-
e01c72c8e50e
```

2. List access.

```
$ manila access-list 2fe736d1-08ac-46f9-a482-8f224405f2a7
+----+-------------+-----------+--------------+-------+
| id | access type | access to | access level | state |
+----+-------------+-----------+--------------+-------+
+----+-------------+-----------+--------------+-------+
```

The access is removed.

4.7.5   Create snapshot

1. Create a snapshot.

```
$ manila snapshot-create --name mysnapshot --description "My Manila snapshot"
 2fe736d1-08ac-46f9-a482-8f224405f2a7
+-------------+-------------------------------------+
| Property    | Value                               |
+-------------+-------------------------------------+
| status      | creating                            |
| share_id    | 2fe736d1-08ac-46f9-a482-8f224405f2a7 |
| name        | mysnapshot                          |
| created_at  | 2015-08-17T21:50:53.295017          |
| share_proto | NFS                                 |
| id          | 1a411703-baef-495f-8e9c-b60e68f2e657 |
| size        | 1                                   |
| share_size  | 1                                   |
| description | My Manila snapshot                  |
+-------------+-------------------------------------+
```

2. List snapshots.

```
$ manila snapshot-list
+-----------------------------------------+-------------------------------------
+-----------+-----------+-----------+
| ID                                      | Share ID                            | Status
 | Name      | Share Size |
+-----------------------------------------+-------------------------------------
+-----------+-----------+-----------+
| 1a411703-baef-495f-8e9c-b60e68f2e657 | 2fe736d1-08ac-46f9-a482-8f224405f2a7 | available
 | mysnapshot | 1        |
+-----------------------------------------+-------------------------------------
+-----------+-----------+-----------+
```

4.7.6   Create share from snapshot

1. Create a share from a snapshot.

```
$ manila create --snapshot-id 1a411703-baef-495f-8e9c-b60e68f2e657 --share-network
  ccd6b453-8b05-4508-bbce-93bfe660451f --name mysharefromsnap NFS 1
+--------------------+-----------------------------------------+
| Property           | Value                                   |
+--------------------+-----------------------------------------+
| status             | creating                                |
| description        | None                                    |
| availability_zone  | nova                                    |
| share_network_id   | ccd6b453-8b05-4508-bbce-93bfe660451f    |
| export_locations   | []                                      |
| host               | ubuntuManila@generic1#GENERIC1          |
| snapshot_id        | 1a411703-baef-495f-8e9c-b60e68f2e657    |
| is_public          | False                                   |
| id                 | bcc5b2a7-862b-418a-9607-5d669619d652    |
| size               | 1                                       |
| name               | mysharefromsnap                         |
| share_type         | default                                 |
| created_at         | 2015-08-17T21:54:43.000000              |
| export_location    | None                                    |
| share_proto        | NFS                                     |
| project_id         | d80a6323e99f4f22a26ad2accd3ec791        |
| metadata           | {}                                      |
+--------------------+-----------------------------------------+
```

2. List shares.

```
$ manila list
+----------------------------------------+-----------------
+-------+------------+-----------+-----------+------------
+-----------------------------------------------------------
+-------------------------------+
| ID                                     | Name          | Size | Share Proto | Status
  | Is Public | Share Type | Export location
  | Host                           |
+----------------------------------------+-----------------
+-------+------------+-----------+-----------+------------
```

```
+-----------------------------------------------------------------
+------------------------------+
| 2fe736d1-08ac-46f9-a482-8f224405f2a7 | myshare          | 1    | NFS        | available
| False     | default    | 10.254.0.3:/shares/share-2fe736d1-08ac-46f9-a482-8f224405f2a7
| ubuntuManila@generic1#GENERIC1 |
| bcc5b2a7-862b-418a-9607-5d669619d652 | mysharefromsnap | 1    | NFS        | creating
| False     | default    | None
| ubuntuManila@generic1#GENERIC1 |
+--------------------------------------+----------------
+-------+--------------+-----------+----------+------------
+-----------------------------------------------------------
+------------------------------+
```

3. Show the share created from snapshot.

```
$ manila show bcc5b2a7-862b-418a-9607-5d669619d652
+-------------------+------------------------------------------------------------------------+
| Property          | Value                                                                  |
+-------------------+------------------------------------------------------------------------+
| status            | available                                                              |
| description       | None                                                                   |
| availability_zone | nova                                                                   |
| share_network_id  | ccd6b453-8b05-4508-bbce-93bfe660451f                                   |
| export_locations  | 10.254.0.3:/shares/share-bcc5b2a7-862b-418a-9607-5d669619d652          |
| host              | ubuntuManila@generic1#GENERIC1                                         |
| snapshot_id       | 1a411703-baef-495f-8e9c-b60e68f2e657                                   |
| is_public         | False                                                                  |
| id                | bcc5b2a7-862b-418a-9607-5d669619d652                                   |
| size              | 1                                                                      |
| name              | mysharefromsnap                                                        |
| share_type        | default                                                                |
| created_at        | 2015-08-17T21:54:43.000000                                             |
| share_proto       | NFS                                                                    |
| project_id        | d80a6323e99f4f22a26ad2accd3ec791                                       |
| metadata          | {}                                                                     |
+-------------------+------------------------------------------------------------------------+
```

4.7.7 Delete share

1. Delete a share.

```
$ manila delete bcc5b2a7-862b-418a-9607-5d669619d652
```

2. List shares.

```
$ manila list
+-------------------------------------+------------------
+------+------------+-----------+----------+-----------
+-----------------------------------------------------------
+------------------------------+

| ID                                   | Name            | Size | Share Proto | Status
 | Is Public | Share Type | Export location
 | Host                       |
+-------------------------------------+------------------
+------+------------+-----------+----------+-----------
+-----------------------------------------------------------
+------------------------------+
| 2fe736d1-08ac-46f9-a482-8f224405f2a7 | myshare          | 1    | NFS         | available
 | False     | default    | 10.254.0.3:/shares/share-2fe736d1-08ac-46f9-a482-8f224405f2a7
 | ubuntuManila@generic1#GENERIC1 |
| bcc5b2a7-862b-418a-9607-5d669619d652 | mysharefromsnap | 1    | NFS         | deleting
 | False     | default    | 10.254.0.3:/shares/share-bcc5b2a7-862b-418a-9607-5d669619d652
 | ubuntuManila@generic1#GENERIC1 |
+-------------------------------------+------------------
+------+------------+-----------+----------+-----------
+-----------------------------------------------------------
+------------------------------+
```

The share is being deleted.

4.7.8 Delete snapshot

1. List snapshots before deleting.

```
$ manila snapshot-list

+-----------------------------------------+----------------------------------------
+------------+------------+------------+
| ID                                      | Share ID                                | Status
 | Name       | Share Size |
+-----------------------------------------+----------------------------------------
+------------+------------+------------+
| 1a411703-baef-495f-8e9c-b60e68f2e657 | 2fe736d1-08ac-46f9-a482-8f224405f2a7 | available
 | mysnapshot | 1          |
+-----------------------------------------+----------------------------------------
+------------+------------+------------+
```

2. Delete a snapshot.

```
$ manila snapshot-delete 1a411703-baef-495f-8e9c-b60e68f2e657xyang@ubuntuManila:~/
devstack$ manila snapshot-list
```

3. List snapshots after deleting.

```
+----+----------+--------+------+------------+
| ID | Share ID | Status | Name | Share Size |
+----+----------+--------+------+------------+
+----+----------+--------+------+------------+
```

The snapshot is deleted.

4.7.9 Extend share

1. Extend share.

```
$ manila extend 2fe736d1-08ac-46f9-a482-8f224405f2a7 2
```

2. Show the share while it is being extended.

```
$ manila show 2fe736d1-08ac-46f9-a482-8f224405f2a7
+------------------+------------------------------------------------------------------+
```

```
| Property           | Value                                                          |
+--------------------+----------------------------------------------------------------+
| status             | extending                                                      |
| description        | My Manila share                                                |
| availability_zone  | nova                                                           |
| share_network_id   | ccd6b453-8b05-4508-bbce-93bfe660451f                           |
| export_locations   | 10.254.0.3:/shares/share-2fe736d1-08ac-46f9-a482-8f224405f2a7 |
| host               | ubuntuManila@generic1#GENERIC1                                 |
| snapshot_id        | None                                                           |
| is_public          | False                                                          |
| id                 | 2fe736d1-08ac-46f9-a482-8f224405f2a7                           |
| size               | 1                                                              |
| name               | myshare                                                        |
| share_type         | default                                                        |
| created_at         | 2015-08-17T21:17:23.000000                                     |
| share_proto        | NFS                                                            |
| project_id         | d80a6323e99f4f22a26ad2accd3ec791                               |
| metadata           | {}                                                             |
+--------------------+----------------------------------------------------------------+
```

3. Show the share after it is extended.

```
$ manila show 2fe736d1-08ac-46f9-a482-8f224405f2a7
+--------------------+----------------------------------------------------------------+
| Property           | Value                                                          |
+--------------------+----------------------------------------------------------------+
| status             | available                                                      |
| description        | My Manila share                                                |
| availability_zone  | nova                                                           |
| share_network_id   | ccd6b453-8b05-4508-bbce-93bfe660451f                           |
| export_locations   | 10.254.0.3:/shares/share-2fe736d1-08ac-46f9-a482-8f224405f2a7 |
| host               | ubuntuManila@generic1#GENERIC1                                 |
| snapshot_id        | None                                                           |
| is_public          | False                                                          |
| id                 | 2fe736d1-08ac-46f9-a482-8f224405f2a7                           |
| size               | 2                                                              |
```

```
| name          | myshare                          |
| share_type    | default                          |
| created_at    | 2015-08-17T21:17:23.000000       |
| share_proto   | NFS                              |
| project_id    | d80a6323e99f4f22a26ad2accd3ec791 |
| metadata      | {}                               |
+---------------+----------------------------------+
```

4.7.10 Shrink share

1. Shrink a share.

```
$ manila shrink 2fe736d1-08ac-46f9-a482-8f224405f2a7 1
```

2. Show the share while it is being shrunk.

```
$ manila show 2fe736d1-08ac-46f9-a482-8f224405f2a7
+-------------------+------------------------------------------------------------+
| Property          | Value                                                      |
+-------------------+------------------------------------------------------------+
| status            | shrinking                                                  |
| description       | My Manila share                                            |
| availability_zone | nova                                                       |
| share_network_id  | ccd6b453-8b05-4508-bbce-93bfe660451f                       |
| export_locations  | 10.254.0.3:/shares/share-2fe736d1-08ac-46f9-a482-8f224405f2a7 |
| host              | ubuntuManila@generic1#GENERIC1                             |
| snapshot_id       | None                                                       |
| is_public         | False                                                      |
| id                | 2fe736d1-08ac-46f9-a482-8f224405f2a7                       |
| size              | 2                                                          |
| name              | myshare                                                    |
| share_type        | default                                                    |
| created_at        | 2015-08-17T21:17:23.000000                                 |
| share_proto       | NFS                                                        |
| project_id        | d80a6323e99f4f22a26ad2accd3ec791                           |
```

```
| metadata         | {}                                                                      |
+------------------+-------------------------------------------------------------------------+
```

3. Show the share after it is being shrunk.

```
$ manila show 2fe736d1-08ac-46f9-a482-8f224405f2a7
+-------------------+-------------------------------------------------------------------+
| Property          | Value                                                             |
+-------------------+-------------------------------------------------------------------+
| status            | available                                                         |
| description       | My Manila share                                                   |
| availability_zone | nova                                                              |
| share_network_id  | ccd6b453-8b05-4508-bbce-93bfe660451f                              |
| export_locations  | 10.254.0.3:/shares/share-2fe736d1-08ac-46f9-a482-8f224405f2a7     |
| host              | ubuntuManila@generic1#GENERIC1                                    |
| snapshot_id       | None                                                              |
| is_public         | False                                                             |
| id                | 2fe736d1-08ac-46f9-a482-8f224405f2a7                              |
| size              | 1                                                                 |
| name              | myshare                                                           |
| share_type        | default                                                           |
| created_at        | 2015-08-17T21:17:23.000000                                        |
| share_proto       | NFS                                                               |
| project_id        | d80a6323e99f4f22a26ad2accd3ec791                                  |
| metadata          | {}                                                                |
+-------------------+-------------------------------------------------------------------+
```

4.8   Configure access and security for instances

When you launch a virtual machine, you can inject a *key pair*, which provides SSH access to your instance. For this to work, the image must contain the `cloud-init` package.

You can create at least one key pair for each project. You can use the key pair for multiple instances that belong to that project. If you generate a key pair with an external tool, you can import it into OpenStack.

Note

A key pair belongs to an individual user, not to a project. To share a key pair across multiple users, each user needs to import that key pair.

If an image uses a static root password or a static key set (neither is recommended), you must not provide a key pair when you launch the instance.

A *security group* is a named collection of network access rules that are use to limit the types of traffic that have access to instances. When you launch an instance, you can assign one or more security groups to it. If you do not create security groups, new instances are automatically assigned to the default security group, unless you explicitly specify a different security group.

The associated *rules* in each security group control the traffic to instances in the group. Any incoming traffic that is not matched by a rule is denied access by default. You can add rules to or remove rules from a security group, and you can modify rules for the default and any other security group.

You can modify the rules in a security group to allow access to instances through different ports and protocols. For example, you can modify rules to allow access to instances through SSH, to ping instances, or to allow UDP traffic; for example, for a DNS server running on an instance. You specify the following parameters for rules:

- **Source of traffic**. Enable traffic to instances from either IP addresses inside the cloud from other group members or from all IP addresses.

- **Protocol**. Choose TCP for SSH, ICMP for pings, or UDP.

- **Destination port on virtual machine**. Define a port range. To open a single port only, enter the same value twice. ICMP does not support ports; instead, you enter values to define the codes and types of ICMP traffic to be allowed.

Rules are automatically enforced as soon as you create or modify them.

 Note

Instances that use the default security group cannot, by default, be accessed from any IP address outside of the cloud. If you want those IP addresses to access the instances, you must modify the rules for the default security group.

You can also assign a floating IP address to a running instance to make it accessible from outside the cloud. See .

4.8.1 Add a key pair

You can generate a key pair or upload an existing public key.

1. To generate a key pair, run the following command.

```
$ nova keypair-add KEY_NAME > MY_KEY.pem
```

This command generates a key pair with the name that you specify for KEY_NAME, writes the private key to the `.pem` file that you specify, and registers the public key to the Nova database.

2. To set the permissions of the `.pem` file so that only you can read and write to it, run the following command.

```
$ chmod 600 MY_KEY.pem
```

4.8.2 Import a key pair

1. If you have already generated a key pair and the public key is located at `~/.ssh/id_rsa.pub`, run the following command to upload the public key.

```
$ nova keypair-add --pub_key ~/.ssh/id_rsa.pub KEY_NAME
```

This command registers the public key at the Nova database and names the key pair the name that you specify for `KEY_NAME`.

2. To ensure that the key pair has been successfully imported, list key pairs as follows:

```
$ nova keypair-list
```

4.8.3 Create and manage security groups

1. To list the security groups for the current project, including descriptions, enter the following command:

   ```
   $ nova secgroup-list
   ```

2. To create a security group with a specified name and description, enter the following command:

   ```
   $ nova secgroup-create SECURITY_GROUP_NAME GROUP_DESCRIPTION
   ```

3. To delete a specified group, enter the following command:

   ```
   $ nova secgroup-delete SECURITY_GROUP_NAME
   ```

 Note

You cannot delete the default security group for a project. Also, you cannot delete a security group that is assigned to a running instance.

4.8.4 Create and manage security group rules

Modify security group rules with the **nova secgroup-*-rule** commands. Before you begin, source the OpenStack RC file. For details, see .

1. To list the rules for a security group, run the following command:

   ```
   $ nova secgroup-list-rules SECURITY_GROUP_NAME
   ```

2. To allow SSH access to the instances, choose one of the following options:

- Allow access from all IP addresses, specified as IP subnet `0.0.0.0/0` in CIDR notation:

```
$ nova secgroup-add-rule SECURITY_GROUP_NAME tcp 22 22 0.0.0.0/0
```

- Allow access only from IP addresses from other security groups (source groups) to access the specified port:

```
$ nova secgroup-add-group-rule --ip_proto tcp --from_port 22 \
    --to_port 22 SECURITY_GROUP_NAME SOURCE_GROUP_NAME
```

3. To allow pinging of the instances, choose one of the following options:

- Allow pinging from all IP addresses, specified as IP subnet `0.0.0.0/0` in CIDR notation.

```
$ nova secgroup-add-rule SECURITY_GROUP_NAME icmp -1 -1 0.0.0.0/0
```

This allows access to all codes and all types of ICMP traffic.

- Allow only members of other security groups (source groups) to ping instances.

```
$ nova secgroup-add-group-rule --ip_proto icmp --from_port -1 \
    --to_port -1 SECURITY_GROUP_NAME SOURCE_GROUP_NAME
```

4. To allow access through a UDP port, such as allowing access to a DNS server that runs on a VM, choose one of the following options:

- Allow UDP access from IP addresses, specified as IP subnet `0.0.0.0/0` in CIDR notation.

```
$ nova secgroup-add-rule SECURITY_GROUP_NAME udp 53 53 0.0.0.0/0
```

- Allow only IP addresses from other security groups (source groups) to access the specified port.

```
$ nova secgroup-add-group-rule --ip_proto udp --from_port 53 \
    --to_port 53 SECURITY_GROUP_NAME SOURCE_GROUP_NAME
```

4.8.5 Delete a security group rule

To delete a security group rule, specify the same arguments that you used to create the rule.

For example, to delete the security group rule that permits SSH access from all IP addresses, run the following command.

```
$ nova secgroup-delete-rule SECURITY_GROUP_NAME tcp 22 22 0.0.0.0/0
```

4.9 Launch instances

Instances are virtual machines that run inside the cloud.

Before you can launch an instance, gather the following parameters:

- The **instance source** can be an image, snapshot, or block storage volume that contains an image or snapshot.

- A **name** for your instance.

- The **flavor** for your instance, which defines the compute, memory, and storage capacity of nova computing instances. A flavor is an available hardware configuration for a server. It defines the size of a virtual server that can be launched.

- Any **user data** files. A user data file is a special key in the metadata service that holds a file that cloud-aware applications in the guest instance can access. For example, one application that uses user data is the cloud-init (https://help.ubuntu.com/community/CloudInit) ↗ system, which is an open-source package from Ubuntu that is available on various Linux distributions and that handles early initialization of a cloud instance.

- Access and security credentials, which include one or both of the following credentials:

- A **key pair** for your instance, which are SSH credentials that are injected into images when they are launched. For the key pair to be successfully injected, the image must contain the `cloud-init` package. Create at least one key pair for each project. If you already have generated a key pair with an external tool, you can import it into OpenStack. You can use the key pair for multiple instances that belong to that project.

- A **security group** that defines which incoming network traffic is forwarded to instances. Security groups hold a set of firewall policies, known as *security group rules*.

- If needed, you can assign a **floating (public) IP address** to a running instance.

- You can also attach a block storage device, or **volume**, for persistent storage.

 Note

Instances that use the default security group cannot, by default, be accessed from any IP address outside of the cloud. If you want those IP addresses to access the instances, you must modify the rules for the default security group.

You can also assign a floating IP address to a running instance to make it accessible from outside the cloud. See .

After you gather the parameters that you need to launch an instance, you can launch it from an *Section 4.9.2, "Launch an instance"* **or a** *Section 4.6, "Manage volumes"*. **You can launch an instance** directly from one of the available OpenStack images or from an image that you have copied to a persistent volume. The OpenStack Image service provides a pool of images that are accessible to members of different projects.

4.9.1 Gather parameters to launch an instance

Before you begin, source the OpenStack RC file.

1. List the available flavors.

   ```
   $ nova flavor-list
   ```

   Note the ID of the flavor that you want to use for your instance:

```
+-----+-----------+-----------+-------+-----------+------+-------+-------------
+-----------+
| ID  | Name      | Memory_MB | Disk  | Ephemeral | Swap | VCPUs | RXTX_Factor | Is_Public
 |
+-----+-----------+-----------+-----------+-------+-----------+------+-------+-------------
+-----------+
| 1   | m1.tiny   | 512       | 1     | 0         |      | 1     | 1.0         | True
 |
```

```
| 2    | m1.small  | 2048    | 20   | 0        |     | 1   | 1.0   | True
|
| 3    | m1.medium | 4096    | 40   | 0        |     | 2   | 1.0   | True
|
| 4    | m1.large  | 8192    | 80   | 0        |     | 4   | 1.0   | True
|
| 5    | m1.xlarge | 16384   | 160  | 0        |     | 8   | 1.0   | True
|
+-----+-----------+---------+------+----------+-----+-----+-------+-------------
+-----------+
```

2. List the available images.

```
$ nova image-list
```

Note the ID of the image from which you want to boot your instance:

```
+--------------------------------------+-----------------------------------+--------
+--------+
| ID                                   | Name                              | Status |
  Server |
+--------------------------------------+-----------------------------------+--------
+--------+
| 397e713c-b95b-4186-ad46-6126863ea0a9 | cirros-0.3.2-x86_64-uec           | ACTIVE |
  |
| df430cc2-3406-4061-b635-a51c16e488ac | cirros-0.3.2-x86_64-uec-kernel    | ACTIVE |
  |
| 3cf852bd-2332-48f4-9ae4-7d926d50945e | cirros-0.3.2-x86_64-uec-ramdisk   | ACTIVE |
  |
+--------------------------------------+-----------------------------------+--------
+--------+
```

You can also filter the image list by using **grep** to find a specific image, as follows:

```
$ nova image-list | grep 'kernel'
```

```
| df430cc2-3406-4061-b635-a51c16e488ac | cirros-0.3.2-x86_64-uec-kernel | ACTIVE |
|
```

3. List the available security groups.

```
$ nova secgroup-list --all-tenants
```

 Note

If you are an admin user, specify the `--all-tenants` parameter to list groups for all tenants.

Note the ID of the security group that you want to use for your instance:

```
+----+---------+-------------+----------------------------------+
| Id | Name    | Description | Tenant_ID                        |
+----+---------+-------------+----------------------------------+
| 2  | default | default     | 66265572db174a7aa66eba661f58eb9e |
| 1  | default | default     | b70d90d65e464582b6b2161cf3603ced |
+----+---------+-------------+----------------------------------+
```

If you have not created any security groups, you can assign the instance to only the default security group.
You can view rules for a specified security group:

```
$ nova secgroup-list-rules default
```

4. List the available key pairs, and note the key pair name that you use for SSH access.

```
$ nova keypair-list
```

4.9.2 Launch an instance

You can launch an instance from various sources.

4.9.2.1 Launch an instance from an image

Follow the steps below to launch an instance from an image.

1. After you gather required parameters, run the following command to launch an instance. Specify the server name, flavor ID, and image ID.

```
$ nova boot --flavor FLAVOR_ID --image IMAGE_ID --key-name KEY_NAME \
  --user-data USER_DATA_FILE --security-groups SEC_GROUP_NAME --meta KEY=VALUE
  \
  INSTANCE_NAME
```

   Optionally, you can provide a key name for access control and a security group for security. You can also include metadata key and value pairs. For example, you can add a description for your server by providing the `--meta description="My Server"` parameter.
   You can pass user data in a local file at instance launch by using the `--user-data USER-DATA-FILE` parameter.

    Important

   > If you boot an instance with an INSTANCE_NAME greater than 63 characters, Compute truncates it automatically when turning it into a host name to ensure the correct work of dnsmasq. The corresponding warning is written into the `nova-network.log` file.

   The following command launches the `MyCirrosServer` instance with the `m1.small` flavor (ID of `1`), `cirros-0.3.2-x86_64-uec` image (ID of `397e713c-b95b-4186-ad46-6126863ea0a9`), `default` security group, `KeyPair01` key, and a user data file called `cloudinit.file`:

```
$ nova boot --flavor 1 --image 397e713c-b95b-4186-ad46-6126863ea0a9 \
  --security-groups default --key-name KeyPair01 --user-data cloudinit.file \
  myCirrosServer
```

   Depending on the parameters that you provide, the command returns a list of server properties.

```
+----------------------------------+------------------------------------------+
| Property                         | Value                                    |
+----------------------------------+------------------------------------------+
| OS-EXT-STS:task_state            | scheduling                               |
| image                            | cirros-0.3.2-x86_64-uec                  |
| OS-EXT-STS:vm_state              | building                                 |
| OS-EXT-SRV-ATTR:instance_name    | instance-00000002                        |
| flavor                           | m1.small                                 |
| id                               | b3cdc6c0-85a7-4904-ae85-71918f734048     |
| security_groups                  | [{u'name': u'default'}]                   |
| user_id                          | 376744b5910b4b4da7d8e6cb483b06a8         |
| OS-DCF:diskConfig                | MANUAL                                   |
| accessIPv4                       |                                          |
| accessIPv6                       |                                          |
| progress                         | 0                                        |
| OS-EXT-STS:power_state           | 0                                        |
| OS-EXT-AZ:availability_zone      | nova                                     |
| config_drive                     |                                          |
| status                           | BUILD                                    |
| updated                          | 2013-07-16T16:25:34Z                     |
| hostId                           |                                          |
| OS-EXT-SRV-ATTR:host             | None                                     |
| key_name                         | KeyPair01                                |
| OS-EXT-SRV-ATTR:hypervisor_hostname | None                                  |
| name                             | myCirrosServer                           |
| adminPass                        | tVs5pL8HcPGw                             |
| tenant_id                        | 66265572db174a7aa66eba661f58eb9e         |
| created                          | 2013-07-16T16:25:34Z                     |
| metadata                         | {u'KEY': u'VALUE'}                        |
+----------------------------------+------------------------------------------+
```

A status of BUILD indicates that the instance has started, but is not yet online.
A status of ACTIVE indicates that the instance is active.

2. Copy the server ID value from the id field in the output. Use the ID to get server details or to delete your server.

3. Copy the administrative password value from the `adminPass` field. Use the password to log in to your server.

 Note

> You can also place arbitrary local files into the instance file system at creation time by using the `--file <dst-path=src-path>` option. You can store up to five files. For example, if you have a special authorized keys file named `special_authorized_keysfile` that you want to put on the instance rather than using the regular SSH key injection, you can use the `--file` option as shown in the following example.

```
$ nova boot --image ubuntu-cloudimage --flavor 1 vm-name \
  --file /root/.ssh/authorized_keys=special_authorized_keysfile
```

4. Check if the instance is online.

```
$ nova list
```

The list shows the ID, name, status, and private (and if assigned, public) IP addresses for all instances in the project to which you belong:

```
+-------------+----------------------+--------+------------+-------------
+------------------+
| ID          | Name                 | Status | Task State | Power State | Networks
  |
+-------------+----------------------+--------+------------+-------------
+------------------+
| 84c6e57d... | myCirrosServer       | ACTIVE | None       | Running     |
 private=10.0.0.3 |
| 8a99547e... | myInstanceFromVolume | ACTIVE | None       | Running     |
 private=10.0.0.4 |
+-------------+----------------------+--------+------------+-------------
+------------------+
```

If the status for the instance is ACTIVE, the instance is online.

5. To view the available options for the **`nova list`** command, run the following command:

```
$ nova help list
```

 Note

> If you did not provide a key pair, security groups, or rules, you can access the instance only from inside the cloud through VNC. Even pinging the instance is not possible.

4.9.2.2 Launch an instance from a volume

You can boot instances from a volume instead of an image.

To complete these tasks, use these parameters on the **`nova boot`** command:

TABLE 4.4: NOVA BOOT

Task	nova boot parameter	Information
Boot an instance from an image and attach a non-bootable volume.	`--block-device`	*Section 4.9.2.2.1, "Boot instance from image and attach non-bootable volume"*
Create a volume from an image and boot an instance from that volume.	`--block-device`	*Section 4.9.2.2.2, "Create volume from image and boot instance"*
Boot from an existing source image, volume, or snapshot.	`--block-device`	*Section 4.9.2.2.2, "Create volume from image and boot instance"*
Attach a swap disk to an instance.	`--swap`	*Section 4.9.2.2.3, "Attach swap or ephemeral disk to an instance"*
Attach an ephemeral disk to an instance.	`--ephemeral`	*Section 4.9.2.2.3, "Attach swap or ephemeral disk to an instance"*

 Note

To attach a volume to a running instance, see *Section 4.6.3, "Attach a volume to an instance"*.

4.9.2.2.1 Boot instance from image and attach non-bootable volume

Create a non-bootable volume and attach that volume to an instance that you boot from an image.

To create a non-bootable volume, do not create it from an image. The volume must be entirely empty with no partition table and no file system.

1. Create a non-bootable volume.

```
$ cinder create --display-name my-volume 8
+--------------------------------+--------------------------------------+
|            Property            |                Value                 |
+--------------------------------+--------------------------------------+
|           attachments          |                 []                   |
|         availability_zone      |                nova                  |
|            bootable            |                false                 |
|            created_at          |       2014-05-09T16:33:11.000000     |
|           description          |                None                  |
|            encrypted           |                False                 |
|               id               | d620d971-b160-4c4e-8652-2513d74e2080 |
|            metadata            |                 {}                   |
|              name              |              my-volume               |
|       os-vol-host-attr:host    |                None                  |
| os-vol-mig-status-attr:migstat |                None                  |
| os-vol-mig-status-attr:name_id |                None                  |
|   os-vol-tenant-attr:tenant_id |    ccef9e62b1e645df98728fb2b3076f27  |
|              size              |                 8                    |
|           snapshot_id          |                None                  |
|           source_volid         |                None                  |
|             status             |              creating                |
|             user_id            |    fef060ae7bfd4024b3edb97dff59017a  |
|           volume_type          |                None                  |
+--------------------------------+--------------------------------------+
```

2. List volumes.

```
$ cinder list
```

```
+------------------+-----------+-----------+------+-------------+----------+-------------+
|       ID         |  Status   |   Name    | Size | Volume Type | Bootable | Attached to |
+------------------+-----------+-----------+------+-------------+----------+-------------+
| d620d971-b16...  | available | my-volume | 8    |    None     |  false   |             |
+------------------+-----------+-----------+------+-------------+----------+-------------+
```

3. Boot an instance from an image and attach the empty volume to the instance.

```
$ nova boot --flavor 2 --image 98901246-af91-43d8-b5e6-a4506aa8f369 \
  --block-device source=volume,id=d620d971-
b160-4c4e-8652-2513d74e2080,dest=volume,shutdown=preserve \
  myInstanceWithVolume

+-------------------------------------+-----------------------------------------------+
| Property                            | Value                                         |
+-------------------------------------+-----------------------------------------------+
| OS-DCF:diskConfig                   | MANUAL                                        |
| OS-EXT-AZ:availability_zone         | nova                                          |
| OS-EXT-SRV-ATTR:host                | -                                             |
| OS-EXT-SRV-ATTR:hypervisor_hostname | -                                             |
| OS-EXT-SRV-ATTR:instance_name       | instance-00000004                             |
| OS-EXT-STS:power_state              | 0                                             |
| OS-EXT-STS:task_state               | scheduling                                    |
| OS-EXT-STS:vm_state                 | building                                      |
| OS-SRV-USG:launched_at              | -                                             |
| OS-SRV-USG:terminated_at            | -                                             |
| accessIPv4                          |                                               |
| accessIPv6                          |                                               |
| adminPass                           | ZaiYeC8iucgU                                  |
| config_drive                        |                                               |
| created                             | 2014-05-09T16:34:50Z                          |
| flavor                              | m1.small (2)                                  |
| hostId                              |                                               |
| id                                  | 1e1797f3-1662-49ff-ae8c-a77e82ee1571          |
| image                               | cirros-0.3.1-x86_64-uec (98901246-af91-... |
| key_name                            | -                                             |
| metadata                            | {}                                            |
```

```
| name                                 | myInstanceWithVolume                  |
| os-extended-volumes:volumes_attached | [{"id": "d620d971-b160-4c4e-8652-2513d7... |
| progress                             | 0                                     |
| security_groups                      | default                               |
| status                               | BUILD                                 |
| tenant_id                            | ccef9e62b1e645df98728fb2b3076f27      |
| updated                              | 2014-05-09T16:34:51Z                  |
| user_id                              | fef060ae7bfd4024b3edb97dff59017a      |
+--------------------------------------+---------------------------------------+
```

4.9.2.2.2 Create volume from image and boot instance

You can create a volume from an existing image, volume, or snapshot. This procedure shows you how to create a volume from an image, and use the volume to boot an instance.

1. List the available images.

```
$ nova image-list
+----------------+------------------------------------+--------+--------+
| ID             | Name                               | Status | Server |
+----------------+------------------------------------+--------+--------+
| 484e05af-a14... | Fedora-x86_64-20-20131211.1-sda   | ACTIVE |        |
| 98901246-af9... | cirros-0.3.1-x86_64-uec           | ACTIVE |        |
| b6e95589-7eb... | cirros-0.3.1-x86_64-uec-kernel    | ACTIVE |        |
| c90893ea-e73... | cirros-0.3.1-x86_64-uec-ramdisk   | ACTIVE |        |
+----------------+------------------------------------+--------+--------+
```

Note the ID of the image that you want to use to create a volume.

2. List the available flavors.

```
$ nova flavor-list
+-----+-----------+----------+------+-----------+------+-------+-------------
+-----------+
| ID  | Name      | Memory_MB | Disk | Ephemeral | Swap | VCPUs | RXTX_Factor | Is_Public
|
```

```
+-----+-----------+----------+------+-----------+------+-------+-------------
+-----------+
| 1   | m1.tiny   | 512      | 1    | 0         |      | 1     | 1.0         | True
|
| 2   | m1.small  | 2048     | 20   | 0         |      | 1     | 1.0         | True
|
| 3   | m1.medium | 4096     | 40   | 0         |      | 2     | 1.0         | True
|
| 4   | m1.large  | 8192     | 80   | 0         |      | 4     | 1.0         | True
|
| 5   | m1.xlarge | 16384    | 160  | 0         |      | 8     | 1.0         | True
|
+-----+-----------+----------+------+-----------+------+-------+-------------
+-----------+
```

Note the ID of the flavor that you want to use to create a volume.

3. To create a bootable volume from an image and launch an instance from this volume, use the `--block-device` parameter.
For example:

```
$ nova boot --flavor FLAVOR --block-device \
  source=SOURCE,id=ID,dest=DEST,size=SIZE,shutdown=PRESERVE,bootindex=INDEX \
  NAME
```

The parameters are:

- `--flavor` FLAVOR. The flavor ID or name.

- `--block-device`
  source = SOURCE,id = ID,dest = DEST,size = SIZE,shutdown = PRESERVE,bootindex = INDEX

  source=SOURCE

  The type of object used to create the block device. Valid values are `volume`, `snapshot`, `image`, and `blank`.

  id=ID

  The ID of the source object.

dest=DEST

> The type of the target virtual device. Valid values are `volume` and `local`.

size=SIZE

> The size of the volume that is created.

shutdown={preserve|remove}

> What to do with the volume when the instance is deleted. `preserve` does not delete the volume. `remove` deletes the volume.

bootindex=INDEX

> Orders the boot disks. Use `0` to boot from this volume.

- `NAME`. The name for the server.

4. Create a bootable volume from an image, before the instance boots. The volume is not deleted when the instance is terminated.

```
$ nova boot --flavor 2 \
  --block-device source=image,id=484e05af-
a14d-4567-812b-28122d1c2260,dest=volume,size=10,shutdown=preserve,bootindex=0 \
  myInstanceFromVolume
+------------------------------------+------------------------------+
| Property                           | Value                        |
+------------------------------------+------------------------------+
| OS-EXT-STS:task_state              | scheduling                   |
| image                              | Attempt to boot from volume  |
|                                    | - no image supplied          |
| OS-EXT-STS:vm_state                | building                     |
| OS-EXT-SRV-ATTR:instance_name      | instance-00000003            |
| OS-SRV-USG:launched_at             | None                         |
| flavor                             | m1.small                     |
| id                                 | 2e65c854-dba9-4f68-8f08-fe3... |
| security_groups                    | [{u'name': u'default'}]      |
| user_id                            | 352b37f5c89144d4ad053413926... |
| OS-DCF:diskConfig                  | MANUAL                       |
| accessIPv4                         |                              |
| accessIPv6                         |                              |
```

```
| progress                                 | 0                            |
| OS-EXT-STS:power_state                    | 0                            |
| OS-EXT-AZ:availability_zone               | nova                         |
| config_drive                             |                              |
| status                                   | BUILD                        |
| updated                                  | 2014-02-02T13:29:54Z         |
| hostId                                   |                              |
| OS-EXT-SRV-ATTR:host                      | None                         |
| OS-SRV-USG:terminated_at                  | None                         |
| key_name                                 | None                         |
| OS-EXT-SRV-ATTR:hypervisor_hostname       | None                         |
| name                                     | myInstanceFromVolume         |
| adminPass                                | TzjqyGsRcJo9                 |
| tenant_id                                | f7ac731cc11f40efbc03a9f9e1d... |
| created                                  | 2014-02-02T13:29:53Z         |
| os-extended-volumes:volumes_attached     | []                           |
| metadata                                 | {}                           |
+------------------------------------------+------------------------------+
```

5. List volumes to see the bootable volume and its attached `myInstanceFromVolume` instance.

```
$ cinder list
+-------------+--------+--------------+------+-------------+----------+-------------+
|     ID      | Status | Display Name | Size | Volume Type | Bootable | Attached to |
+-------------+--------+--------------+------+-------------+----------+-------------+
| 2fff50ab... | in-use |              |  10  |    None     |   true   | 2e65c854... |
+-------------+--------+--------------+------+-------------+----------+-------------+
```

4.9.2.2.3 Attach swap or ephemeral disk to an instance

Use the nova `boot --swap` parameter to attach a swap disk on boot or the nova `boot --ephemeral` parameter to attach an ephemeral disk on boot. When you terminate the instance, both disks are deleted.

Boot an instance with a 512 MB swap disk and 2 GB ephemeral disk.

```
$ nova boot --flavor FLAVOR --image IMAGE_ID --swap 512 --ephemeral size=2 NAME
```

 Note

The flavor defines the maximum swap and ephemeral disk size. You cannot exceed these maximum values.

4.9.2.3 Launch an instance using ISO image

4.9.2.3.1 Boot an instance from an ISO image

OpenStack supports booting instances using ISO images. But before you make such instances functional, use the **nova boot** command with the following parameters to boot an instance.

```
$ nova boot \
    --image ubuntu-14.04.2-server-amd64.iso \
    --block-device source=blank,dest=volume,size=10,shutdown=preserve \
    --nic net-id = NETWORK_UUID \
    --flavor 2 INSTANCE_NAME
+-----------------------------------+-------------------------------------------+
| Property                          | Value                                     |
+-----------------------------------+-------------------------------------------+
| OS-DCF:diskConfig                 | MANUAL                                    |
| OS-EXT-AZ:availability_zone       | nova                                      |
| OS-EXT-SRV-ATTR:host              | -                                         |
| OS-EXT-SRV-ATTR:hypervisor_hostname | -                                       |
| OS-EXT-SRV-ATTR:instance_name     | instance-00000004                         |
| OS-EXT-STS:power_state            | 0                                         |
| OS-EXT-STS:task_state             | scheduling                                |
| OS-EXT-STS:vm_state               | building                                  |
| OS-SRV-USG:launched_at            | -                                         |
| OS-SRV-USG:terminated_at          | -                                         |
| accessIPv4                        |                                           |
| accessIPv6                        |                                           |
```

```
| adminPass                             | ZaiYeC8iucgU                         |
| config_drive                          |                                      |
| created                               | 2015-06-01T16:34:50Z                 |
| flavor                                | m1.small (2)                         |
| hostId                                |                                      |
| id                                    | 1e1797f3-1662-49ff-ae8c-a77e82ee1571 |
| image                                 | ubuntu-14.04.2-server-amd64.iso      |
| key_name                              | -                                    |
| metadata                              | {}                                   |
| name                                  | INSTANCE_NAME                        |
| os-extended-volumes:volumes_attached  | []                                   |
| progress                              | 0                                    |
| security_groups                       | default                              |
| status                                | BUILD                                |
| tenant_id                             | ccef9e62b1e645df98728fb2b3076f27     |
| updated                               | 2014-05-09T16:34:51Z                 |
| user_id                               | fef060ae7bfd4024b3edb97dff59017a     |
+---------------------------------------+--------------------------------------+
```

In this command, `ubuntu-14.04.2-server-amd64.iso` is the ISO image, and `INSTANCE_NAME` is the name of the new instance. `NETWORK_UUID` is a valid network id in your system.

 Note

You need the Block Storage service, and the parameter `shutdown=preserve` is also mandatory, thus the volume will be preserved after the shutdown of the instance.

After the instance is successfully launched, connect to the instance using a remote console and follow the instructions to install the system as using ISO images on regular computers. When the installation is finished and system is rebooted, the instance asks you again to install the operating system, which means your instance is not usable. If you have problems with image creation, check the Virtual Machine Image Guide (http://docs.openstack.org/image-guide/create-images-manually.html) ↗ for reference.

4.9.2.3.2 Make the instances booted from ISO image functional

Now complete the following steps to make your instances created using ISO image actually functional.

1. Delete the instance using the following command.

```
$ nova delete INSTANCE_NAME
```

2. After you delete the instance, the system you have just installed using your ISO image remains, because the parameter `shutdown=preserve` was set, so run the following command.

```
$ cinder list
+----------------+----------+------------+------+-------------+----------
+------------+
|       ID       |  Status  |    Name    | Size | Volume Type | Bootable | Attached
 to |
+----------------+----------+------------+------+-------------+----------
+------------+
| d620d971-b16... | available | 655ef3e4-... |  8  |    None     |  false  |
    |
+----------------+----------+------------+------+-------------+----------
+------------+
```

You get a list with all the volumes in your system. In this list, you can find the volume that is attached to your ISO created instance, with the false bootable property.

3. Upload the volume to glance.

```
$ cinder upload-to-image VOLUME_UUID IMAGE_NAME
$ glance image-list
+------------------+------------+-------------+------------------+------------+--------+
| ID               | Name       | Disk Format | Container Format | Size       | Status |
+------------------+------------+-------------+------------------+------------+--------+
| 74303284-f802-... | IMAGE_NAME | iso         | bare             | 764321792  | active |
+------------------+------------+-------------+------------------+------------+--------+
```

The `VOLUME_UUID` is the uuid of the volume that is attached to your ISO created instance, and the `IMAGE_NAME` is the name that you give to your new image.

4. After the image is successfully uploaded, you can use the new image to boot instances. The instances launched using this image contain the system that you have just installed using the ISO image.

4.10   Manage instances and hosts

Instances are virtual machines that run inside the cloud on physical compute nodes. The Compute service manages instances. A host is the node on which a group of instances resides.

This section describes how to perform the different tasks involved in instance management, such as adding floating IP addresses, stopping and starting instances, and terminating instances. This section also discusses node management tasks.

4.10.1   Manage IP addresses

Each instance has a private, fixed IP address and can also have a public, or floating IP address. Private IP addresses are used for communication between instances, and public addresses are used for communication with networks outside the cloud, including the Internet.

When you launch an instance, it is automatically assigned a private IP address that stays the same until you explicitly terminate the instance. Rebooting an instance has no effect on the private IP address.

A pool of floating IP addresses, configured by the cloud administrator, is available in OpenStack Compute. The project quota defines the maximum number of floating IP addresses that you can allocate to the project. After you allocate a floating IP address to a project, you can:

- Associate the floating IP address with an instance of the project. Only one floating IP address can be allocated to an instance at any given time.

- Disassociate a floating IP address from an instance in the project.

- Delete a floating IP from the project which automatically deletes that IP's associations.

Use the `nova floating-ip-*` commands to manage floating IP addresses.

4.10.1.1 List floating IP address information

To list all pools that provide floating IP addresses, run:

```
$ nova floating-ip-pool-list
+--------+
| name   |
+--------+
| public |
| test   |
+--------+
```

 Note

> If this list is empty, the cloud administrator must configure a pool of floating IP addresses.

To list all floating IP addresses that are allocated to the current project, run:

```
$ nova floating-ip-list
+--------------+-------------------------------------------+----------+--------+
| Ip           | Instance Id                               | Fixed Ip | Pool   |
+--------------+-------------------------------------------+----------+--------+
| 172.24.4.225 | 4a60ff6a-7a3c-49d7-9515-86ae501044c6      | 10.0.0.2 | public |
| 172.24.4.226 | None                                      | None     | public |
+--------------+-------------------------------------------+----------+--------+
```

For each floating IP address that is allocated to the current project, the command outputs the floating IP address, the ID for the instance to which the floating IP address is assigned, the associated fixed IP address, and the pool from which the floating IP address was allocated.

4.10.1.2 Associate floating IP addresses

You can assign a floating IP address to a project and to an instance.

1. Run the following command to allocate a floating IP address to the current project. By default, the floating IP address is allocated from the public pool. The command outputs the allocated IP address:

```
$ nova floating-ip-create
+--------------+-------------+----------+---------+
| IP           | Instance Id | Fixed IP | Pool    |
+--------------+-------------+----------+---------+
| 172.24.4.225 | None        | None     | public  |
+--------------+-------------+----------+---------+
```

 Note

> If more than one IP address pool is available, you can specify from which pool to allocate the IP address, using the pool's name. For example, to allocate a floating IP address from the `test` pool, run:
>
> ```
> $ nova floating-ip-create test
> ```

2. List all project instances with which a floating IP address could be associated.

```
$ nova list
+----------------------+------+---------+------------+-------------+------------------+
| ID                   | Name | Status  | Task State | Power State | Networks         |
+----------------------+------+---------+------------+-------------+------------------+
| d5c854f9-d3e5-4f...  | VM1  | ACTIVE  | -          | Running     | private=10.0.0.3 |
| 42290b01-0968-43...  | VM2  | SHUTOFF | -          | Shutdown    | private=10.0.0.4 |
+----------------------+------+---------+------------+-------------+------------------+
```

3. Associate an IP address with an instance in the project, as follows:

```
$ nova floating-ip-associate INSTANCE_NAME_OR_ID FLOATING_IP_ADDRESS
```

For example:

```
$ nova floating-ip-associate VM1 172.24.4.225
```

The instance is now associated with two IP addresses:

```
$ nova list
+------------------+------+--------+------------+-------------
+-----------------------------+
| ID               | Name | Status | Task State | Power State | Networks
     |
+------------------+------+--------+------------+-------------
+-----------------------------+
| d5c854f9-d3e5... | VM1  | ACTIVE | -          | Running     | private=10.0.0.3,
 172.24.4.225|
| 42290b01-0968... | VM2  | SHUTOFF| -          | Shutdown    | private=10.0.0.4
     |
+------------------+------+--------+------------+-------------
+-----------------------------+
```

After you associate the IP address and configure security group rules for the instance, the instance is publicly available at the floating IP address.

 Note

If an instance is connected to multiple networks, you can associate a floating IP address with a specific fixed IP address using the optional `--fixed-address` parameter:

```
$ nova floating-ip-associate --fixed-address FIXED_IP_ADDRESS \
    INSTANCE_NAME_OR_ID FLOATING_IP_ADDRESS
```

4.10.1.3 Disassociate floating IP addresses

To disassociate a floating IP address from an instance:

```
$ nova floating-ip-disassociate INSTANCE_NAME_OR_ID FLOATING_IP_ADDRESS
```

To remove the floating IP address from a project:

```
$ nova floating-ip-delete FLOATING_IP_ADDRESS
```

The IP address is returned to the pool of IP addresses that is available for all projects. If the IP address is still associated with a running instance, it is automatically disassociated from that instance.

4.10.2 Change the size of your server

Change the size of a server by changing its flavor.

1. Show information about your server, including its size, which is shown as the value of the flavor property:

```
$ nova show myCirrosServer
+------------------------------------+------------------------------------+
| Property                           | Value                              |
+------------------------------------+------------------------------------+
| status                             | ACTIVE                             |
| updated                            | 2013-07-18T15:08:20Z               |
| OS-EXT-STS:task_state              | None                               |
| OS-EXT-SRV-ATTR:host               | devstack                           |
| key_name                           | None                               |
| image                              | cirros-0.3.2-x86_64-uec (397e71... |
| private network                    | 10.0.0.3                           |
| hostId                             | 6e1e69b71ac9b1e6871f91e2dfc9a9b9...|
| OS-EXT-STS:vm_state                | active                             |
| OS-EXT-SRV-ATTR:instance_name      | instance-00000005                  |
| OS-EXT-SRV-ATTR:hypervisor_hostname| devstack                           |
| flavor                             | m1.small (2)                       |
| id                                 | 84c6e57d-a6b1-44b6-81eb-fcb36afd31b5|
| security_groups                    | [{u'name': u'default'}]            |
| user_id                            | 376744b5910b4b4da7d8e6cb483b06a8   |
| name                               | myCirrosServer                     |
| created                            | 2013-07-18T15:07:59Z               |
```

```
| tenant_id                   | 66265572db174a7aa66eba661f58eb9e  |
| OS-DCF:diskConfig           | MANUAL                            |
| metadata                    | {u'description': u'Small test ima...|
| accessIPv4                  |                                   |
| accessIPv6                  |                                   |
| progress                    | 0                                 |
| OS-EXT-STS:power_state      | 1                                 |
| OS-EXT-AZ:availability_zone | nova                              |
| config_drive                |                                   |
+-------------------------------------+-------------------------------------------+
```

The size (flavor) of the server is `m1.small (2)`.

2. List the available flavors with the following command:

```
$ nova flavor-list
+-----+-----------+-----------+------+-----------+------+-------+--------------+-----------
+
| ID  | Name      | Memory_MB | Disk | Ephemeral | Swap | VCPUs | RXTX_Factor |
  Is_Public|
+-----+-----------+-----------+------+-----------+------+-------+--------------+-----------
+
| 1   | m1.tiny   | 512       | 1    | 0         |      | 1     | 1.0         | True
  |
| 2   | m1.small  | 2048      | 20   | 0         |      | 1     | 1.0         | True
  |
| 3   | m1.medium | 4096      | 40   | 0         |      | 2     | 1.0         | True
  |
| 4   | m1.large  | 8192      | 80   | 0         |      | 4     | 1.0         | True
  |
| 5   | m1.xlarge | 16384     | 160  | 0         |      | 8     | 1.0         | True
  |
+-----+-----------+-----------+------+-----------+------+-------+--------------+-----------
+
```

3. To resize the server, use the **nova resize** command and add the server ID or name and the new flavor. Include the `--poll` parameter to display the resize progress. For example:

```
$ nova resize myCirrosServer 4 --poll


Instance resizing... 100% complete
Finished
```

 Note

> By default, the **nova resize** command gives the guest operating system a chance to perform a controlled shutdown before the instance is powered off and the instance is resized. The shutdown behavior is configured by the `shutdown_timeout` parameter that can be set in the `nova.conf` file. Its value stands for the overall period (in seconds) a guest operation system is allowed to complete the shutdown. The default timeout is 60 seconds. See Description of Compute configuration options (http://docs.openstack.org/liberty/config-reference/content/list-of-compute-config-options.html) ↗ for details.
>
> The timeout value can be overridden on a per image basis by means of `os_shutdown_timeout` that is an image metadata setting allowing different types of operating systems to specify how much time they need to shut down cleanly.

4. Show the status for your server.

```
$ nova list
+----------------------+----------------+--------
+----------------------------------------+
| ID                   | Name           | Status | Networks
   |
+----------------------+----------------+--------
+----------------------------------------+
| 84c6e57d-a6b1-44b... | myCirrosServer | RESIZE | private=172.16.101.6,
  public=10.4.113.6 |
+----------------------+----------------+--------
+----------------------------------------+
```

When the resize completes, the status becomes VERIFY_RESIZE.

5. Confirm the resize,for example:

```
$ nova resize-confirm 84c6e57d-a6b1-44b6-81eb-fcb36afd31b5
```

The server status becomes ACTIVE.

6. If the resize fails or does not work as expected, you can revert the resize. For example:

```
$ nova resize-revert 84c6e57d-a6b1-44b6-81eb-fcb36afd31b5
```

The server status becomes ACTIVE.

4.10.3   Stop and start an instance

Use one of the following methods to stop and start an instance.

4.10.3.1   Pause and unpause an instance

To pause an instance, run the following command:

```
$ nova pause INSTANCE_NAME
```

This command stores the state of the VM in RAM. A paused instance continues to run in a frozen state.

To unpause an instance, run the following command:

```
$ nova unpause INSTANCE_NAME
```

4.10.3.2   Suspend and resume an instance

To initiate a hypervisor-level suspend operation, run the following command:

```
$ nova suspend INSTANCE_NAME
```

To resume a suspended instance, run the following command:

```
$ nova resume INSTANCE_NAME
```

4.10.3.3 Shelve and unshelve an instance

Shelving is useful if you have an instance that you are not using, but would like retain in your list of servers. For example, you can stop an instance at the end of a work week, and resume work again at the start of the next week. All associated data and resources are kept; however, anything still in memory is not retained. If a shelved instance is no longer needed, it can also be entirely removed.

You can run the following shelving tasks:

- Shelve an instance - Shuts down the instance, and stores it together with associated data and resources (a snapshot is taken if not volume backed). Anything in memory is lost.

```
$ nova shelve SERVERNAME
```

 Note

By default, the **nova shelve** command gives the guest operating system a chance to perform a controlled shutdown before the instance is powered off. The shutdown behavior is configured by the `shutdown_timeout` parameter that can be set in the `nova.conf` file. Its value stands for the overall period (in seconds) a guest operation system is allowed to complete the shutdown. The default timeout is 60 seconds. See Description of Compute configuration options (http://docs.openstack.org/liberty/config-reference/content/list-of-compute-config-options.html) ↗ for details.

The timeout value can be overridden on a per image basis by means of `os_shutdown_timeout` that is an image metadata setting allowing different types of operating systems to specify how much time they need to shut down cleanly.

- Unshelve an instance - Restores the instance.

```
$ nova unshelve SERVERNAME
```

- Remove a shelved instance - Removes the instance from the server; data and resource associations are deleted. If an instance is no longer needed, you can move the instance off the hypervisor in order to minimize resource usage.

```
$ nova shelve-offload SERVERNAME
```

4.10.4 Search for an instance using IP address

You can search for an instance using the IP address parameter, `--ip`, with the **nova list** command.

```
$ nova list --ip IP_ADDRESS
```

The following example shows the results of a search on `10.0.0.4`.

```
$ nova list --ip 10.0.0.4
+-----------------+-----------------------+--------+------------+-------------
+-----------------+
| ID              | Name                  | Status | Task State | Power State | Networks
     |
+-----------------+-----------------------+--------+------------+-------------
+-----------------+
| 8a99547e-7385... | myInstanceFromVolume  | ACTIVE | None       | Running     |
 private=10.0.0.4 |
+-----------------+-----------------------+--------+------------+-------------
+-----------------+
```

4.10.5 Reboot an instance

You can soft or hard reboot a running instance. A soft reboot attempts a graceful shut down and restart of the instance. A hard reboot power cycles the instance.

By default, when you reboot an instance, it is a soft reboot.

```
$ nova reboot SERVER
```

To perform a hard reboot, pass the `--hard` parameter, as follows:

```
$ nova reboot --hard SERVER
```

It is also possible to reboot a running instance into rescue mode. For example, this operation may be required, if a filesystem of an instance becomes corrupted with prolonged use.

Note

Pause, suspend, and stop operations are not allowed when an instance is running in rescue mode, as triggering these actions causes the loss of the original instance state, and makes it impossible to unrescue the instance.

Rescue mode provides a mechanism for access, even if an image renders the instance inaccessible. By default, it starts an instance from the initial image attaching the current boot disk as a secondary one.

To perform an instance reboot into rescue mode, run the following command:

```
$ nova rescue SERVER
```

 Note

On running the **nova rescue** command, an instance performs a soft shutdown first. This means that the guest operating system has a chance to perform a controlled shutdown before the instance is powered off. The shutdown behavior is configured by the `shutdown_timeout` parameter that can be set in the `nova.conf` file. Its value stands for the overall period (in seconds) a guest operation system is allowed to complete the shutdown. The default timeout is 60 seconds. See Description of Compute configuration options (http://docs.openstack.org/liberty/config-reference/content/list-of-compute-config-options.html) ↗ for details.

The timeout value can be overridden on a per image basis by means of `os_shutdown_timeout` that is an image metadata setting allowing different types of operating systems to specify how much time they need to shut down cleanly.

To restart the instance from the normal boot disk, run the following command:

```
$ nova unrescue SERVER
```

If you want to rescue an instance with a specific image, rather than the default one, use the --rescue_image_ref parameter:

```
$ nova rescue --rescue_image_ref IMAGE_ID SERVER
```

4.10.6   Delete an instance

When you no longer need an instance, you can delete it.

1. List all instances:

```
$ nova list
+-------------+----------------------+--------+------------+-------------
+-----------------+
| ID          | Name                 | Status | Task State | Power State | Networks
   |
+-------------+----------------------+--------+------------+-------------
+-----------------+
| 84c6e57d... | myCirrosServer       | ACTIVE | None       | Running     |
 private=10.0.0.3 |
| 8a99547e... | myInstanceFromVolume | ACTIVE | None       | Running     |
 private=10.0.0.4 |
| d7efd3e4... | newServer            | ERROR  | None       | NOSTATE     |
   |
+-------------+----------------------+--------+------------+-------------
+-----------------+
```

2. Run the **nova delete** command to delete the instance. The following example shows deletion of the newServer instance, which is in ERROR state:

```
$ nova delete newServer
```

The command does not notify that your server was deleted.

3. To verify that the server was deleted, run the **nova list** command:

```
$ nova list
+-------------+----------------------+--------+------------+-------------
+-----------------+
| ID          | Name                 | Status | Task State | Power State | Networks
   |
+-------------+----------------------+--------+------------+-------------
+-----------------+
```

```
| 84c6e57d... | myCirrosServer       | ACTIVE | None        | Running     |
private=10.0.0.3 |
| 8a99547e... | myInstanceFromVolume | ACTIVE | None        | Running     |
private=10.0.0.4 |
+-------------+----------------------+--------+-------------+-------------
+-----------------+
```

The deleted instance does not appear in the list.

4.10.7   Access an instance through a console

VNC or SPICE is used to view the console output of an instance, regardless of whether or not the console log has output. This allows relaying keyboard and mouse activity to and from an instance.

There are three remote console access methods commonly used with OpenStack:

novnc

> An in-browser VNC client implemented using HTML5 Canvas and WebSockets

spice

> A complete in-browser client solution for interaction with virtualized instances

xvpvnc

> A Java client offering console access to an instance

Example:

To access an instance through a remote console, run the following command:

```
$ nova get-vnc-console INSTANCE_NAME VNC_TYPE
```

The command returns a URL from which you can access your instance:

```
+--------+-----------------------------------------------------------------------+
| Type   | Url                                                                   |
+--------+-----------------------------------------------------------------------+
| xvpvnc | http://192.168.5.96:6081/console?token=c83ae3a3-15c4-4890-8d45-aefb494a8d6c |
+--------+-----------------------------------------------------------------------+
```

VNC_TYPE can be replaced by any of the above values as connection types.

When using SPICE to view the console of an instance, a browser plugin can be used directly on the instance page, or the `get-vnc-console` command can be used with it, as well, by returning a token-authenticated address, as in the example above.

For further information and comparisons (including security considerations), see the Security Guide (http://docs.openstack.org/security-guide/compute.html) ↗.

4.10.8   Manage bare-metal nodes

The bare-metal driver for OpenStack Compute manages provisioning of physical hardware by using common cloud APIs and tools such as Orchestration (Heat). The use case for this driver is for single tenant clouds such as a high-performance computing cluster, or for deploying OpenStack itself.

If you use the bare-metal driver, you must create a network interface and add it to a bare-metal node. Then, you can launch an instance from a bare-metal image.

You can list and delete bare-metal nodes. When you delete a node, any associated network interfaces are removed. You can list and remove network interfaces that are associated with a bare-metal node.

4.10.8.1   Commands

The following commands can be used to manage bare-metal nodes.

`baremetal-interface-add`

>   Adds a network interface to a bare-metal node.

`baremetal-interface-list`

>   Lists network interfaces associated with a bare-metal node.

`baremetal-interface-remove`

>   Removes a network interface from a bare-metal node.

`baremetal-node-create`

>   Creates a bare-metal node.

`baremetal-node-delete`

>   Removes a bare-metal node and any associated interfaces.

```
baremetal-node-list
```
Lists available bare-metal nodes.

```
baremetal-node-show
```
Shows information about a bare-metal node.

4.10.8.2 Create a bare-metal node

When you create a bare-metal node, your PM address, user name, and password should match the information in your hardware's BIOS/IPMI configuration.

```
$ nova baremetal-node-create --pm_address PM_ADDRESS --pm_user PM_USERNAME \
  --pm_password PM_PASSWORD $(hostname -f) 1 512 10 aa:bb:cc:dd:ee:ff
```

The following example shows the command and results from creating a node with the PM address `1.2.3.4`, the PM user name ipmi, and password `ipmi`.

```
$ nova baremetal-node-create --pm_address 1.2.3.4 --pm_user ipmi \
  --pm_password ipmi $(hostname -f) 1 512 10 aa:bb:cc:dd:ee:ff
+------------------+-------------------+
| Property         | Value             |
+------------------+-------------------+
| instance_uuid    | None              |
| pm_address       | 1.2.3.4           |
| interfaces       | []                |
| prov_vlan_id     | None              |
| cpus             | 1                 |
| memory_mb        | 512               |
| prov_mac_address | aa:bb:cc:dd:ee:ff |
| service_host     | ubuntu            |
| local_gb         | 10                |
| id               | 1                 |
| pm_user          | ipmi              |
| terminal_port    | None              |
+------------------+-------------------+
```

4.10.8.3 Add a network interface to the node

For each NIC on the node, you must create an interface, specifying the interface's MAC address.

```
$ nova baremetal-interface-add 1 aa:bb:cc:dd:ee:ff
+-------------+-------------------+
| Property    | Value             |
+-------------+-------------------+
| datapath_id | 0                 |
| id          | 1                 |
| port_no     | 0                 |
| address     | aa:bb:cc:dd:ee:ff |
+-------------+-------------------+
```

4.10.8.4 Launch an instance from a bare-metal image

A bare-metal instance is an instance created directly on a physical machine, without any virtu-alization layer running underneath it. Nova retains power control via IPMI. In some situations, Nova may retain network control via Neutron and OpenFlow.

```
$ nova boot --image my-baremetal-image --flavor my-baremetal-flavor test
+---------------------------+--------------------------------------+
| Property                  | Value                                |
+---------------------------+--------------------------------------+
| status                    | BUILD                                |
| id                        | cc302a8f-cd81-484b-89a8-b75eb3911b1b |
+---------------------------+--------------------------------------+

... wait for instance to become active ...
```

 Note

Set the `--availability_zone` parameter to specify which zone or node to use to start the server. Separate the zone from the host name with a comma. For example:

```
$ nova boot --availability_zone zone:HOST,NODE
```

host is optional for the `--availability_zone` parameter. You can simply specify `zone:,node`, still including the comma.

4.10.8.5   List bare-metal nodes and interfaces

Use the **nova baremetal-node-list** command to view all bare-metal nodes and interfaces. When a node is in use, its status includes the UUID of the instance that runs on it:

```
$ nova baremetal-node-list

+----+--------+------+-----------+---------+-------------------+------+------------+
+-------------+-------------+---------------+
| ID | Host   | CPUs | Memory_MB | Disk_GB | MAC Address       | VLAN | PM Address | PM
 Username | PM Password | Terminal Port |
+----+--------+------+-----------+---------+-------------------+------+------------+
+-------------+-------------+---------------+
| 1  | ubuntu | 1    | 512       | 10      | aa:bb:cc:dd:ee:ff | None | 1.2.3.4    | ipmi
 |              | None        |               |
+----+--------+------+-----------+---------+-------------------+------+------------+
+-------------+-------------+---------------+
```

4.10.8.6   Show details for a bare-metal node

Use the **nova baremetal-node-show** command to view the details for a bare-metal node:

```
$ nova baremetal-node-show 1

+-----------------+--------------------------------------+
| Property        | Value                                |
+-----------------+--------------------------------------+
| instance_uuid   | cc302a8f-cd81-484b-89a8-b75eb3911b1b |
| pm_address      | 1.2.3.4                              |
| interfaces      | [{u'datapath_id': u'0', u'id': 1,    |
|                 | u'port_no': 0,                       |
|                 | u'address': u'aa:bb:cc:dd:ee:ff'}]   |
| prov_vlan_id    | None                                 |
| cpus            | 1                                    |
```

```
| memory_mb       | 512               |                                     |
| prov_mac_address | aa:bb:cc:dd:ee:ff |                                     |
| service_host    | ubuntu            |                                     |
| local_gb        | 10                |                                     |
| id              | 1                 |                                     |
| pm_user         | ipmi              |                                     |
| terminal_port   | None              |                                     |
+-----------------+-----------------------------------------------------+
```

4.11   Provide user data to instances

A user data file is a special key in the metadata service that holds a file that cloud-aware applications in the guest instance can access. For example, one application that uses *user data* is the cloud-init (https://help.ubuntu.com/community/CloudInit) ↗ system, which is an open-source package from Ubuntu that is available on various Linux distributions and which handles early initialization of a cloud instance.

You can place user data in a local file and pass it through the `--user-data <user-data-file>` parameter at instance creation.

```
$ nova boot --image ubuntu-cloudimage --flavor 1 --user-data mydata.file
```

4.12   Use snapshots to migrate instances

To use snapshots to migrate instances from OpenStack projects to clouds, complete these steps. In the source project:

1. Section 4.12.1, "Create a snapshot of the instance"

2. Section 4.12.2, "Download the snapshot as an image"

In the destination project:

1. Section 4.12.3, "Import the snapshot to the new environment"

2. *Section 4.12.4, "Boot a new instance from the snapshot"*

 Note

Some cloud providers allow only administrators to perform this task.

4.12.1 Create a snapshot of the instance

1. Shut down the source VM before you take the snapshot to ensure that all data is flushed to disk. If necessary, list the instances to view the instance name:

```
$ nova list
+-----------------------------------------+-------------+--------
+-----------------------------+
| ID                                      | Name        | Status | Networks
   |
+-----------------------------------------+-------------+--------
+-----------------------------+
| c41f3074-c82a-4837-8673-fa7e9fea7e11 | myInstance | ACTIVE | private=10.0.0.3
   |
+-----------------------------------------+-------------+--------
+-----------------------------+

$ nova stop example
```

2. Use the **nova list** command to confirm that the instance shows a SHUTOFF status:

```
$ nova list
+-----------------------------------------+-------------+---------
+-------------------+
| ID                                      | Name        | Status   | Networks
   |
+-----------------------------------------+-------------+---------
+-------------------+
| c41f3074-c82a-4837-8673-fa7e9fea7e11 | myInstance | SHUTOFF |
 private=10.0.0.3 |
```

```
+---------------------------------------------+--------------+---------
+------------------+
```

3. Use the **nova image-create** command to take a snapshot:

```
$ nova image-create --poll myInstance myInstanceSnapshot
Instance snapshotting... 50% complete
```

4. Use the **nova image-list** command to check the status until the status is `ACTIVE`:

```
$ nova image-list
+--------------------------------------+----------------------------------+---------
+--------+
| ID                                   | Name                             | Status |
 Server |
+--------------------------------------+----------------------------------+---------
+--------+
| 657ebb01-6fae-47dc-986a-e49c4dd8c433 | cirros-0.3.2-x86_64-uec          | ACTIVE |
 |
| 72074c6d-bf52-4a56-a61c-02a17bf3819b | cirros-0.3.2-x86_64-uec-kernel   | ACTIVE |
 |
| 3c5e5f06-637b-413e-90f6-ca7ed015ec9e | cirros-0.3.2-x86_64-uec-ramdisk  | ACTIVE |
 |
| f30b204e-1ce6-40e7-b8d9-b353d4d84e7d | myInstanceSnapshot               | ACTIVE |
 |
+--------------------------------------+----------------------------------+---------
+--------+
```

4.12.2   Download the snapshot as an image

1. Get the image ID:

```
$ nova image-list
+------------------+------------------+--------+------------------------------------+
| ID               | Name             | Status | Server                             |
+------------------+------------------+--------+------------------------------------+
```

```
| f30b204e-1ce6... | myInstanceSnapshot| ACTIVE | c41f3074-c82a-4837-8673-fa7e9fea7e11 |
+------------------+-------------------+--------+--------------------------------------+
```

2. Download the snapshot by using the image ID that was returned in the previous step:

```
$ glance image-download --file snapshot.raw f30b204e-1ce6-40e7-b8d9-
b353d4d84e7d
```

 Note

The **glance image-download** command requires the image ID and cannot use the image name. Check there is sufficient space on the destination file system for the image file.

3. Make the image available to the new environment, either through HTTP or direct upload to a machine (`scp`).

4.12.3   Import the snapshot to the new environment

In the new project or cloud environment, import the snapshot:

```
$ glance image-create --copy-from IMAGE_URL
```

4.12.4   Boot a new instance from the snapshot

In the new project or cloud environment, use the snapshot to create the new instance:

```
$ nova boot --flavor m1.tiny --image myInstanceSnapshot myNewInstance
```

4.13   Store metadata on a configuration drive

You can configure OpenStack to write metadata to a special configuration drive that attaches to the instance when it boots. The instance can mount this drive and read files from it to get information that is normally available through the metadata service (http://docs.openstack.org/admin-guide-cloud/compute-networking-nova.html#metadata-service) ↗. This metadata is different from the user data.

One use case for using the configuration drive is to pass a networking configuration when you do not use DHCP to assign IP addresses to instances. For example, you might pass the IP address configuration for the instance through the configuration drive, which the instance can mount and access before you configure the network settings for the instance.

Any modern guest operating system that is capable of mounting an ISO 9660 or VFAT file system can use the configuration drive.

4.13.1   Requirements and guidelines

To use the configuration drive, you must follow the following requirements for the compute host and image.

Compute host requirements

- The following hypervisors support the configuration drive: libvirt, XenServer, Hyper-V, and VMware.
  Also, the Bare Metal service supports the configuration drive.

- To use configuration drive with libvirt, XenServer, or VMware, you must first install the genisoimage package on each compute host. Otherwise, instances do not boot properly. Use the `mkisofs_cmd` flag to set the path where you install the genisoimage program. If genisoimage is in same path as the `nova-compute` service, you do not need to set this flag.

- To use configuration drive with Hyper-V, you must set the `mkisofs_cmd` value to the full path to an `mkisofs.exe` installation. Additionally, you must set the `qemu_img_cmd` value in the `hyperv` configuration section to the full path to an **qemu-img** command installation.

- To use configuration drive with the Bare Metal service, you do not need to prepare anything because the Bare Metal service treats the configuration drive properly.

Image requirements

- An image built with a recent version of the cloud-init package can automatically access metadata passed through the configuration drive. The cloud-init package version 0.7.1 works with Ubuntu and Fedora based images, such as Red Hat Enterprise Linux.

- If an image does not have the cloud-init package installed, you must customize the image to run a script that mounts the configuration drive on boot, reads the data from the drive, and takes appropriate action such as adding the public key to an account. You can read more details about how data is organized on the configuration drive.

- If you use Xen with a configuration drive, use the `xenapi_disable_agent` configuration parameter to disable the agent.

Guidelines

- Do not rely on the presence of the EC2 metadata in the configuration drive, because this content might be removed in a future release. For example, do not rely on files in the `ec2` directory.

- When you create images that access configuration drive data and multiple directories are under the `openstack` directory, always select the highest API version by date that your consumer supports. For example, if your guest image supports the 2012-03-05, 2012-08-05, and 2013-04-13 versions, try 2013-04-13 first and fall back to a previous version if 2013-04-13 is not present.

4.13.2   Enable and access the configuration drive

1. To enable the configuration drive, pass the `--config-drive true` parameter to the **nova boot** command.
   The following example enables the configuration drive and passes user data, two files, and two key/value metadata pairs, all of which are accessible from the configuration drive:

```
$ nova boot --config-drive true --image my-image-name --key-name mykey \
   --flavor 1 --user-data ./my-user-data.txt myinstance \
   --file /etc/network/interfaces=/home/myuser/instance-interfaces \
   --file known_hosts=/home/myuser/.ssh/known_hosts \
   --meta role=webservers --meta essential=false
```

You can also configure the Compute service to always create a configuration drive by setting the following option in the `/etc/nova/nova.conf` file:

```
force_config_drive=true
```

 Note

> If a user passes the `--config-drive true` flag to the **nova boot** command, an administrator cannot disable the configuration drive.

2. If your guest operating system supports accessing disk by label, you can mount the configuration drive as the `/dev/disk/by-label/configurationDriveVolumeLabel` device. In the following example, the configuration drive has the `config-2` volume label:

```
# mkdir -p /mnt/config
# mount /dev/disk/by-label/config-2 /mnt/config
```

 Note

Ensure that you use at least version 0.3.1 of CirrOS for configuration drive support.

If your guest operating system does not use `udev`, the `/dev/disk/by-label` directory is not present.

You can use the **blkid** command to identify the block device that corresponds to the configuration drive. For example, when you boot the CirrOS image with the `m1.tiny` flavor, the device is `/dev/vdb`:

```
# blkid -t LABEL="config-2" -odevice
```

```
/dev/vdb
```

Once identified, you can mount the device:

```
# mkdir -p /mnt/config
# mount /dev/vdb /mnt/config
```

4.13.2.1 Configuration drive contents

In this example, the contents of the configuration drive are as follows:

```
ec2/2009-04-04/meta-data.json
ec2/2009-04-04/user-data
ec2/latest/meta-data.json
ec2/latest/user-data
openstack/2012-08-10/meta_data.json
openstack/2012-08-10/user_data
openstack/content
openstack/content/0000
openstack/content/0001
openstack/latest/meta_data.json
openstack/latest/user_data
```

The files that appear on the configuration drive depend on the arguments that you pass to the **nova boot** command.

4.13.2.2 OpenStack metadata format

The following example shows the contents of the `openstack/2012-08-10/meta_data.json` and `openstack/latest/meta_data.json` files. These files are identical. The file contents are formatted for readability.

```
{
    "availability_zone": "nova",
    "files": [
        {
            "content_path": "/content/0000",
            "path": "/etc/network/interfaces"
        },
        {
            "content_path": "/content/0001",
            "path": "known_hosts"
        }
    ],
```

```
    "hostname": "test.novalocal",
    "launch_index": 0,
    "name": "test",
    "meta": {
        "role": "webservers",
        "essential": "false"
    },
    "public_keys": {
        "mykey": "ssh-rsa AAAAB3NzaClyc2EAAAADAQABAAAAgQDBqUfVvCSez0/Wfpd8dLLgZXV9GtXQ7hnMN
+Z0OWQUyebVEHeylCXuin0uY1cAJMhUq8j98SiW+cU0sU4J3x5l2+xilbodDm1BtFWVeLIOQINpfV1n8fKjHB
+ynPpe1F6tMDvrFGU1Js44t30BrujMXBe8Rq44cCk6wqyjATA3rQ== Generated by Nova\n"
    },
    "uuid": "83679162-1378-4288-a2d4-70e13ec132aa"
}
```

Note the effect of the `--file /etc/network/interfaces=/home/myuser/instance-inter-faces` argument that was passed to the **nova boot** command. The contents of this file are contained in the `openstack/content/0000` file on the configuration drive, and the path is specified as `/etc/network/interfaces` in the `meta_data.json` file.

4.13.2.3   EC2 metadata format

The following example shows the contents of the `ec2/2009-04-04/meta-data.json` and the `ec2/latest/meta-data.json` files. These files are identical. The file contents are formatted to improve readability.

```
{
    "ami-id": "ami-00000001",
    "ami-launch-index": 0,
    "ami-manifest-path": "FIXME",
    "block-device-mapping": {
        "ami": "sda1",
        "ephemeral0": "sda2",
        "root": "/dev/sda1",
        "swap": "sda3"
    },
```

```
    "hostname": "test.novalocal",
    "instance-action": "none",
    "instance-id": "i-00000001",
    "instance-type": "m1.tiny",
    "kernel-id": "aki-00000002",
    "local-hostname": "test.novalocal",
    "local-ipv4": null,
    "placement": {
        "availability-zone": "nova"
    },
    "public-hostname": "test.novalocal",
    "public-ipv4": "",
    "public-keys": {
        "0": {
            "openssh-key": "ssh-rsa AAAAB3NzaC1yc2EAAAADAQABAAAAgQDBqUfVvCSez0/
Wfpd8dLLgZXV9GtXQ7hnMN+Z0OWQUyebVEHey1CXuin0uY1cAJMhUq8j98SiW
+cU0sU4J3x5l2+xi1bodDm1BtFWVeLIOQINpfV1n8fKjHB
+ynPpe1F6tMDvrFGUlJs44t30BrujMXBe8Rq44cCk6wqyjATA3rQ== Generated by Nova\n"
        }
    },
    "ramdisk-id": "ari-00000003",
    "reservation-id": "r-7lfps8wj",
    "security-groups": [
        "default"
    ]
}
```

4.13.2.4   User data

The openstack/2012-08-10/user_data, openstack/latest/user_data, ec2/2009-04-04/user-data, and ec2/latest/user-data file are present only if the --user-data flag and the contents of the user data file are passed to the **nova boot** command.

4.13.2.5   Configuration drive format

The default format of the configuration drive as an ISO 9660 file system. To explicitly specify the ISO 9660 format, add the following line to the `/etc/nova/nova.conf` file:

```
config_drive_format=iso9660
```

By default, you cannot attach the configuration drive image as a CD drive instead of as a disk drive. To attach a CD drive, add the following line to the `/etc/nova/nova.conf` file:

```
config_drive_cdrom=true
```

For legacy reasons, you can configure the configuration drive to use VFAT format instead of ISO 9660. It is unlikely that you would require VFAT format because ISO 9660 is widely supported across operating systems. However, to use the VFAT format, add the following line to the `/etc/nova/nova.conf` file:

```
config_drive_format=vfat
```

If you choose VFAT, the configuration drive is 64 MB.

 Note

> In current version (Liberty) of OpenStack Compute, live migration with `config_drive` on local disk is forbidden due to the bug in libvirt of copying a read-only disk. However, if we use VFAT as the format of `config_drive`, the function of live migration works well.

4.14   Create and manage networks

Before you run commands, set the following environment variables:

```
export OS_USERNAME=admin
export OS_PASSWORD=password
export OS_TENANT_NAME=admin
export OS_AUTH_URL=http://localhost:5000/v2.0
```

4.14.1 Create networks

1. List the extensions of the system:

```
$ neutron ext-list -c alias -c name


+-----------------+---------------------------+
| alias           | name                      |
+-----------------+---------------------------+
| agent_scheduler | Agent Schedulers          |
| binding         | Port Binding              |
| quotas          | Quota management support  |
| agent           | agent                     |
| provider        | Provider Network          |
| router          | Neutron L3 Router         |
| lbaas           | LoadBalancing service     |
| extraroute      | Neutron Extra Route       |
+-----------------+---------------------------+
```

2. Create a network:

```
$ neutron net-create net1


Created a new network:
+---------------------------+--------------------------------------+
| Field                     | Value                                |
+---------------------------+--------------------------------------+
| admin_state_up            | True                                 |
| id                        | 2d627131-c841-4e3a-ace6-f2dd75773b6d |
| name                      | net1                                 |
| provider:network_type     | vlan                                 |
| provider:physical_network | physnet1                             |
| provider:segmentation_id  | 1001                                 |
| router:external           | False                                |
| shared                    | False                                |
| status                    | ACTIVE                               |
```

```
| subnets                   |                                      |
| tenant_id                 | 3671f46ec35e4bbca6ef92ab7975e463     |
+---------------------------+--------------------------------------+
```

 Note

Some fields of the created network are invisible to non-admin users.

3. Create a network with specified provider network type.

```
$ neutron net-create net2 --provider:network-type local


Created a new network:
+---------------------------+--------------------------------------+
| Field                     | Value                                |
+---------------------------+--------------------------------------+
| admin_state_up            | True                                 |
| id                        | 524e26ea-fad4-4bb0-b504-1ad0dc770e7a |
| name                      | net2                                 |
| provider:network_type     | local                                |
| provider:physical_network |                                      |
| provider:segmentation_id  |                                      |
| router:external           | False                                |
| shared                    | False                                |
| status                    | ACTIVE                               |
| subnets                   |                                      |
| tenant_id                 | 3671f46ec35e4bbca6ef92ab7975e463     |
+---------------------------+--------------------------------------+
```

Just as shown previously, the unknown option `--provider:network-type` is used to create a `local` provider network.

4.14.2 Create subnets

Create a subnet:

```
$ neutron subnet-create net1 192.168.2.0/24 --name subnet1

Created a new subnet:
+------------------+----------------------------------------------------+
| Field            | Value                                              |
+------------------+----------------------------------------------------+
| allocation_pools | {"start": "192.168.2.2", "end": "192.168.2.254"}   |
| cidr             | 192.168.2.0/24                                     |
| dns_nameservers  |                                                    |
| enable_dhcp      | True                                               |
| gateway_ip       | 192.168.2.1                                        |
| host_routes      |                                                    |
| id               | 15a09f6c-87a5-4d14-b2cf-03d97cd4b456               |
| ip_version       | 4                                                  |
| name             | subnet1                                            |
| network_id       | 2d627131-c841-4e3a-ace6-f2dd75773b6d               |
| tenant_id        | 3671f46ec35e4bbca6ef92ab7975e463                   |
+------------------+----------------------------------------------------+
```

The `subnet-create` command has the following positional and optional parameters:

- The name or ID of the network to which the subnet belongs.
  In this example, `net1` is a positional argument that specifies the network name.

- The CIDR of the subnet.
  In this example, `192.168.2.0/24` is a positional argument that specifies the CIDR.

- The subnet name, which is optional.
  In this example, `--name subnet1` specifies the name of the subnet.

For information and examples on more advanced use of neutron's `subnet` sub-command, see the Cloud Administrator Guide (http://docs.openstack.org/admin-guide-cloud/networking_use.html#advanced-networking-operations) ↗.

4.14.3 Create routers

1. Create a router:

```
$ neutron router-create router1

Created a new router:
+----------------------+--------------------------------------+
| Field                | Value                                |
+----------------------+--------------------------------------+
| admin_state_up       | True                                 |
| external_gateway_info |                                     |
| id                   | 6e1f11ed-014b-4c16-8664-f4f615a3137a |
| name                 | router1                              |
| status               | ACTIVE                               |
| tenant_id            | 7b5970fbe7724bf9b74c245e66b92abf     |
+----------------------+--------------------------------------+
```

Take note of the unique router identifier returned, this will be required in subsequent steps.

2. Link the router to the external provider network:

```
$ neutron router-gateway-set ROUTER NETWORK
```

Replace ROUTER with the unique identifier of the router, replace NETWORK with the unique identifier of the external provider network.

3. Link the router to the subnet:

```
$ neutron router-interface-add ROUTER SUBNET
```

Replace ROUTER with the unique identifier of the router, replace SUBNET with the unique identifier of the subnet.

4.14.4 Create ports

1. Create a port with specified IP address:

```
$ neutron port-create net1 --fixed-ip ip_address=192.168.2.40

Created a new port:
+----------------------
+-----------------------------------------------------------------------+
| Field               | Value
    |
+----------------------
+-----------------------------------------------------------------------+
| admin_state_up      | True
    |
| binding:capabilities | {"port_filter": false}
    |
| binding:vif_type    | ovs
    |
| device_id           |
    |
| device_owner        |
    |
| fixed_ips           | {"subnet_id": "15a09f6c-87a5-4d14-b2cf-03d97cd4b456",
"ip_address... |
| id                  | f7a08fe4-e79e-4b67-bbb8-a5002455a493
    |
| mac_address         | fa:16:3e:97:e0:fc
    |
| name                |
    |
| network_id          | 2d627131-c841-4e3a-ace6-f2dd75773b6d
    |
| status              | DOWN
    |
| tenant_id           | 3671f46ec35e4bbca6ef92ab7975e463
    |
```

```
+--------------------

+---------------------------------------------------------------+
```

In the previous command, `net1` is the network name, which is a positional argument. `--fixed-ip ip_address=192.168.2.40` is an option which specifies the port's fixed IP address we wanted.

 Note

When creating a port, you can specify any unallocated IP in the subnet even if the address is not in a pre-defined pool of allocated IP addresses (set by your cloud provider).

2. Create a port without specified IP address:

```
$ neutron port-create net1

Created a new port:
+--------------------

+---------------------------------------------------------------+
| Field               | Value

    |

+--------------------

+---------------------------------------------------------------+
| admin_state_up      | True

    |
| binding:capabilities | {"port_filter": false}

    |
| binding:vif_type    | ovs

    |
| device_id           |

    |
| device_owner        |

    |
| fixed_ips           | {"subnet_id": "15a09f6c-87a5-4d14-b2cf-03d97cd4b456",
  "ip_address... |
```

```
| id                    | baf13412-2641-4183-9533-de8f5b91444c
    |
| mac_address           | fa:16:3e:f6:ec:c7
    |
| name                  |
    |
| network_id            | 2d627131-c841-4e3a-ace6-f2dd75773b6d
    |
| status                | DOWN
    |
| tenant_id             | 3671f46ec35e4bbca6ef92ab7975e463
    |
+----------------------
+----------------------------------------------------------------+
```

 Note

Note that the system allocates one IP address if you do not specify an IP address in the **neutron port-create** command.

3. Query ports with specified fixed IP addresses:

```
$ neutron port-list --fixed-ips ip_address=192.168.2.2 \
  ip_address=192.168.2.40


+----------------+------+------------------
+----------------------------------------------------+
| id             | name | mac_address       | fixed_ips
    |
+----------------+------+------------------
+----------------------------------------------------+
| baf13412-26... |      | fa:16:3e:f6:ec:c7 | {"subnet_id"... ..."ip_address":
  "192.168.2.2"} |
| f7a08fe4-e7... |      | fa:16:3e:97:e0:fc | {"subnet_id"... ..."ip_address":
  "192.168.2.40"}|
```

```
+-----------------+------+-----------------
+------------------------------------------+
```

`--fixed-ips ip_address=192.168.2.2 ip_address=192.168.2.40` is one unknown option.

How to find unknown options The unknown options can be easily found by watching the output of **create_xxx** or **show_xxx** command. For example, in the port creation command, we see the fixed_ips fields, which can be used as an unknown option.

4.15   Manage objects and containers

The OpenStack Object Storage service provides the `swift` client, which is a command-line interface (CLI). Use this client to list objects and containers, upload objects to containers, and download or delete objects from containers. You can also gather statistics and update metadata for accounts, containers, and objects.

This client is based on the native swift client library, `client.py`, which seamlessly re-authenticates if the current token expires during processing, retries operations multiple times, and provides a processing concurrency of 10.

4.15.1   Create and manage containers

* To create a container, run the following command and replace `CONTAINER` with the name of your container.

```
$ swift post CONTAINER
```

* To list all containers, run the following command:

```
$ swift list
```

* To check the status of containers, run the following command:

```
$ swift stat
```

```
Account: AUTH_7b5970fbe7724bf9b74c245e77c03bcg
```

```
Containers: 2
Objects: 3
Bytes: 268826
Accept-Ranges: bytes
X-Timestamp: 1392683866.17952
Content-Type: text/plain; charset=utf-8
```

You can also use the **swift stat** command with the ACCOUNT or CONTAINER names as parameters.

```
$ swift stat CONTAINER
```

```
Account: AUTH_7b5970fbe7724bf9b74c245e77c03bcg
Container: storage1
Objects: 2
Bytes: 240221
Read ACL:
Write ACL:
Sync To:
Sync Key:
Accept-Ranges: bytes
X-Timestamp: 1392683866.20180
Content-Type: text/plain; charset=utf-8
```

4.15.2   Manage access

- Users have roles on accounts. For example, a user with the admin role has full access to all containers and objects in an account. You can set access control lists (ACLs) at the container level and support lists for read and write access, which you set with the X-Container-Read and X-Container-Write headers.

  To give a user read access, use the **swift post** command with the -r parameter. To give a user write access, use the -w parameter.

  The following example enables the testuser user to read objects in the container:

```
$ swift post -r 'testuser'
```

You can also use this command with a list of users.

- If you use StaticWeb middleware to enable Object Storage to serve public web content, use `.r:`, followed by a list of allowed referrers.
  The following command gives object access to all referring domains:

```
$ swift post -r '.r:*'
```

4.15.3 Manage objects

- To upload an object to a container, run the following command:

```
$ swift upload CONTAINER OBJECT_FILENAME
```

To upload in chunks, for large files, run the following command:

```
$ swift upload -S CHUNK_SIZE CONTAINER OBJECT_FILENAME
```

- To check the status of the object, run the following command:

```
$ swift stat CONTAINER OBJECT_FILENAME
```

```
Account: AUTH_7b5970fbe7724bf9b74c245e77c03bcg
Container: storage1
Object: images
Content Type: application/octet-stream
Content Length: 211616
Last Modified: Tue, 18 Feb 2014 00:40:36 GMT
ETag: 82169623d55158f70a0d720f238ec3ef
Meta Orig-Filename: images.jpg
Accept-Ranges: bytes
X-Timestamp: 1392684036.33306
```

- To list the objects in a container, run the following command:

```
$ swift list CONTAINER
```

- To download an object from a container, run the following command:

```
$ swift download CONTAINER OBJECT_FILENAME
```

4.15.4 Environment variables required to run examples

To run the cURL command examples for the Object Storage API requests, set these environment variables:

publicURL

The public URL that is the HTTP endpoint from where you can access Object Storage. It includes the Object Storage API version number and your account name. For example, `https://23.253.72.207/v1/my_account`.

token

The authentication token for Object Storage.

To obtain these values, run the **swift stat -v** command.

As shown in this example, the public URL appears in the `StorageURL` field, and the token appears in the `Auth Token` field:

```
StorageURL: https://23.253.72.207/v1/my_account
Auth Token: {token}
Account: my_account
Containers: 2
Objects: 3
Bytes: 47
Meta Book: MobyDick
X-Timestamp: 1389453423.35964
X-Trans-Id: txee55498935404a2caad89-0052dd3b77
Content-Type: text/plain; charset=utf-8
Accept-Ranges: bytes
```

4.15.5 Object versioning

You can store multiple versions of your content so that you can recover from unintended over-writes. Object versioning is an easy way to implement version control, which you can use with any type of content.

 Note

> You cannot version a large-object manifest file, but the large-object manifest file can point to versioned segments.

We strongly recommend that you put non-current objects in a different container than the container where current object versions reside.

4.15.5.1 To enable and use object versioning

1. To enable object versioning, ask your cloud provider to set the `allow_versions` option to `TRUE` in the container configuration file.

2. Create an `archive` container to store older versions of objects:

   ```
   $ curl -i $publicURL/archive -X PUT -H "Content-Length: 0" -H "X-Auth-Token: $token"
   ```

   ```
   HTTP/1.1 201 Created
   Content-Length: 0
   Content-Type: text/html; charset=UTF-8
   X-Trans-Id: tx46f8c29050834d88b8d7e-0052e1859d
   Date: Thu, 23 Jan 2014 21:11:57 GMT
   ```

3. Create a `current` container to store current versions of objects.
   Include the `X-Versions-Location` header. This header defines the container that holds the non-current versions of your objects. You must UTF-8-encode and then URL-encode the container name before you include it in the `X-Versions-Location` header. This header enables object versioning for all objects in the `current` container. Changes to objects in the `current` container automatically create non-current versions in the `archive` container.

```
$ curl -i $publicURL/current -X PUT -H "Content-Length: 0" -H \
  "X-Auth-Token: $token" -H "X-Versions-Location: archive"
```

```
HTTP/1.1 201 Created
Content-Length: 0
Content-Type: text/html; charset=UTF-8
X-Trans-Id: txb91810fb717347d09eec8-0052e18997
Date: Thu, 23 Jan 2014 21:28:55 GMT
```

4. Create the first version of an object in the `current` container:

```
$ curl -i $publicURL/current/my_object --data-binary 1 -X PUT -H \
  "Content-Length: 0" -H "X-Auth-Token: $token"
```

```
HTTP/1.1 201 Created
Last-Modified: Thu, 23 Jan 2014 21:31:22 GMT
Content-Length: 0
Etag: d41d8cd98f00b204e9800998ecf8427e
Content-Type: text/html; charset=UTF-8
X-Trans-Id: tx5992d536a4bd4fec973aa-0052e18a2a
Date: Thu, 23 Jan 2014 21:31:22 GMT
```

Nothing is written to the non-current version container when you initially `PUT` an object in the `current` container. However, subsequent `PUT` requests that edit an object trigger the creation of a version of that object in the `archive` container.

These non-current versions are named as follows:

```
<length><object_name><timestamp>
```

Where `length` is the 3-character, zero-padded hexadecimal character length of the object, `<object_name>` is the object name, and `<timestamp>` is the time when the object was initially created as a current version.

5. Create a second version of the object in the `current` container:

```
$ curl -i $publicURL/current/my_object --data-binary 2 -X PUT -H \
```

```
"Content-Length: 0" -H "X-Auth-Token: $token"
```

```
HTTP/1.1 201 Created
Last-Modified: Thu, 23 Jan 2014 21:41:32 GMT
Content-Length: 0
Etag: d41d8cd98f00b204e9800998ecf8427e
Content-Type: text/html; charset=UTF-8
X-Trans-Id: tx468287ce4fc94eada96ec-0052e18c8c
Date: Thu, 23 Jan 2014 21:41:32 GMT
```

6. Issue a GET request to a versioned object to get the current version of the object. You do not have to do any request redirects or metadata lookups.

List older versions of the object in the archive container:

```
$ curl -i $publicURL/archive?prefix=009my_object -X GET -H \
   "X-Auth-Token: $token"
```

```
HTTP/1.1 200 OK
Content-Length: 30
X-Container-Object-Count: 1
Accept-Ranges: bytes
X-Timestamp: 1390513280.79684
X-Container-Bytes-Used: 0
Content-Type: text/plain; charset=utf-8
X-Trans-Id: tx9a441884997542d3a5868-0052e18d8e
Date: Thu, 23 Jan 2014 21:45:50 GMT


  009my_object/1390512682.92052
```

 Note

A POST request to a versioned object updates only the metadata for the object and does not create a new version of the object. New versions are created only when the content of the object changes.

7. Issue a DELETE request to a versioned object to remove the current version of the object and replace it with the next-most current version in the non-current container.

```
$ curl -i $publicURL/current/my_object -X DELETE -H \
    "X-Auth-Token: $token"
```

```
HTTP/1.1 204 No Content
Content-Length: 0
Content-Type: text/html; charset=UTF-8
X-Trans-Id: tx006d944e02494e229b8ee-0052e18edd
Date: Thu, 23 Jan 2014 21:51:25 GMT
```

List objects in the archive container to show that the archived object was moved back to the current container:

```
$ curl -i $publicURL/archive?prefix=009my_object -X GET -H \
    "X-Auth-Token: $token"
```

```
HTTP/1.1 204 No Content
Content-Length: 0
X-Container-Object-Count: 0
Accept-Ranges: bytes
X-Timestamp: 1390513280.79684
X-Container-Bytes-Used: 0
Content-Type: text/html; charset=UTF-8
X-Trans-Id: tx044f2a05f56f4997af737-0052e18eed
Date: Thu, 23 Jan 2014 21:51:41 GMT
```

This next-most current version carries with it any metadata last set on it. If you want to completely remove an object and you have five versions of it, you must DELETE it five times.

8. To disable object versioning for the current container, remove its X-Versions-Location metadata header by sending an empty key value.

```
$ curl -i $publicURL/current -X PUT -H "Content-Length: 0" -H \
    "X-Auth-Token: $token" -H "X-Versions-Location: "
```

```
HTTP/1.1 202 Accepted

Content-Length: 76

Content-Type: text/html; charset=UTF-8

X-Trans-Id: txe2476de217134549996d0-0052e19038

Date: Thu, 23 Jan 2014 21:57:12 GMT


<html><h1>Accepted</h1><p>The request is accepted for processing.</p></html>
```

4.15.6 Serialized response formats

By default, the Object Storage API uses a `text/plain` response format. In addition, both JSON and XML data serialization response formats are supported.

 Note

> To run the cURL command examples, you must export environment variables. For more information, see the section *Section 4.15.4, "Environment variables required to run examples"*.

To define the response format, use one of these methods:

Method	Description
format = `format` query parameter	Append this parameter to the URL for a `GET` request, where `format` is `json` or `xml`.

`Accept` request header	Include this header in the `GET` request. The valid header values are:
	
	• text/plain
	  Plain text response format. The default.
	
	• application/jsontext
	  JSON data serialization response format.
	
	• application/xml
	  XML data serialization response format.
	
	• text/xml

Method	Description
	XML data serialization response format.

4.15.6.1 Example 1. JSON example with format query parameter

For example, this request uses the `format` query parameter to ask for a JSON response:

```
$ curl -i $publicURL?format=json -X GET -H "X-Auth-Token: $token"
```

```
HTTP/1.1 200 OK
Content-Length: 96
X-Account-Object-Count: 1
X-Timestamp: 1389453423.35964
X-Account-Meta-Subject: Literature
X-Account-Bytes-Used: 14
X-Account-Container-Count: 2
Content-Type: application/json; charset=utf-8
Accept-Ranges: bytes
X-Trans-Id: tx274a77a8975c4a66aeb24-0052d95365
Date: Fri, 17 Jan 2014 15:59:33 GMT
```

Object Storage lists container names with additional information in JSON format:

```
[
    {
        "count":0,
        "bytes":0,
        "name":"janeausten"
    },
    {
        "count":1,
        "bytes":14,
        "name":"marktwain"
    }
]
```

4.15.6.2 Example 2. XML example with Accept header

This request uses the `Accept` request header to ask for an XML response:

```
$ curl -i $publicURL -X GET -H "X-Auth-Token: $token" -H \
  "Accept: application/xml; charset=utf-8"
```

```
HTTP/1.1 200 OK
Content-Length: 263
X-Account-Object-Count: 3
X-Account-Meta-Book: MobyDick
X-Timestamp: 1389453423.35964
X-Account-Bytes-Used: 47
X-Account-Container-Count: 2
Content-Type: application/xml; charset=utf-8
Accept-Ranges: bytes
X-Trans-Id: txf0b4c9727c3e491694019-0052e03420
Date: Wed, 22 Jan 2014 21:12:00 GMT
```

Object Storage lists container names with additional information in XML format:

```
<?xml version="1.0" encoding="UTF-8"?>
<account name="AUTH_73f0aa26640f4971864919d0eb0f0880">
    <container>
        <name>janeausten</name>
        <count>2</count>
        <bytes>33</bytes>
    </container>
    <container>
        <name>marktwain</name>
        <count>1</count>
        <bytes>14</bytes>
    </container>
</account>
```

The remainder of the examples in this guide use standard, non-serialized responses. However, all `GET` requests that perform list operations accept the `format` query parameter or `Accept` request header.

4.15.7 Page through large lists of containers or objects

If you have a large number of containers or objects, you can use the `marker`, `limit`, and `end_marker` parameters to control how many items are returned in a list and where the list starts or ends.

- **marker**

    When you request a list of containers or objects, Object Storage returns a maximum of 10,000 names for each request. To get subsequent names, you must make another request with the `marker` parameter. Set the `marker` parameter to the name of the last item returned in the previous list. You must URL-encode the `marker` value before you send the HTTP request. Object Storage returns a maximum of 10,000 names starting after the last item returned.

- **limit**

    To return fewer than 10,000 names, use the `limit` parameter. If the number of names returned equals the specified `limit` (or 10,000 if you omit the `limit` parameter), you can assume there are more names to list. If the number of names in the list is exactly divisible by the `limit` value, the last request has no content.

- **end_marker**

    Limits the result set to names that are less than the `end_marker` parameter value. You must URL-encode the `end_marker` value before you send the HTTP request.

4.15.7.1 To page through a large list of containers

Assume the following list of container names:

```
apples
bananas
kiwis
oranges
pears
```

1. Use a `limit` of two:

```
# curl -i $publicURL/?limit=2 -X GET -H "X-Auth-Token: $token"
```

```
apples
bananas
```

Because two container names are returned, there are more names to list.

2. Make another request with a `marker` parameter set to the name of the last item returned:

```
# curl -i $publicURL/?limit=2&amp;marker=bananas -X GET -H \
   "X-Auth-Token: $token"
```

```
kiwis
oranges
```

Again, two items are returned, and there might be more.

3. Make another request with a `marker` of the last item returned:

```
# curl -i $publicURL/?limit=2&amp;marker=oranges -X GET -H \"
   X-Auth-Token: $token"
```

```
pears
```

You receive a one-item response, which is fewer than the `limit` number of names. This indicates that this is the end of the list.

4. Use the `end_marker` parameter to limit the result set to object names that are less than the `end_marker` parameter value:

```
# curl -i $publicURL/?end_marker=oranges -X GET -H \"
  X-Auth-Token: $token"
```

```
apples
bananas
kiwis
```

You receive a result set of all container names before the `end-marker` value.

4.15.8 Pseudo-hierarchical folders and directories

Although you cannot nest directories in OpenStack Object Storage, you can simulate a hierarchical structure within a single container by adding forward slash characters (/) in the object name. To navigate the pseudo-directory structure, you can use the `delimiter` query parameter. This example shows you how to use pseudo-hierarchical folders and directories.

 Note

> In this example, the objects reside in a container called `backups`. Within that container, the objects are organized in a pseudo-directory called `photos`. The container name is not displayed in the example, but it is a part of the object URLs. For instance, the URL of the picture `me.jpg` is `https://storage.swiftdrive.com/v1/CF_xer7_343/back-ups/photos/me.jpg`.

4.15.8.1 List pseudo-hierarchical folders request: HTTP

To display a list of all the objects in the storage container, use `GET` without a `delimiter` or `prefix`.

```
$ curl -X GET -i -H "X-Auth-Token: $token" \
  $publicurl/v1/AccountString/backups
```

The system returns status code 2xx (between 200 and 299, inclusive) and the requested list of the objects.

```
photos/animals/cats/persian.jpg
photos/animals/cats/siamese.jpg
photos/animals/dogs/corgi.jpg
photos/animals/dogs/poodle.jpg
photos/animals/dogs/terrier.jpg
photos/me.jpg
photos/plants/fern.jpg
photos/plants/rose.jpg
```

Use the delimiter parameter to limit the displayed results. To use `delimiter` with pseudo-directories, you must use the parameter slash (/).

```
$ curl -X GET -i -H "X-Auth-Token: $token" \
 $publicurl/v1/AccountString/backups?delimiter=/
```

The system returns status code 2xx (between 200 and 299, inclusive) and the requested matching objects. Because you use the slash, only the pseudo-directory photos/ displays. The returned values from a slash delimiter query are not real objects. The value will refer to a real object if it does not end with a slash. The pseudo-directories have no content-type, rather, each pseudo-directory has its own subdir entry in the response of JSON and XML results. For example:

```
[
  {
    "subdir": "photos/"
  }
]


[
  {
    "subdir": "photos/animals/"
  },
  {
    "hash": "b249a153f8f38b51e92916bbc6ea57ad",
    "last_modified": "2015-12-03T17:31:28.187370",
    "bytes": 2906,
    "name": "photos/me.jpg",
    "content_type": "image/jpeg"
  },
  {
    "subdir": "photos/plants/"
  }
]
```

```
<?xml version="1.0" encoding="UTF-8"?>
<container name="backups">
  <subdir name="photos/">
    <name>photos/</name>
  </subdir>
```

```
</container>

<?xml version="1.0" encoding="UTF-8"?>
<container name="backups">
  <subdir name="photos/animals/">
    <name>photos/animals/</name>
  </subdir>
  <object>
    <name>photos/me.jpg</name>
    <hash>b249a153f8f38b51e92916bbc6ea57ad</hash>
    <bytes>2906</bytes>
    <content_type>image/jpeg</content_type>
    <last_modified>2015-12-03T17:31:28.187370</last_modified>
  </object>
  <subdir name="photos/plants/">
    <name>photos/plants/</name>
  </subdir>
</container>
```

Use the `prefix` and `delimiter` parameters to view the objects inside a pseudo-directory, including further nested pseudo-directories.

```
$ curl -X GET -i -H "X-Auth-Token: $token" \
 $publicurl/v1/AccountString/backups?prefix=photos/&delimiter=/
```

The system returns status code 2xx (between 200 and 299, inclusive) and the objects and pseudo-directories within the top level pseudo-directory.

```
photos/animals/
photos/me.jpg
photos/plants/
```

You can create an unlimited number of nested pseudo-directories. To navigate through them, use a longer `prefix` parameter coupled with the `delimiter` parameter. In this sample output, there is a pseudo-directory called `dogs` within the pseudo-directory `animals`. To navigate directly to the files contained within `dogs`, enter the following command:

```
$ curl -X GET -i -H "X-Auth-Token: $token" \
```

```
$publicurl/v1/AccountString/backups?prefix=photos/animals/dogs/&delimiter=/
```

The system returns status code 2xx (between 200 and 299, inclusive) and the objects and pseudo-directories within the nested pseudo-directory.

```
photos/animals/dogs/corgi.jpg
photos/animals/dogs/poodle.jpg
photos/animals/dogs/terrier.jpg
```

4.15.9 Discoverability

Your Object Storage system might not enable all features that this document describes. These features are:

- *Section 4.15.10, "Large objects"*

- *Section 4.15.11, "Auto-extract archive files"*

- *Section 4.15.12, "Bulk delete"*

- *Section 4.15.13, "Create static website"*

To discover which features are enabled in your Object Storage system, use the `/info` request. To use the `/info` request, send a `GET` request using the `/info` path to the Object Store endpoint as shown in this example:

```
$ curl https://storage.example.com/info
```

This example shows a truncated response body:

```
{
   "swift":{
      "version":"1.11.0"
   },
   "staticweb":{

   },
   "tempurl":{
```

```
    }
  }
```

This output shows that the Object Storage system has enabled the static website and temporary URL features.

 Note

> In some cases, the `/info` request will return an error. This could be because your service provider has disabled the `/info` request function, or because you are using an older version that does not support it.

4.15.10   Large objects

To discover whether your Object Storage system supports this feature, see *Section 4.15.9, "Discoverability"* or check with your service provider.

By default, the content of an object cannot be greater than 5 GB. However, you can use a number of smaller objects to construct a large object. The large object is comprised of two types of objects:

- `Segment objects` store the object content. You can divide your content into segments and upload each segment into its own segment object. Segment objects do not have any special features. You create, update, download, and delete segment objects just as you do with normal objects.

- A `manifest object` links the segment objects into one logical large object. When you download a manifest object, Object Storage concatenates and returns the contents of the segment objects in the response body. This behavior extends to the response headers returned by `GET` and `HEAD` requests. The `Content-Length` response header contains the total size of all segment objects.
  Object Storage takes the `ETag` value of each segment, concatenates them together, and returns the MD5 checksum of the result to calculate the `ETag` response header value. The manifest object types are:

Static large objects
> The manifest object content is an ordered list of the names of the segment objects in JSON format. See *Section 4.15.10.1, "Static large objects"*.

Dynamic large objects

The manifest object has no content but it has a `X-Object-Manifest` metadata header. The value of this header is `CONTAINER/PREFIX`, where `CONTAINER` is the name of the container where the segment objects are stored, and `PREFIX` is a string that all segment objects have in common. See *Section 4.15.10.2, "Dynamic large objects"*.

 Note

If you use a manifest object as the source of a `COPY` request, the new object is a normal, and not a segment, object. If the total size of the source segment objects exceeds 5 GB, the `COPY` request fails. However, you can make a duplicate of the manifest object and this new object can be larger than 5 GB.

4.15.10.1 · Static large objects

To create a static large object, divide your content into pieces and create (upload) a segment object to contain each piece.

You must record the `ETag` response header value that the `PUT` operation returns. Alternatively, you can calculate the MD5 checksum of the segment before you perform the upload and include this value in the `ETag` request header. This action ensures that the upload cannot corrupt your data.

List the name of each segment object along with its size and MD5 checksum in order.

Create a manifest object. Include the `?multipart-manifest=put` query string at the end of the manifest object name to indicate that this is a manifest object.

The body of the `PUT` request on the manifest object comprises a JSON list where each element contains these attributes:

path

The container and object name in the format: `CONTAINER_NAME/OBJECT_NAME`.

etag

The MD5 checksum of the content of the segment object. This value must match the `ETag` of that object.

size_bytes

The size of the segment object. This value must match the `Content-Length` of that object.

4.15.10.1.1 Static large object manifest list

This example shows three segment objects. You can use several containers and the object names do not have to conform to a specific pattern, in contrast to dynamic large objects.

```
[
    {
        "path": "mycontainer/objseg1",
        "etag": "0228c7926b8b642dfb29554cd1f00963",
        "size_bytes": 1468006
    },
    {
        "path": "mycontainer/pseudodir/seg-obj2",
        "etag": "5bfc9ea51a00b790717eeb934fb77b9b",
        "size_bytes": 1572864
    },
    {
        "path": "other-container/seg-final",
        "etag": "b9c3da507d2557c1ddc51f27c54bae51",
        "size_bytes": 256
    }
]
```

The `Content-Length` request header must contain the length of the JSON content and not the length of the segment objects. However, after the `PUT` operation completes, the `Content-Length` metadata is set to the total length of all the object segments. A similar situation applies to the `ETag`. If used in the `PUT` operation, it must contain the MD5 checksum of the JSON content. The `ETag` metadata value is then set to be the MD5 checksum of the concatenated `ETag` values of the object segments. You can also set the `Content-Type` request header and custom object metadata.

When the `PUT` operation sees the `?multipart-manifest=put` query parameter, it reads the request body and verifies that each segment object exists and that the sizes and ETags match. If there is a mismatch, the `PUT` operation fails.

If everything matches, the API creates the manifest object and sets the `X-Static-Large-Object` metadata to `true` to indicate that the manifest is a static object manifest.

Normally when you perform a `GET` operation on the manifest object, the response body contains the concatenated content of the segment objects. To download the manifest list, use the `?multipart-manifest=get` query parameter. The list in the response is not formatted the same as the manifest that you originally used in the `PUT` operation.

If you use the `DELETE` operation on a manifest object, the manifest object is deleted. The segment objects are not affected. However, if you add the `?multipart-manifest=delete` query parameter, the segment objects are deleted and if all are successfully deleted, the manifest object is also deleted.

To change the manifest, use a `PUT` operation with the `?multipart-manifest=put` query parameter. This request creates a manifest object. You can also update the object metadata in the usual way.

4.15.10.2   Dynamic large objects

Before you can upload objects that are larger than 5 GB, you must segment them. You upload the segment objects like you do with any other object and create a dynamic large manifest object. The manifest object tells Object Storage how to find the segment objects that comprise the large object. You can still access each segment individually, but when you retrieve the manifest object, the API concatenates the segments. You can include any number of segments in a single large object.

To ensure the download works correctly, you must upload all the object segments to the same container and prefix each object name so that the segments sort in correct concatenation order.

You also create and upload a manifest file. The manifest file is a zero-byte file with the extra `X-Object-Manifest CONTAINER/PREFIX` header. The `CONTAINER` is the container the object segments are in and `PREFIX` is the common prefix for all the segments. You must UTF-8-encode and then URL-encode the container and common prefix in the `X-Object-Manifest` header.

It is best to upload all the segments first and then create or update the manifest. With this method, the full object is not available for downloading until the upload is complete. Also, you can upload a new set of segments to a second location and update the manifest to point to this new location. During the upload of the new segments, the original manifest is still available to download the first set of segments.

4.15.10.2.1   Upload segment of large object request: HTTP

```
PUT /API_VERSION/ACCOUNT/CONTAINER/OBJECT HTTP/1.1
Host: storage.example.com
X-Auth-Token: eaaafd18-0fed-4b3a-81b4-663c99ec1cbb
ETag: 8a964ee2a5e88be344f36c22562a6486
Content-Length: 1
X-Object-Meta-PIN: 1234
```

No response body is returned.

The 2``nn`` response code indicates a successful write. nn is a value from 00 to 99.

The Length Required (411) response code indicates that the request does not include a required Content-Length or Content-Type header.

The Unprocessable Entity (422) response code indicates that the MD5 checksum of the data written to the storage system does NOT match the optional ETag value.

You can continue to upload segments, like this example shows, before you upload the manifest.

4.15.10.2.2   Upload next segment of large object request: HTTP

```
PUT /API_VERSION/ACCOUNT/CONTAINER/OBJECT HTTP/1.1
Host: storage.example.com
X-Auth-Token: eaaafd18-0fed-4b3a-81b4-663c99ec1cbb
ETag: 8a964ee2a5e88be344f36c22562a6486
Content-Length: 1
X-Object-Meta-PIN: 1234
```

Next, upload the manifest. This manifest specifies the container where the object segments reside. Note that if you upload additional segments after you create the manifest, the concatenated object becomes that much larger but you do not need to recreate the manifest file for subsequent additional segments.

4.15.10.2.3   Upload manifest request: HTTP

```
PUT /API_VERSION/ACCOUNT/CONTAINER/OBJECT HTTP/1.1
Host: storage.clouddrive.com
```

```
X-Auth-Token: eaaafd18-0fed-4b3a-81b4-663c99ec1cbb
Content-Length: 0
X-Object-Meta-PIN: 1234
X-Object-Manifest: CONTAINER/PREFIX
```

4.15.10.2.4   Upload manifest response: HTTP

```
[...]
```

A GET or HEAD request on the manifest returns a Content-Type response header value that is the same as the Content-Type request header value in the PUT request that created the manifest. To change the Content- Type, reissue the PUT request.

4.15.10.3   Extra transaction information

You can use the X-Trans-Id-Extra request header to include extra information to help you debug any errors that might occur with large object upload and other Object Storage transactions.

The Object Storage API appends the first 32 characters of the X-Trans-Id-Extra request header value to the transaction ID value in the generated X-Trans-Id response header. You must UTF-8-encode and then URL-encode the extra transaction information before you include it in the X-Trans-Id-Extra request header.

For example, you can include extra transaction information when you upload large objects such as images.

When you upload each segment and the manifest, include the same value in the X-Trans-Id-Extra request header. If an error occurs, you can find all requests that are related to the large object upload in the Object Storage logs.

You can also use X-Trans-Id-Extra strings to help operators debug requests that fail to receive responses. The operator can search for the extra information in the logs.

4.15.10.4 Comparison of static and dynamic large objects

While static and dynamic objects have similar behavior, this table describes their differences:

Description	Static large object	Dynamic large object
End-to-end integrity	Assured. The list of segments includes the MD5 checksum (`ETag`) of each segment. You cannot upload the manifest object if the `ETag` in the list differs from the uploaded segment object. If a segment is somehow lost, an attempt to download the manifest object results in an error.	Not guaranteed. The eventual consistency model means that although you have uploaded a segment object, it might not appear in the container listing until later. If you download the manifest before it appears in the container, it does not form part of the content returned in response to a `GET` request.
Upload order	You must upload the segment objects before upload the manifest object.	You can upload manifest and segment objects in any order. You are recommended to upload the manifest object after the segments in case a premature download of the manifest occurs. However, this is not enforced.
Removal or addition of segment objects	You cannot add or remove segment objects from the manifest. However, you can create a completely new manifest object of the same name with a different manifest list.	You can upload new segment objects or remove existing segments. The names must simply match the `PREFIX` supplied in `X-Object-Manifest`.
Segment object size and number	Segment objects must be at least 1 MB in size (by default). The final segment object can	Segment objects can be any size.

Description	Static large object	Dynamic large object
	be any size. At most, 1000 segments are supported (by default).	
Segment object container name	The manifest list includes the container name of each object. Segment objects can be in different containers.	All segment objects must be in the same container.
Manifest object metadata	The object has `X-Static-Large-Object` set to `true`. You do not set this metadata directly. Instead the system sets it when you `PUT` a static manifest object.	The `X-Object-Manifest` value is the `CONTAINER/PREFIX`, which indicates where the segment objects are located. You supply this request header in the `PUT` operation.
Copying the manifest object	Include the `?multipart-manifest=get` query string in the `COPY` request. The new object contains the same manifest as the original. The segment objects are not copied. Instead, both the original and new manifest objects share the same set of segment objects.	The `COPY` operation does not create a manifest object. To duplicate a manifest object, use the `GET` operation to read the value of `X-Object-Manifest` and use this value in the `X-Object-Manifest` request header in a `PUT` operation. This creates a new manifest object that shares the same set of segment objects as the original manifest object.

4.15.11 Auto-extract archive files

To discover whether your Object Storage system supports this feature, see *Section 4.15.9, "Discoverability"*. Alternatively, check with your service provider.

Use the auto-extract archive feature to upload a tar archive file.

The Object Storage system extracts files from the archive file and creates an object.

4.15.11.1 Auto-extract archive request

To upload an archive file, make a `PUT` request. Add the `extract-archive=format` query parameter to indicate that you are uploading a tar archive file instead of normal content.

Valid values for the `format` variable are `tar`, `tar.gz`, or `tar.bz2`.

The path you specify in the `PUT` request is used for the location of the object and the prefix for the resulting object names.

In the `PUT` request, you can specify the path for:

- An account

- Optionally, a specific container

- Optionally, a specific object prefix

For example, if the first object in the tar archive is `/home/file1.txt` and you specify the `/v1/12345678912345/mybackup/castor/` path, the operation creates the `castor/home/file1.txt` object in the `mybackup` container in the `12345678912345` account.

4.15.11.2 Create an archive for auto-extract

You must use the tar utility to create the tar archive file.

You can upload regular files but you cannot upload other items (for example, empty directories or symbolic links).

You must UTF-8-encode the member names.

The archive auto-extract feature supports these formats:

- The POSIX.1-1988 Ustar format.

- The GNU tar format. Includes the long name, long link, and sparse extensions.

- The POSIX.1-2001 pax format.
  Use gzip or bzip2 to compress the archive.
  Use the `extract-archive` query parameter to specify the format. Valid values for this parameter are `tar`, `tar.gz`, or `tar.bz2`.

4.15.11.3 Auto-extract archive response

When Object Storage processes the request, it performs multiple sub-operations. Even if all sub-operations fail, the operation returns a 201 `Created` status. Some sub-operations might succeed while others fail. Examine the response body to determine the results of each auto-extract archive sub-operation.

You can set the `Accept` request header to one of these values to define the response format:

`text/plain`

    Formats response as plain text. If you omit the `Accept` header, `text/plain` is the default.

`application/json`

    Formats response as JSON.

`application/xml`

    Formats response as XML.

`text/xml`

    Formats response as XML.

The following auto-extract archive files example shows a `text/plain` response body where no failures occurred:

```
Number Files Created: 10
Errors:
```

The following auto-extract archive files example shows a `text/plain` response where some failures occurred. In this example, the Object Storage system is configured to reject certain character strings so that the 400 Bad Request error occurs for any objects that use the restricted strings.

```
Number Files Created: 8
Errors:
/v1/12345678912345/mycontainer/home/xx%3Cyy, 400 Bad Request
/v1/12345678912345/mycontainer/../image.gif, 400 Bad Request
```

The following example shows the failure response in `application/json` format.

```
{
```

```
"Number Files Created":1,
"Errors":[
   [
      "/v1/12345678912345/mycontainer/home/xx%3Cyy",
      "400 Bad Request"
   ],
   [
      "/v1/12345678912345/mycontainer/../image.gif",
      "400 Bad Request"
   ]
]
}
```

4.15.12   Bulk delete

To discover whether your Object Storage system supports this feature, see *Section 4.15.9, "Discoverability"*. Alternatively, check with your service provider.

With bulk delete, you can delete up to 10,000 objects or containers (configurable) in one request.

4.15.12.1   Bulk delete request

To perform a bulk delete operation, add the `bulk-delete` query parameter to the path of a `POST` or `DELETE` operation.

 Note

The `DELETE` operation is supported for backwards compatibility.

The path is the account, such as `/v1/12345678912345`, that contains the objects and containers.

In the request body of the `POST` or `DELETE` operation, list the objects or containers to be deleted. Separate each name with a newline character. You can include a maximum of 10,000 items (configurable) in the list.

In addition, you must:

- UTF-8-encode and then URL-encode the names.

- To indicate an object, specify the container and object name as: `CONTAINER_NAME`/`OBJECT_NAME`.

- To indicate a container, specify the container name as: `CONTAINER_NAME`. Make sure that the container is empty. If it contains objects, Object Storage cannot delete the container.

- Set the `Content-Type` request header to `text/plain`.

4.15.12.2 Bulk delete response

When Object Storage processes the request, it performs multiple sub-operations. Even if all sub-operations fail, the operation returns a 200 status. The bulk operation returns a response body that contains details that indicate which sub-operations have succeeded and failed. Some sub-operations might succeed while others fail. Examine the response body to determine the results of each delete sub-operation.

You can set the `Accept` request header to one of the following values to define the response format:

`text/plain`
> Formats response as plain text. If you omit the `Accept` header, `text/plain` is the default.

`application/json`
> Formats response as JSON.

`application/xml` **or** `text/xml`
> Formats response as XML.

The response body contains the following information:

- The number of files actually deleted.

- The number of not found objects.

- Errors. A list of object names and associated error statuses for the objects that failed to delete. The format depends on the value that you set in the `Accept` header.

The following bulk delete response is in `application/xml` format. In this example, the `my-container` container is not empty, so it cannot be deleted.

```
<delete>
    <number_deleted>2</number_deleted>
    <number_not_found>4</number_not_found>
    <errors>
        <object>
            <name>/v1/12345678912345/mycontainer</name>
            <status>409 Conflict</status>
        </object>
    </errors>
</delete>
```

4.15.13 Create static website

To discover whether your Object Storage system supports this feature, see *Section 4.15.9, "Discoverability"*. Alternatively, check with your service provider.

You can use your Object Storage account to create a static website. This static website is created with Static Web middleware and serves container data with a specified index file, error file resolution, and optional file listings. This mode is normally active only for anonymous requests, which provide no authentication token. To use it with authenticated requests, set the header `X-Web-Mode` to `TRUE` on the request.

The Static Web filter must be added to the pipeline in your `/etc/swift/proxy-server.conf` file below any authentication middleware. You must also add a Static Web middleware configuration section.

See the Cloud Administrator Guide for an example of the static web configuration syntax (http://docs.openstack.org/liberty/config-reference/content/object-storage-static-web.html)↗.

See the Cloud Administrator Guide for a complete example of the /etc/swift/proxy-server.conf file (http://docs.openstack.org/liberty/config-reference/content/proxy-server-conf.html)↗ (including static web).

Your publicly readable containers are checked for two headers, `X-Container-Meta-Web-Index` and `X-Container-Meta-Web-Error`. The `X-Container-Meta-Web-Error` header is discussed below, in the section called *Section 4.15.13.1.5, "Set error pages for static website"*.

Use `X-Container-Meta-Web-Index` to determine the index file (or default page served, such as `index.html`) for your website. When someone initially enters your site, the `index.html` file displays automatically. If you create sub-directories for your site by creating pseudo-directories in your container, the index page for each sub-directory is displayed by default. If your pseudo-directory does not have a file with the same name as your index file, visits to the sub-directory return a 404 error.

You also have the option of displaying a list of files in your pseudo-directory instead of a web page. To do this, set the `X-Container-Meta-Web-Listings` header to `TRUE`. You may add styles to your file listing by setting `X-Container-Meta-Web-Listings-CSS` to a style sheet (for example, `lists.css`).

4.15.13.1   Static Web middleware through Object Storage

The following sections show how to use Static Web middleware through Object Storage.

4.15.13.1.1   Make container publicly readable

Make the container publicly readable. Once the container is publicly readable, you can access your objects directly, but you must set the index file to browse the main site URL and its sub-directories.

```
$ swift post -r '.r:*' container
```

4.15.13.1.2   Set site index file

Set the index file. In this case, `index.html` is the default file displayed when the site appears.

```
$ swift post -m 'web-index:index.html' container
```

4.15.13.1.3   Enable file listing

Turn on file listing. If you do not set the index file, the URL displays a list of the objects in the container. Instructions on styling the list with a CSS follow.

```
$ swift post -m 'web-listings: true' container
```

4.15.13.1.4   Enable CSS for file listing

Style the file listing using a CSS.

```
$ swift post -m 'web-listings-css:listings.css' container
```

4.15.13.1.5   Set error pages for static website

You can create and set custom error pages for visitors to your website; currently, only 401 (Unauthorized) and 404 (Not Found) errors are supported. To do this, set the metadata header, `X-Container-Meta-Web-Error`.

Error pages are served with the status code pre-pended to the name of the error page you set. For instance, if you set `X-Container-Meta-Web-Error` to `error.html`, 401 errors will display the page `401error.html`. Similarly, 404 errors will display `404error.html`. You must have both of these pages created in your container when you set the `X-Container-Meta-Web-Error` metadata, or your site will display generic error pages.

You only have to set the `X-Container-Meta-Web-Error` metadata once for your entire static website.

4.15.13.1.6   Set error pages for static website request

```
$ swift post -m 'web-error:error.html' container
```

Any 2`nn` response indicates success.

4.16   Create and manage stacks

The Orchestration service enables you to orchestrate multiple composite cloud applications. This service supports use of both the Amazon Web Services (AWS) CloudFormation template format through both a Query API that is compatible with CloudFormation and the native OpenStack *Heat Orchestration Template (HOT)* format through a REST API.

These flexible template languages enable application developers to describe and automate the deployment of infrastructure, services, and applications. The templates enable creation of most OpenStack resource types, such as instances, floating IP addresses, volumes, security groups, and users. The resources, once created, are referred to as stacks.

The template languages are described in the Template Guide (http://docs.openstack.org/developer/heat/template_guide/index.html)↗ in the Heat developer documentation (http://docs.openstack.org/developer/heat/)↗.

4.16.1   Create a stack from an example template file

- To create a stack, or template, from an example template file (https://git.openstack.org/cgit/openstack/heat-templates)↗, run the following command:

```
$ heat stack-create mystack --template-file /PATH_TO_HEAT_TEMPLATES/
WordPress_Single_Instance.template \
  --parameters
 "InstanceType=m1.large;DBUsername=USERNAME;DBPassword=PASSWORD;KeyName=HEAT_KEY;LinuxDistribution=F17"
```

The `--parameters` values that you specify depend on the parameters that are defined in the template. If a website hosts the template file, you can specify the URL with the `--template-url` parameter instead of the `--template-file` parameter.
The command returns the following output:

```
+-------------------+---------------+--------------------+--------------------
+
| id                | stack_name    | stack_status       | creation_time
  |
+-------------------+---------------+--------------------+--------------------
+
| 4c712026-dcd5...  | mystack       | CREATE_IN_PROGRESS | 2013-04-03T23:22:08Z
  |
+-------------------+---------------+--------------------+--------------------
+
```

Note

When you run the **heat stack-create** command with the --poll option, it prints the **heat stack-show** output first, and then continuously prints the events in log format until the stack completes its action with success or failure.

- You can also use the **template-validate** command to validate a template file without creating a stack from it.

 Note

Previous versions of the heat client used **validate** instead of **template-validate**, but it has been deprecated in favor of **template-validate**.

To do so, run the following command:

```
$ heat template-validate --template-file /PATH_TO_HEAT_TEMPLATES/
WordPress_Single_Instance.template
```

If validation fails, the response returns an error message.

4.16.2   Get information about stacks

To explore the state and history of a particular stack, you can run a number of commands.

- To see which stacks are visible to the current user, run the following command:

```
$ heat stack-list
+------------------+----------------+------------------+----------------------+
| id               | stack_name     | stack_status     | creation_time        |
+------------------+----------------+------------------+----------------------+
| 4c712026-dcd5... | mystack        | CREATE_COMPLETE  | 2013-04-03T23:22:08Z |
| 7edc7480-bda5... | my-otherstack  | CREATE_FAILED    | 2013-04-03T23:28:20Z |
```

```
+--------------------+--------------------+------------------+---------------------+
```

- To show the details of a stack, run the following command:

```
$ heat stack-show mystack
```

- A stack consists of a collection of resources. To list the resources and their status, run the following command:

```
$ heat resource-list mystack
+--------------------+--------------------+----------------+---------------------+
| logical_resource_id | resource_type      | resource_status | updated_time        |
+--------------------+--------------------+----------------+---------------------+
| WikiDatabase       | AWS::EC2::Instance | CREATE_COMPLETE | 2013-04-03T23:25:56Z |
+--------------------+--------------------+----------------+---------------------+
```

- To show the details for a specific resource in a stack, run the following command:

```
$ heat resource-show mystack WikiDatabase
```

- Some resources have associated metadata which can change throughout the lifecycle of a resource. Show the metadata by running the following command:

```
$ heat resource-metadata mystack WikiDatabase
```

- A series of events is generated during the lifecycle of a stack. To display lifecycle events, run the following command:

```
$ heat event-list mystack
+--------------------+----+----------------------+----------------
+--------------------+
| logical_resource_id | id | resource_status_reason | resource_status | event_time
     |
+--------------------+----+----------------------+----------------
+--------------------+
| WikiDatabase       | 1  | state changed         | IN_PROGRESS     |
 2013-04-03T23:22:09Z |
| WikiDatabase       | 2  | state changed         | CREATE_COMPLETE |
 2013-04-03T23:25:56Z |
```

```
+----------------------+----+-------------------------+----------------
+----------------------+
```

- To show the details for a particular event, run the following command:

```
$ heat event-show WikiDatabase 1
```

4.16.3 Update a stack

To update an existing stack from a modified template file, run a command like the following command:

```
$ heat stack-update mystack --template-file \
  /path/to/heat/templates/WordPress_Single_Instance_v2.template \
  --parameters
 "InstanceType=m1.large;DBUsername=wp;DBPassword=verybadpassword;KeyName=heat_key;LinuxDistribution=F17"
+-----------------------------------------+-----------------+-----------------
+----------------------+
| id                                      | stack_name      | stack_status    | creation_time
 |
+-----------------------------------------+-----------------+-----------------
+----------------------+
| 4c712026-dcd5-4664-90b8-0915494c1332 | mystack         | UPDATE_COMPLETE | 2013-04-03T23:22:08Z
 |
| 7edc7480-bda5-4e1c-9d5d-f567d3b6a050 | my-otherstack | CREATE_FAILED   | 2013-04-03T23:28:20Z
 |
+-----------------------------------------+-----------------+-----------------
+----------------------+
```

Some resources are updated in-place, while others are replaced with new resources.

4.17 Measure cloud resources

Telemetry measures cloud resources in OpenStack. It collects data related to billing. Currently, this metering service is available through only the **ceilometer** command-line client.

To model data, Telemetry uses the following abstractions:

Meter

Measures a specific aspect of resource usage, such as the existence of a running instance, or ongoing performance, such as the CPU utilization for an instance. Meters exist for each type of resource. For example, a separate `cpu_util` meter exists for each instance. The lifecycle of a meter is decoupled from the existence of its related resource. The meter persists after the resource goes away.

A meter has the following attributes:

- String name

- A unit of measurement

- A type, which indicates whether values increase monotonically (cumulative), are interpreted as a change from the previous value (delta), or are stand-alone and relate only to the current duration (gauge)

Sample

An individual data point that is associated with a specific meter. A sample has the same attributes as the associated meter, with the addition of time stamp and value attributes. The value attribute is also known as the sample `volume`.

Statistic

A set of data point aggregates over a time duration. (In contrast, a sample represents a single data point.) The Telemetry service employs the following aggregation functions:

- **count**. The number of samples in each period.

- **max**. The maximum number of sample volumes in each period.

- **min**. The minimum number of sample volumes in each period.

- **avg**. The average of sample volumes over each period.

- **sum**. The sum of sample volumes over each period.

Alarm

A set of rules that define a monitor and a current state, with edge-triggered actions associated with target states. Alarms provide user-oriented Monitoring-as-a-Service and a general purpose utility for OpenStack. Orchestration auto scaling is a typical use case. Alarms follow a tristate model of `ok`, `alarm`, and `insufficient data`. For conventional threshold-oriented alarms, a static threshold value and comparison operator govern state transitions. The comparison operator compares a selected meter statistic against an evaluation window of configurable length into the recent past.

This example uses the **heat** client to create an auto-scaling stack and the **ceilometer** client to measure resources.

1. Create an auto-scaling stack by running the following command. The `-f` option specifies the name of the stack template file, and the `-P` option specifies the KeyName parameter as heat_key:

```
$ heat stack-create -f cfn/F17/AutoScalingCeilometer.yaml -P "KeyName=heat_key"
```

2. List the heat resources that were created:

```
$ heat resource-list


+---------------------------+--------------------------------------------------+------------------
+----------------------+
| resource_name            | resource_type                                   |resource_status |
  updated_time           |
+---------------------------+--------------------------------------------------+------------------
+----------------------+
| CfnUser                  | AWS::IAM::User                                  |CREATE_COMPLETE |
  2013-10-02T05:53:41Z |
| WebServerKeys            | AWS::IAM::AccessKey                              |CREATE_COMPLETE |
  2013-10-02T05:53:42Z |
| LaunchConfig             | AWS::AutoScaling::LaunchConfiguration            |CREATE_COMPLETE |
  2013-10-02T05:53:43Z |
| ElasticLoadBalancer      | AWS::ElasticLoadBalancing::LoadBalancer         |UPDATE_COMPLETE |
  2013-10-02T05:55:58Z |
| WebServerGroup           | AWS::AutoScaling::AutoScalingGroup              |CREATE_COMPLETE |
  2013-10-02T05:55:58Z |
| WebServerScaleDownPolicy | AWS::AutoScaling::ScalingPolicy                 |CREATE_COMPLETE |
  2013-10-02T05:56:00Z |
| WebServerScaleUpPolicy   | AWS::AutoScaling::ScalingPolicy                 |CREATE_COMPLETE |
  2013-10-02T05:56:00Z |
```

```
| CPUAlarmHigh              | OS::Ceilometer::Alarm                    |CREATE_COMPLETE |
 2013-10-02T05:56:02Z |
| CPUAlarmLow               | OS::Ceilometer::Alarm                    |CREATE_COMPLETE |
 2013-10-02T05:56:02Z |
+------------------------+--------------------------------+------------------
+--------------------+
```

3. List the alarms that are set:

```
$ ceilometer alarm-list
+------------------------------------+------------------------------
+------------------+---------+------------+--------------------------------+
| Alarm ID                           | Name                        | State
 | Enabled | Continuous | Alarm condition            |
+------------------------------------+------------------------------
+------------------+---------+------------+--------------------------------+
| 4f896b40-0859-460b-9c6a-b0d329814496 | as-CPUAlarmLow-i6qqgkf2fubs  | insufficient data
 | True    | False      | cpu_util &lt; 15.0 during 1x 60s |
| 75d8ecf7-afc5-4bdc-95ff-19ed9ba22920 | as-CPUAlarmHigh-sf4muyfruy5m | insufficient data
 | True    | False      | cpu_util &gt; 50.0 during 1x 60s |
+------------------------------------+------------------------------
+------------------+---------+------------+--------------------------------+
```

4. List the meters that are set:

```
$ ceilometer meter-list
+--------------+------------+----------+------------------------------------
+----------------------------------+------------------------------+
| Name         | Type       | Unit     | Resource ID                        | User ID
                         | Project ID                    |
+--------------+------------+----------+------------------------------------
+----------------------------------+------------------------------+
| cpu          | cumulative | ns       | 3965b41b-81b0-4386-bea5-6ec37c8841c1 |
 d1a2996d3b1f4e0e8645ba9650308011 | bf03bf32e3884d489004ac995ff7a61c |
| cpu          | cumulative | ns       | 62520a83-73c7-4084-be54-275fe770ef2c |
 d1a2996d3b1f4e0e8645ba9650308011 | bf03bf32e3884d489004ac995ff7a61c |
```

```
| cpu_util      | gauge      | %         | 3965b41b-81b0-4386-bea5-6ec37c8841c1 |
   d1a2996d3b1f4e0e8645ba9650308011 | bf03bf32e3884d489004ac995ff7a61c |
+-------------+-----------+---------+-------------------------------------
+---------------------------------------------------+
```

5. List samples:

```
$ ceilometer sample-list -m cpu_util
+-----------------------------------------+----------+-------+---------------+------
+--------------------+
| Resource ID                             | Name     | Type  | Volume        | Unit |
  Timestamp           |
+-----------------------------------------+----------+-------+---------------+------
+--------------------+
| 3965b41b-81b0-4386-bea5-6ec37c8841c1 | cpu_util | gauge | 3.98333333333 | %    |
  2013-10-02T10:50:12 |
+-----------------------------------------+----------+-------+---------------+------
+--------------------+
```

6. View statistics:

```
$ ceilometer statistics -m cpu_util
+--------+-------------------+---------------------+-------+---------------
+---------------+---------------+---------------+----------+--------------------
+--------------------+
| Period | Period Start      | Period End          | Count | Min
   | Sum           | Avg           | Duration | Duration Start       | Duration End
   |
+--------+-------------------+---------------------+-------+---------------
+---------------+---------------+---------------+----------+--------------------
+--------------------+
| 0      | 2013-10-02T10:50:12 | 2013-10-02T10:50:12 | 1     | 3.98333333333 |
  3.98333333333 | 3.98333333333 | 3.98333333333 | 0.0      | 2013-10-02T10:50:12 |
  2013-10-02T10:50:12 |
+--------+-------------------+---------------------+-------+---------------
+---------------+---------------+---------------+----------+--------------------
+--------------------+
```

4.18 Create and manage databases

The Database service provides scalable and reliable cloud provisioning functionality for both relational and non-relational database engines. Users can quickly and easily use database features without the burden of handling complex administrative tasks.

4.18.1 Create and access a database

Assume that you have installed the Database service and populated your data store with images for the type and versions of databases that you want, and that you can create and access a database.

This example shows you how to create and access a MySQL 5.5 database.

4.18.1.1 Create and access a database

1. **Determine which flavor to use for your database**

   When you create a database instance, you must specify a nova flavor. The flavor indicates various characteristics of the instance, such as RAM, root volume size, and so on. The default nova flavors are not sufficient to create database instances. You might need to create or obtain some new nova flavors that work for databases.

   The first step is to list flavors by using the **nova flavor-list** command.

   Here are the default flavors, although you may have additional custom flavors in your environment:

```
$ nova flavor-list


+-----+----------+-----------+------+-----------+------+-------+--------------
+-----------+
| ID  | Name     | Memory_MB | Disk | Ephemeral | Swap | VCPUs | RXTX_Factor | Is_Public
 |
+-----+----------+-----------+------+-----------+------+-------+--------------
+-----------+
| 1   | m1.tiny  | 512       | 1    | 0         |      | 1     | 1.0         | True
 |
```

```
| 2    | m1.small  | 2048    | 20  | 0          |    | 1    | 1.0   | True
|

| 3    | m1.medium | 4096    | 40  | 0          |    | 2    | 1.0   | True
|

| 4    | m1.large  | 8192    | 80  | 0          |    | 4    | 1.0   | True
|

| 5    | m1.xlarge | 16384   | 160 | 0          |    | 8    | 1.0   | True
|

+------+-----------+---------+-----+------------+------+------+-------+-------------
+-----------+
```

Now take a look at the minimum requirements for various database instances:

Database	RAM (MB)	Disk (GB)	VCPUs
MySQL	512	5	1
Cassandra	2048	5	1
MongoDB	1024	5	1
Redis	512	5	1

- If you have a custom flavor that meets the needs of the database that you want to create, proceed to *Step 2* and use that flavor.

- If your environment does not have a suitable flavor, an administrative user must create a custom flavor by using the **nova flavor-create** command.

MySQL example. This example creates a flavor that you can use with a MySQL database. This example has the following attributes:

- Flavor name: `mysql_minimum`

- Flavor ID: You must use an ID that is not already in use. In this example, IDs 1 through 5 are in use, so use ID `6`.

- RAM: `512`

- Root volume size in GB: 5

- Virtual CPUs: 1

```
$ nova flavor-create mysql-minimum 6 512 5 1
+----+---------------+-----------+------+-----------+------+-------+-------------
+-----------+
| ID | Name          | Memory_MB | Disk | Ephemeral | Swap | VCPUs | RXTX_Factor |
 Is_Public |
+----+---------------+-----------+------+-----------+------+-------+-------------
+-----------+
| 6  | mysql-minimum | 512       | 5    | 0         |      | 1     | 1.0         | True
    |
+----+---------------+-----------+------+-----------+------+-------+-------------
+-----------+
```

2. **Create a database instance**

   This example creates a database instance with the following characteristics:

   - Name of the instance: mysql_instance_1

   - Database flavor: 6

   In addition, this command specifies these options for the instance:

   - A volume size of 5 (5 GB).

   - The myDB database.

   - The database is based on the mysql data store and the mysql-5.5 datastore_version.

   - The userA user with the password password.

```
$ trove create mysql_instance_1 6 --size 5 --databases myDB \
    --users userA:password --datastore_version mysql-5.5 \
    --datastore mysql
+-------------------
+------------------------------------------------------------------------------
```

```
t----------------------------------------------------------------------------------------
+
|     Property     |
                              Value
                                           |
+-------------------
+----------------------------------------------------------------------------------------
+
|     created      |
                         2014-05-29T21:26:21
                                           |
|    datastore     |
          {u'version': u'mysql-5.5', u'type': u'mysql'}
                                           |
| datastore_version |
                             mysql-5.5
                                           |
|     flavor       | {u'id': u'6', u'links': [{u'href': u'https://controller:8779/
v1.0/46d0bc4fc32e4b9e8520f8fc62199f58/flavors/6', u'rel': u'self'}, {u'href': u'https://
controller:8779/flavors/6', u'rel': u'bookmark'}]} |
|       id         |
              5599dad6-731e-44df-bb60-488da3da9cfe

|      name        |
                         mysql_instance_1
                                           |
|     status       |
                              BUILD
                                           |
|     updated      |
                         2014-05-29T21:26:21
                                           |
|     volume       |
                           {u'size': 5}
                                           |
```

```
                +------------------
                +-----------------------------------------------------
                +
```

3. **Get the IP address of the database instance**

First, use the **trove list** command to list all instances and their IDs:

```
$ trove list
+-------------------------------------+-------------------+-----------
+-----------------+---------+-----------+------+
|               id                    |       name        | datastore | datastore_version
 | status | flavor_id | size |
+-------------------------------------+-------------------+-----------
+-----------------+---------+-----------+------+
| 5599dad6-731e-44df-bb60-488da3da9cfe | mysql_instance_1 |   mysql   |     mysql-5.5
 | BUILD |    6    |  5  |
+-------------------------------------+-------------------+-----------
+-----------------+---------+-----------+------+
```

This command returns the instance ID of your new instance.

You can now pass in the instance ID with the **trove show** command to get the IP address of the instance. In this example, replace INSTANCE_ID with 5599dad6-731e-44df-bb60-488da3da9cfe.

```
$ trove show INSTANCE_ID

+-------------------+-----------------------------------------------+
|    Property       |                   Value                       |
+-------------------+-----------------------------------------------+
|    created        |            2014-05-29T21:26:21                |
|    datastore      |                   mysql                       |
| datastore_version |                 mysql-5.5                     |
|    flavor         |                     6                         |
|     id            |   5599dad6-731e-44df-bb60-488da3da9cfe        |
|     ip            |                172.16.200.2                   |
|    name           |              mysql_instance_1                 |
|    status         |                   BUILD                       |
```

```
|       updated       |       2014-05-29T21:26:54       |
|       volume        |               5               |
+--------------------+--------------------------------+
```

This command returns the IP address of the database instance.

4. **Access the new database**

   You can now access the new database you just created (myDB) by using typical database access commands. In this MySQL example, replace IP_ADDRESS with 172.16.200.2.

```
$ mysql -u userA -ppassword -h IP_ADDRESS myDB
```

4.18.2   Backup and restore a database

You can use Database services to backup a database and store the backup artifact in the Object Storage service. Later on, if the original database is damaged, you can use the backup artifact to restore the database. The restore process creates a database instance.

This example shows you how to back up and restore a MySQL database.

1. **Backup the database instance**

   As background, assume that you have created a database instance with the following characteristics:

   - Name of the database instance: guest1

   - Flavor ID: 10

   - Root volume size: 2

   - Databases: db1 and db2

   - Users: The user1 user with the password password

   First, get the ID of the guest1 database instance by using the **trove list** command:

```
$ trove list


+-----------------------------------------------+--------+----------+--------------------+-------------
+-----------+------+
```

```
|                    id                   | name | datastore | datastore_version | status
| flavor_id | size |
+-----------------------------------------+--------+-----------+--------------------+---------
+-----------+------+
| 97b4b853-80f6-414f-ba6f-c6f455a79ae6 | guest1 |   mysql   |     mysql-5.5      | ACTIVE
|    10     |  2   |
+-----------------------------------------+--------+-----------+--------------------+---------
+-----------+------+
```

Back up the database instance by using the **trove backup-create** command. In this example, the backup is called backup1. In this example, replace INSTANCE_ID with 97b4b853-80f6-414f-ba6f-c6f455a79ae6:

 Note

This command syntax pertains only to python-troveclient version 1.0.6 and later. Earlier versions require you to pass in the backup name as the first argument.

```
$ trove backup-create INSTANCE_ID backup1


+-------------+-------------------------------------------+
|  Property   |                   Value                   |
+-------------+-------------------------------------------+
|   created   |            2014-03-18T17:09:07            |
| description |                   None                    |
|     id      |    8af30763-61fd-4aab-8fe8-57d528911138   |
| instance_id |    97b4b853-80f6-414f-ba6f-c6f455a79ae6   |
| locationRef |                   None                    |
|    name     |                  backup1                  |
|  parent_id  |                   None                    |
|    size     |                   None                    |
|   status    |                   NEW                     |
|   updated   |            2014-03-18T17:09:07            |
+-------------+-------------------------------------------+
```

Note that the command returns both the ID of the original instance (`instance_id`) and the ID of the backup artifact (`id`).

Later on, use the **trove backup-list** command to get this information:

```
$ trove backup-list

+-------------------------------------------+-------------------------------------------+---------
+-----------+-----------+--------------------+
|                   id                      |                instance_id                | name |
   status  | parent_id |      updated        |
+-------------------------------------------+-------------------------------------------+---------
+-----------+-----------+--------------------+
| 8af30763-61fd-4aab-8fe8-57d528911138 | 97b4b853-80f6-414f-ba6f-c6f455a79ae6 | backup1 |
 COMPLETED |    None   | 2014-03-18T17:09:11 |
+-------------------------------------------+-------------------------------------------+---------
+-----------+-----------+--------------------+
```

You can get additional information about the backup by using the **trove backup-show** command and passing in the `BACKUP_ID`, which is `8af30763-61fd-4aab-8fe8-57d528911138`.

```
$ trove backup-show BACKUP_ID


+-------------+--------------------------------------------------+
|  Property   |                     Value                        |
+-------------+--------------------------------------------------+
|   created   |              2014-03-18T17:09:07                 |
| description |                     None                         |
|     id      |                   8af...138                      |
| instance_id |                   97b...ae6                      |
| locationRef | http://10.0.0.1:.../.../8af...138.xbstream.gz.enc |
|    name     |                   backup1                        |
|  parent_id  |                     None                         |
|    size     |                     0.17                         |
|   status    |                   COMPLETED                      |
|   updated   |              2014-03-18T17:09:11                 |
+-------------+--------------------------------------------------+
```

2. **Restore a database instance**

Now assume that your guest1 database instance is damaged and you need to restore it. In this example, you use the **trove create** command to create a new database instance called guest2.

- You specify that the new guest2 instance has the same flavor (10) and the same root volume size (2) as the original guest1 instance.

- You use the --backup argument to indicate that this new instance is based on the backup artifact identified by BACKUP_ID. In this example, replace BACKUP_ID with 8af30763-61fd-4aab-8fe8-57d528911138.

```
$ trove create guest2 10 --size 2 --backup BACKUP_ID


+------------------+------------------------------------------------+
|     Property     |                    Value                       |
+------------------+------------------------------------------------+
|      created     |             2014-03-18T17:12:03                |
|     datastore    | {u'version': u'mysql-5.5', u'type': u'mysql'}|
|datastore_version |                  mysql-5.5                     |
|      flavor      | {u'id': u'10', u'links': [{u'href': ...]}      |
|        id        |     ac7a2b35-a9b4-4ff6-beac-a1bcee86d04b       |
|       name       |                   guest2                       |
|      status      |                   BUILD                        |
|      updated     |             2014-03-18T17:12:03                |
|      volume      |                 {u'size': 2}                   |
+------------------+------------------------------------------------+
```

3. **Verify backup**

Now check that the new guest2 instance has the same characteristics as the original guest1 instance.

Start by getting the ID of the new guest2 instance.

```
$ trove list


+----------+--------+----------+-------------------+--------+-----------
+------+
```

```
|    id    |  name  | datastore | datastore_version | status | flavor_id |
 size |
+----------+--------+-----------+-------------------+--------+-----------+
+------+
| 97b...ae6 | guest1 |   mysql   |     mysql-5.5     | ACTIVE |    10     | 2
    |
| ac7...04b | guest2 |   mysql   |     mysql-5.5     | ACTIVE |    10     | 2
    |
+----------+--------+-----------+-------------------+--------+-----------+
+------+
```

Use the **trove show** command to display information about the new guest2 instance. Pass in guest2's `INSTANCE_ID`, which is `ac7a2b35-a9b4-4ff6-beac-a1bcee86d04b`.

```
$ trove show INSTANCE_ID


+------------------+----------------------------------------+
|     Property     |                 Value                  |
+------------------+----------------------------------------+
|     created      |          2014-03-18T17:12:03           |
|     datastore    |                 mysql                  |
| datastore_version |              mysql-5.5                 |
|      flavor      |                  10                    |
|        id        | ac7a2b35-a9b4-4ff6-beac-a1bcee86d04b   |
|        ip        |               10.0.0.3                 |
|       name       |                guest2                  |
|      status      |                ACTIVE                  |
|     updated      |          2014-03-18T17:12:06           |
|      volume      |                  2                     |
|   volume_used    |                 0.18                   |
+------------------+----------------------------------------+
```

Note that the data store, flavor ID, and volume size have the same values as in the original `guest1` instance.

Use the **trove database-list** command to check that the original databases (`db1` and `db2`) are present on the restored instance.

```
$ trove database-li0st INSTANCE_ID

+--------------------+
|        name        |
+--------------------+
|        db1         |
|        db2         |
| performance_schema |
|        test        |
+--------------------+
```

Use the **trove user-list** command to check that the original user (user1) is present on the restored instance.

```
$ trove user-list INSTANCE_ID

+--------+------+-----------+
|  name  | host | databases |
+--------+------+-----------+
| user1  |  %   | db1, db2  |
+--------+------+-----------+
```

4. **Notify users**

   Tell the users who were accessing the now-disabled guest1 database instance that they can now access guest2. Provide them with guest2's name, IP address, and any other information they might need. (You can get this information by using the **trove show** command.)

5. **Clean up**

   At this point, you might want to delete the disabled guest1 instance, by using the **trove delete** command.

```
$ trove delete INSTANCE_ID
```

4.18.3 Use incremental backups

Incremental backups let you chain together a series of backups. You start with a regular backup. Then, when you want to create a subsequent incremental backup, you specify the parent backup.

Restoring a database instance from an incremental backup is the same as creating a database instance from a regular backup—the Database service handles the complexities of applying the chain of incremental backups.

This example shows you how to use incremental backups with a MySQL database.

Assumptions. Assume that you have created a regular backup for the following database instance:

- Instance name: `guest1`

- ID of the instance (`INSTANCE_ID`): `792a6a56-278f-4a01-9997-d997fa126370`

- ID   of   the   regular   backup   artifact   (`BACKUP_ID`): `6dc3a9b7-1f3e-4954-8582-3f2e4942cddd`

4.18.3.1 Create and use incremental backups

1. **Create your first incremental backup**

   Use the **trove backup-create** command and specify:

   - The `INSTANCE_ID` of the database instance you are doing the incremental backup for (in this example, `792a6a56-278f-4a01-9997-d997fa126370`)

   - The name of the incremental backup you are creating: `backup1.1`

   - The `BACKUP_ID` of the parent backup. In this case, the parent is the regular backup, with an ID of `6dc3a9b7-1f3e-4954-8582-3f2e4942cddd`

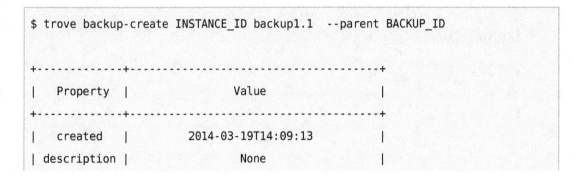

```
$ trove backup-create INSTANCE_ID backup1.1  --parent BACKUP_ID


+-------------+----------------------------------------+
|  Property   |                 Value                  |
+-------------+----------------------------------------+
|   created   |         2014-03-19T14:09:13            |
| description |                 None                   |
```

```
|     id      | 1d474981-a006-4f62-b25f-43d7b8a7097e |
| instance_id | 792a6a56-278f-4a01-9997-d997fa126370 |
| locationRef |                 None                 |
|    name     |              backup1.1               |
|  parent_id  | 6dc3a9b7-1f3e-4954-8582-3f2e4942cddd |
|    size     |                 None                 |
|   status    |                 NEW                  |
|   updated   |         2014-03-19T14:09:13          |
+-------------+--------------------------------------+
```

Note that this command returns both the ID of the database instance you are incrementally backing up (`instance_id`) and a new ID for the new incremental backup artifact you just created (`id`).

2. **Create your second incremental backup**

   The name of your second incremental backup is `backup1.2`. This time, when you specify the parent, pass in the ID of the incremental backup you just created in the previous step (`backup1.1`). In this example, it is `1d474981-a006-4f62-b25f-43d7b8a7097e`.

```
$ trove backup-create INSTANCE_ID  backup1.2  --parent BACKUP_ID


+-------------+--------------------------------------+
|  Property   |                Value                 |
+-------------+--------------------------------------+
|   created   |         2014-03-19T14:09:13          |
| description |                 None                 |
|     id      | bb84a240-668e-49b5-861e-6a98b67e7a1f |
| instance_id | 792a6a56-278f-4a01-9997-d997fa126370 |
| locationRef |                 None                 |
|    name     |              backup1.2               |
|  parent_id  | 1d474981-a006-4f62-b25f-43d7b8a7097e |
|    size     |                 None                 |
|   status    |                 NEW                  |
|   updated   |         2014-03-19T14:09:13          |
+-------------+--------------------------------------+
```

3. **Restore using incremental backups**

Now assume that your `guest1` database instance is damaged and you need to restore it from your incremental backups. In this example, you use the **trove create** command to create a new database instance called `guest2`.

To incorporate your incremental backups, you simply use the `--backup` parameter to pass in the `BACKUP_ID` of your most recent incremental backup. The Database service handles the complexities of applying the chain of all previous incremental backups.

```
$ trove create guest2 10 --size 1 --backup BACKUP_ID


+-------------------
+----------------------------------------------------------+
|     Property      |                    Value
 |
+-------------------
+----------------------------------------------------------+
|     created       |              2014-03-19T14:10:56
 |
|    datastore      |        {u'version': u'mysql-5.5', u'type': u'mysql'}
 |
| datastore_version |                    mysql-5.5
 |
|     flavor        | {u'id': u'10', u'links':
 |
|                   | [{u'href': u'https://10.125.1.135:8779/v1.0/
 |
|                   | 626734041baa4254ae316de52a20b390/flavors/10', u'rel':
 |
|                   | u'self'}, {u'href': u'https://10.125.1.135:8779/
 |
|                   | flavors/10', u'rel': u'bookmark'}]}
 |
|       id          |        a3680953-eea9-4cf2-918b-5b8e49d7e1b3
 |
|      name         |                    guest2
 |
```

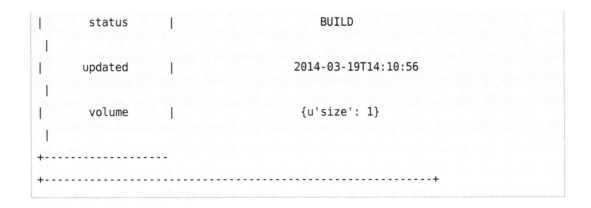

```
|      status      |                    BUILD
   |
|      updated     |              2014-03-19T14:10:56
   |
|      volume      |                {u'size': 1}
   |
+-------------------
+-----------------------------------------------------------+
```

4.18.4 Manage database configuration

You can manage database configuration tasks by using configuration groups. Configuration groups let you set configuration options, in bulk, on one or more databases.

This example assumes you have created a MySQL database and shows you how to use a configuration group to configure it. Although this example sets just one option on one database, you can use these same procedures to set multiple options on multiple database instances throughout your environment. This can provide significant time savings in managing your cloud.

4.18.4.1 Bulk-configure a database or databases

1. **List available options**

   First, determine which configuration options you can set. Different data store versions have different configuration options.

   List the names and IDs of all available versions of the `mysql` data store:

   ```
   $ trove datastore-version-list mysql

   +------------------------------------------+-----------+
   |                   id                     |   name    |
   +------------------------------------------+-----------+
   | eeb574ce-f49a-48b6-820d-b2959fcd38bb     | mysql-5.5 |
   +------------------------------------------+-----------+
   ```

Pass in the data store version ID with the **trove configuration-parameter-list** command to get the available options:

```
$ trove configuration-parameter-list DATASTORE_VERSION_ID


+--------------------------------+---------+---------+----------------------
+------------------+
|            name                |  type   |  min    |         max          |
 restart_required |
+--------------------------------+---------+---------+----------------------
+------------------+
|    auto_increment_increment    | integer |    1    |        65535         |      False
 |
|    auto_increment_offset       | integer |    1    |        65535         |      False
 |
|         autocommit             | integer |    0    |          1           |      False
 |
|    bulk_insert_buffer_size     | integer |    0    | 18446744073709547520 |      False
 |
|     character_set_client       | string  |         |                      |      False
 |
|   character_set_connection     | string  |         |                      |      False
 |
|    character_set_database      | string  |         |                      |      False
 |
|   character_set_filesystem     | string  |         |                      |      False
 |
|    character_set_results       | string  |         |                      |      False
 |
|     character_set_server       | string  |         |                      |      False
 |
|     collation_connection       | string  |         |                      |      False
 |
|      collation_database        | string  |         |                      |      False
 |
```

collation_server	string				False
connect_timeout	integer	1	65535		False
expire_logs_days	integer	1	65535		False
innodb_buffer_pool_size	integer	0	68719476736		True
innodb_file_per_table	integer	0	1		True
innodb_flush_log_at_trx_commit	integer	0	2		False
innodb_log_buffer_size	integer	1048576	4294967296		True
innodb_open_files	integer	10	4294967296		True
innodb_thread_concurrency	integer	0	1000		False
interactive_timeout	integer	1	65535		False
join_buffer_size	integer	0	4294967296		False
key_buffer_size	integer	0	4294967296		False
local_infile	integer	0	1		False
max_allowed_packet	integer	1024	1073741824		False
max_connect_errors	integer	1	18446744073709547520		False
max_connections	integer	1	65535		False
max_user_connections	integer	1	100000		False
myisam_sort_buffer_size	integer	4	18446744073709547520		False

```
|         server_id          | integer |   1   |        100000        |    True
     |
|       sort_buffer_size      | integer | 32768 | 18446744073709547520 |    False
     |
|        sync_binlog          | integer |   0   | 18446744073709547520 |    False
     |
|        wait_timeout         | integer |   1   |       31536000       |    False
     |
+-----------------------------+---------+-------+----------------------+-------------------------
+------------------+
```

In this example, the **configuration-parameter-list** command returns a list of options that work with MySQL 5.5.

2. **Create a configuration group**

   A configuration group contains a comma-separated list of key-value pairs. Each pair consists of a configuration option and its value.

   You can create a configuration group by using the **trove configuration-create** command. The general syntax for this command is:

   ```
   $ trove configuration-create NAME VALUES --datastore DATASTORE_NAME
   ```

   - *NAME*. The name you want to use for this group.

   - *VALUES*. The list of key-value pairs.

   - *DATASTORE_NAME*. The name of the associated data store.

   Set *VALUES* as a JSON dictionary, for example:

   ```
   {"myFirstKey" : "someString", "mySecondKey" : someInt}
   ```

   This example creates a configuration group called `group1`. `group1` contains just one key and value pair, and this pair sets the `sync_binlog` option to `1`.

   ```
   $ trove configuration-create group1 '{"sync_binlog" : 1}' --datastore mysql

   +----------------------+----------------------------------------+
   |       Property       |                 Value                  |
   ```

```
+---------------------+--------------------------------------+
| datastore_version_id | eeb574ce-f49a-48b6-820d-b2959fcd38bb |
| description         |                 None                 |
| id                  | 9a9ef3bc-079b-476a-9cbf-85aa64f898a5 |
| name                |                group1                |
| values              |          {"sync_binlog": 1}          |
+---------------------+--------------------------------------+
```

3. **Examine your existing configuration**

   Before you use the newly-created configuration group, look at how the sync_binlog option is configured on your database. Replace the following sample connection values with values that connect to your database:

   ```
   $ mysql -u user7 -ppassword -h 172.16.200.2 myDB7
    Welcome to the MySQL monitor. Commands end with ; or \g.
    ...
   mysql> show variables like 'sync_binlog';
   +---------------+-------+
   | Variable_name | Value |
   +---------------+-------+
   | sync_binlog   | 0     |
   +---------------+-------+
   ```

   As you can see, the sync_binlog option is currently set to 0 for the myDB7 database.

4. **Change the database configuration using a configuration group**

   You can change a database's configuration by attaching a configuration group to a database instance. You do this by using the **trove configuration-attach** command and passing in the ID of the database instance and the ID of the configuration group.

   Get the ID of the database instance:

   ```
   $ trove list

   +-------------+------------------+-----------+-------------------+--------+-----------
   +------+
   |     id      |       name       | datastore | datastore_version | status | flavor_id |
     size |
   ```

```
+-------------+------------------+----------+--------------------+--------+----------
+------+
| 26a265dd... | mysql_instance_7 |  mysql   |     mysql-5.5      | ACTIVE |    6     |
  5   |
+-------------+------------------+----------+--------------------+--------+----------
+------+
```

Get the ID of the configuration group:

```
$ trove configuration-list

+-------------+--------+-------------+---------------------+
|    id       | name   | description |datastore_version_id |
+-------------+--------+-------------+---------------------+
| 9a9ef3bc... | group1 |    None     |     eeb574ce...     |
+-------------+--------+-------------+---------------------+
```

Attach the configuration group to the database instance:

 Note

> This command syntax pertains only to python-troveclient version 1.0.6 and later.
> Earlier versions require you to pass in the configuration group ID as the first argu-
> ment.

```
$ trove configuration-attach DB_INSTANCE_ID CONFIG_GROUP_ID
```

5. **Re-examine the database configuration**

   Display the `sync_binlog` setting again:

```
mysql> show variables like 'sync_binlog';
+---------------+-------+
| Variable_name | Value |
+---------------+-------+
| sync_binlog   | 1     |
+---------------+-------+
```

As you can see, the `sync_binlog` option is now set to `1`, as specified in the `group1` configuration group.

Conclusion. Using a configuration group to set a single option on a single database is obviously a trivial example. However, configuration groups can provide major efficiencies when you consider that:

- A configuration group can specify a large number of option values.

- You can apply a configuration group to hundreds or thousands of database instances in your environment.

Used in this way, configuration groups let you modify your database cloud configuration, on the fly, on a massive scale.

Maintenance. There are also a number of useful maintenance features for working with configuration groups. You can:

- Disassociate a configuration group from a database instance, using the **trove configuration-detach** command.

- Modify a configuration group on the fly, using the **trove configuration-patch** command.

- Find out what instances are using a configuration group, using the **trove configuration-instances** command.

- Delete a configuration group, using the **trove configuration-delete** command. You might want to do this if no instances use a group.

4.18.5   Set up database replication

You can create a replica of an existing database instance. When you make subsequent changes to the original instance, the system automatically applies those changes to the replica.

- Replicas are read-only.

- When you create a replica, do not specify the `--users` or `--databases` options.

- You can choose a smaller volume or flavor for a replica than for the original, but the replica's volume must be big enough to hold the data snapshot from the original.

This example shows you how to replicate a MySQL database instance.

4.18.5.1 Set up replication

1. **Get the instance ID**

   Get the ID of the original instance you want to replicate:

   ```
   $ trove list
   +-----------+---------+-----------+------------------+--------+-----------+------+
   |    id     | name    | datastore | datastore_version | status | flavor_id | size |
   +-----------+---------+-----------+------------------+--------+-----------+------+
   | 97b...ae6 | base_1  |   mysql   |     mysql-5.5    | ACTIVE |    10     |  2   |
   +-----------+---------+-----------+------------------+--------+-----------+------+
   ```

2. **Create the replica**

   Create a new instance that will be a replica of the original instance. You do this by passing in the `--replica_of` option with the **trove create** command. This example creates a replica called `replica_1`. `replica_1` is a replica of the original instance, `base_1`:

   ```
   $ trove create replica_1 6 --size=5 --datastore_version mysql-5.5 \
     --datastore mysql --replica_of ID_OF_ORIGINAL_INSTANCE
   ```

3. **Verify replication status**

   Pass in `replica_1`'s instance ID with the **trove show** command to verify that the newly created `replica_1` instance is a replica of the original `base_1`. Note that the `replica_of` property is set to the ID of `base_1`.

   ```
   $ trove show INSTANCE_ID_OF_REPLICA_1
   +-------------------+--------------------------------------+
   | Property          | Value                                |
   +-------------------+--------------------------------------+
   | created           | 2014-09-16T11:16:49                  |
   | datastore         | mysql                                |
   | datastore_version | mysql-5.5                            |
   | flavor            | 6                                    |
   | id                | 49c6eff6-ef91-4eff-91c0-efbda7e83c38 |
   ```

```
| name              | replica_1                            |
| replica_of        | 97b4b853-80f6-414f-ba6f-c6f455a79ae6 |
| status            | BUILD                                |
| updated           | 2014-09-16T11:16:49                  |
| volume            | 5                                    |
+-------------------+--------------------------------------+
```

Now pass in `base_1`'s instance ID with the **trove show** command to list the replica(s) associated with the original instance. Note that the `replicas` property is set to the ID of `replica_1`. If there are multiple replicas, they appear as a comma-separated list.

```
$ trove show INSTANCE_ID_OF_BASE_1
+-------------------+--------------------------------------+
| Property          | Value                                |
+-------------------+--------------------------------------+
| created           | 2014-09-16T11:04:56                  |
| datastore         | mysql                                |
| datastore_version | mysql-5.5                            |
| flavor            | 6                                    |
| id                | 97b4b853-80f6-414f-ba6f-c6f455a79ae6 |
| ip                | 172.16.200.2                         |
| name              | base_1                               |
| replicas          | 49c6eff6-ef91-4eff-91c0-efbda7e83c38 |
| status            | ACTIVE                               |
| updated           | 2014-09-16T11:05:06                  |
| volume            | 5                                    |
| volume_used       | 0.11                                 |
+-------------------+--------------------------------------+
```

4. **Detach the replica**

   If the original instance goes down, you can detach the replica. The replica becomes a standalone database instance. You can then take the new standalone instance and create a new replica of that instance.

   You detach a replica using the **trove detach-replica** command:

```
$ trove detach-replica INSTANCE_ID_OF_REPLICA
```

4.18.6 Set up database clustering

You can store data across multiple machines by setting up MongoDB sharded clusters.
Each cluster includes:

- One or more *shards*. Each shard consists of a three member replica set (three instances organized as a replica set).

- One or more *query routers*. A query router is the machine that your application actually connects to. This machine is responsible for communicating with the config server to figure out where the requested data is stored. It then accesses and returns the data from the appropriate shard(s).

- One or more *config servers*. Config servers store the metadata that links requested data with the shard that contains it.

This example shows you how to set up a MongoDB sharded cluster.

 Note

Before you begin. Make sure that:

- The administrative user has registered a MongoDB datastore type and version.

- The administrative user has created an appropriate *Section 4.18.1, "Create and access a database"*.

4.18.6.1 Set up clustering

1. **Create a cluster**

Create a cluster by using the **trove cluster-create** command. This command creates a one-shard cluster. Pass in:

- The name of the cluster.

- The name and version of the datastore you want to use.

- The three instances you want to include in the replication set for the first shard. Specify each instance by using the `--instance` argument and the associated flavor ID and volume size. Use the same flavor ID and volume size for each instance. In this example, flavor `7` is a custom flavor that meets the MongoDB minimum requirements.

```
$ trove cluster-create cluster1 mongodb "2.4" \
  --instance flavor_id=7,volume=2 --instance flavor_id=7,volume=2 \
  --instance flavor_id=7,volume=2
+-------------------+---------------------------------------+
| Property          | Value                                 |
+-------------------+---------------------------------------+
| created           | 2014-08-16T01:46:51                   |
| datastore         | mongodb                               |
| datastore_version | 2.4                                   |
| id                | aa6ef0f5-dbef-48cd-8952-573ad881e717 |
| name              | cluster1                              |
| task_description  | Building the initial cluster.         |
| task_name         | BUILDING                              |
| updated           | 2014-08-16T01:46:51                   |
+-------------------+---------------------------------------+
```

2. **Display cluster information**

   Display information about a cluster by using the **trove cluster-show** command. Pass in the ID of the cluster.

   The cluster ID displays when you first create a cluster. (If you need to find it later on, use the **trove cluster-list** command to list the names and IDs of all the clusters in your system.)

```
$ trove cluster-show CLUSTER_ID
+-------------------+---------------------------------------+
```

```
| Property           | Value                                   |
+--------------------+-----------------------------------------+
| created            | 2014-08-16T01:46:51                     |
| datastore          | mongodb                                 |
| datastore_version  | 2.4                                     |
| id                 | aa6ef0f5-dbef-48cd-8952-573ad881e717 |
| ip                 | 10.0.0.2                                |
| name               | cluster1                                |
| task_description   | No tasks for the cluster.               |
| task_name          | NONE                                    |
| updated            | 2014-08-16T01:59:33                     |
+--------------------+-----------------------------------------+
```

 Note

Your application connects to this IP address. The trove **cluster-show** command displays the IP address of the query router. This is the IP address your application uses to retrieve data from the database.

3. **List cluster instances**

List the instances in a cluster by using the **trove cluster-instances** command.

```
$ trove cluster-instances CLUSTER_ID
+--------------------------------------+--------------+-----------+------+
| ID                                   | Name         | Flavor ID | Size |
+--------------------------------------+--------------+-----------+------+
| 45532fc4-661c-4030-8ca4-18f02aa2b337 | cluster1-rs1-1 | 7       |    2 |
| 7458a98d-6f89-4dfd-bb61-5cf1dd65c121 | cluster1-rs1-2 | 7       |    2 |
| b37634fb-e33c-4846-8fe8-cf2b2c95e731 | cluster1-rs1-3 | 7       |    2 |
+--------------------------------------+--------------+-----------+------+
```

Naming conventions for replication sets and instances. Note that the `Name` column displays an instance name that includes the replication set name. The replication set names and instance names are automatically generated, following these rules:

- **Replication set name.** This name consists of the cluster name, followed by the string -rs*n*, where *n* is 1 for the first replication set you create, 2 for the second replication set, and so on. In this example, the cluster name is `cluster1`, and there is only one replication set, so the replication set name is `cluster1-rs1`.

- **Instance name.** This name consists of the replication set name followed by the string -*n*, where *n* is 1 for the first instance in a replication set, 2 for the second instance, and so on. In this example, the instance names are `cluster1-rs1-1`, `cluster1-rs1-2`, and `cluster1-rs1-3`.

4. **List clusters**

   List all the clusters in your system, using the **trove cluster-list** command.

```
$ trove cluster-list
+---------------------------------------+----------+-----------+-------------------+----------+
| ID                                    | Name     | Datastore | Datastore Version | Task     |
                                                                                    Name     |
+---------------------------------------+----------+-----------+-------------------+----------+
| aa6ef0f5-dbef-48cd-8952-573ad881e717  | cluster1 | mongodb   | 2.4               | NONE     |
                                                                                             |
| b8829c2a-b03a-49d3-a5b1-21ec974223ee  | cluster2 | mongodb   | 2.4               |          |
  BUILDING  |
+---------------------------------------+----------+-----------+-------------------+----------+
```

5. **Delete a cluster**

   Delete a cluster, using the **trove cluster-delete** command.

```
$ trove cluster-delete CLUSTER_ID
```

4.18.6.1.1 Query routers and config servers

Each cluster includes at least one query router and one config server. Query routers and config servers count against your quota. When you delete a cluster, the system deletes the associated query router(s) and config server(s).

5 OpenStack Python SDK

The OpenStack Python Software Development Kit (SDK) is used to write Python automation scripts that create and manage resources in your OpenStack cloud. The SDK implements Python bindings to the OpenStack API, which enables you to perform automation tasks in Python by making calls on Python objects, rather than making REST calls directly. All OpenStack command-line tools are implemented using the Python SDK.

You should also be familiar with:

- RESTful web services

- HTTP/1.1

- JSON and XML data serialization formats

5.1 Installing OpenStack SDK

Each OpenStack project has its own Python library. These libraries are bundled with the command-line clients. For example, the Python bindings for the Compute API are bundled with the python-novaclient package.

For details about how to install the clients, see .

5.2 Authenticate

When using the SDK, you must authenticate against an OpenStack endpoint before you can use OpenStack services. Each project uses a slightly different syntax for authentication.

You must typically authenticate against a specific version of a service. For example, a client might need to authenticate against Identity v2.0.

Python scripts that use the OpenStack SDK must have access to the credentials contained in the OpenStack RC file. Because credentials are sensitive information, do not include them in your scripts. This guide assumes that users source the PROJECT-openrc.sh file and access the credentials by using the environment variables in the Python scripts.

5.2.1 Authenticate against an Identity endpoint

To authenticate against the Identity v2.0 endpoint, instantiate a keystoneclient.v_20.client.Client (http://docs.openstack.org/developer/python-keystoneclient/api/keystoneclient.v2_0.client.html#keystoneclient.v2_0.client.Client) ↗ object:

```
from os import environ as env
import keystoneclient.v2_0.client as ksclient
keystone = ksclient.Client(auth_url=env['OS_AUTH_URL'],
                           username=env['OS_USERNAME'],
                           password=env['OS_PASSWORD'],
                           tenant_name=env['OS_TENANT_NAME'],
                           region_name=env['OS_REGION_NAME'])
```

After you instantiate a `Client` object, you can retrieve the token by accessing its `auth_token` attribute object:

```
import keystoneclient.v2_0.client as ksclient
keystone = ksclient.Client(...)
print keystone.auth_token
```

If the OpenStack cloud is configured to use public-key infrastructure (PKI) tokens, the Python script output looks something like this:

```
MIIQUQYJKoZIhvcNAQcCoIIQQjCCED4CAQExCTAHBgUrDgMCGjCCDqcGCSqGSIb3DQEHAaCCDpgE
gg6UeyJhY2Nlc3MiOiB7InRva2VuIjogeyJpc3N1ZWRfYXQiOiAiMjAxMy0xMC0yMFQxNjo1NjoyNi
4zNTg2MjUiLCAiZXhwaXJlcyI6ICIyMDEzLTEwLTIxVDE2OjU2OjI2WiIsICJpZCI6ICJwbGFjZWhv
...
R3g14FJ0BxtTPbo6WarZ+sA3PZwdgIDyGNI-0Oqv-8ih4gJC9C6wBCel1dUXJ0Mn7BN-SfuxkooVk6
e090bcKjTWet3CC8IEj7a6LyLRVTdvmKGA5-pgp2mS5fb3G2mIad4Zeeb-zQn9V3Xf9WUGxuiVu1Hn
fhuUpJT-s9mU7+WEC3-8qkcBjEpqVCvMpmM4INI=
```

 Note

This example shows a subset of a PKI token. A complete token is over 5000 characters long.

5.2.2 Authenticate against an Image service endpoint

To authenticate against an Image service endpoint, instantiate a glanceclient.v2.client.Client (http://docs.openstack.org/developer/python-glanceclient/api/glanceclient.v2.client.html#glanceclient.v2.client.Client) ↗ object:

```
from os import environ as env
import glanceclient.v2.client as glclient
import keystoneclient.v2_0.client as ksclient

keystone = ksclient.Client(auth_url=env['OS_AUTH_URL'],
                           username=env['OS_USERNAME'],
                           password=env['OS_PASSWORD'],
                           tenant_name=env['OS_TENANT_NAME'],
                           region_name=env['OS_REGION_NAME'])
glance_endpoint = keystone.service_catalog.url_for(service_type='image')
glance = glclient.Client(glance_endpoint, token=keystone.auth_token)
```

5.2.3 Authenticate against a Compute endpoint

To authenticate against a Compute endpoint, instantiate a novaclient.v_1_1.client.Client (http://docs.openstack.org/developer/python-novaclient/api/novaclient.v1_1.client.html#novaclient.v1_1.client.Client) ↗ object:

```
from os import environ as env
import novaclient.v1_1.client as nvclient
nova = nvclient.Client(auth_url=env['OS_AUTH_URL'],
                       username=env['OS_USERNAME'],
                       api_key=env['OS_PASSWORD'],
                       project_id=env['OS_TENANT_NAME'],
                       region_name=env['OS_REGION_NAME'])
```

Alternatively, you can instantiate a `novaclient.client.Client` object and pass the version number:

```
from os import environ as env
import novaclient.client
```

```
nova = novaclient.client.Client("1.1", auth_url=env['OS_AUTH_URL'],
                                username=env['OS_USERNAME'],
                                api_key=env['OS_PASSWORD'],
                                project_id=env['OS_TENANT_NAME'],
                                region_name=env['OS_REGION_NAME'])
```

If you authenticate against an endpoint that uses a custom authentication back end, you must load the authentication plug-in and pass it to the constructor.

The Rackspace public cloud is an OpenStack deployment that uses a custom authentication back end. To authenticate against this cloud, you must install the rackspace-novaclient (https://pypi.python.org/pypi/rackspace-novaclient/) ⏶ library that contains the Rackspace authentication plug-in, called `rackspace`. The following Python code shows the additional modifications required to instantiate a `Client` object that can authenticate against the Rackspace custom authentication back end.

```
import novaclient.auth_plugin
import novaclient.v1_1.client as nvclient
from os import environ as env
auth_system = 'rackspace'
auth_plugin = novaclient.auth_plugin.load_plugin('rackspace')
nova = nvclient.Client(auth_url=env['OS_AUTH_URL'],
                       username=env['OS_USERNAME'],
                       api_key=env['OS_PASSWORD'],
                       project_id=env['OS_TENANT_NAME'],
                       region_name=env['OS_REGION_NAME'],
                       auth_system='rackspace',
                       auth_plugin=auth_plugin)
```

If you set the `OS_AUTH_SYSTEM` environment variable, check for this variable in your Python script to determine whether you need to load a custom authentication back end:

```
import novaclient.auth_plugin
import novaclient.v1_1.client as nvclient
from os import environ as env
auth_system = env.get('OS_AUTH_SYSTEM', 'keystone')
if auth_system != "keystone":
  auth_plugin = novaclient.auth_plugin.load_plugin(auth_system)
```

```
else:
  auth_plugin = None
nova = nvclient.Client(auth_url=env['OS_AUTH_URL'],
                       username=env['OS_USERNAME'],
                       api_key=env['OS_PASSWORD'],
                       project_id=env['OS_TENANT_NAME'],
                       region_name=env['OS_REGION_NAME'],
                       auth_system=auth_system,
                       auth_plugin=auth_plugin)
```

5.2.4   Authenticate against a Networking endpoint

To authenticate against a Networking endpoint, instantiate a neutronclient.v_2_0.client.Client object:

```
from os import environ as env
from neutronclient.v2_0 import client as neutronclient
neutron = neutronclient.Client(auth_url=env['OS_AUTH_URL'],
                               username=env['OS_USERNAME'],
                               password=env['OS_PASSWORD'],
                               tenant_name=env['OS_TENANT_NAME'],
                               region_name=env['OS_REGION_NAME'])
```

You can also authenticate by explicitly specifying the endpoint and token:

```
from os import environ as env
import keystoneclient.v2_0.client as ksclient
from neutronclient.v2_0 import client as neutronclient
keystone = ksclient.Client(auth_url=env['OS_AUTH_URL'],
                           username=env['OS_USERNAME'],
                           password=env['OS_PASSWORD'],
                           tenant_name=env['OS_TENANT_NAME'],
                           region_name=env['OS_REGION_NAME'])
endpoint_url = keystone.service_catalog.url_for(service_type='network')
token = keystone.auth_token
neutron = neutronclient.Client(endpoint_url=endpoint_url, token=token)
```

5.3 Manage images

When working with images in the SDK, you will call both `glance` and `nova` methods.

5.3.1 List images

To list the available images, call the `glanceclient.v2.images.Controller.list` method:

```
import glanceclient.v2.client as glclient
glance = glclient.Client(...)
images = glance.images.list()
```

The images method returns a Python generator, as shown in the following interaction with the Python interpreter:

```
>>> images = glance.images.list()
>>> images
<generator object list at 0x105e9c2d0>
>>> list(images)
[{u'checksum': u'f8a2eeee2dc65b3d9b6e63678955bd83',
  u'container_format': u'ami',
  u'created_at': u'2013-10-20T14:28:10Z',
  u'disk_format': u'ami',
  u'file': u'/v2/images/dbc9b2db-51d7-403d-b680-3f576380b00c/file',
  u'id': u'dbc9b2db-51d7-403d-b680-3f576380b00c',
  u'kernel_id': u'c002c82e-2cfa-4952-8461-2095b69c18a6',
  u'min_disk': 0,
  u'min_ram': 0,
  u'name': u'cirros-0.3.2-x86_64-uec',
  u'protected': False,
  u'ramdisk_id': u'4c1c9b4f-3fe9-425a-a1ec-1d8fd90b4db3',
  u'schema': u'/v2/schemas/image',
  u'size': 25165824,
  u'status': u'active',
  u'tags': [],
  u'updated_at': u'2013-10-20T14:28:11Z',
```

```
   u'visibility': u'public'},
 {u'checksum': u'69c33642f44ca552ba4bb8b66ad97e85',
  u'container_format': u'ari',
  u'created_at': u'2013-10-20T14:28:09Z',
  u'disk_format': u'ari',
  u'file': u'/v2/images/4c1c9b4f-3fe9-425a-a1ec-1d8fd90b4db3/file',
  u'id': u'4c1c9b4f-3fe9-425a-a1ec-1d8fd90b4db3',
  u'min_disk': 0,
  u'min_ram': 0,
  u'name': u'cirros-0.3.2-x86_64-uec-ramdisk',
  u'protected': False,
  u'schema': u'/v2/schemas/image',
  u'size': 3714968,
  u'status': u'active',
  u'tags': [],
  u'updated_at': u'2013-10-20T14:28:10Z',
  u'visibility': u'public'},
 {u'checksum': u'c352f4e7121c6eae958bc1570324f17e',
  u'container_format': u'aki',
  u'created_at': u'2013-10-20T14:28:08Z',
  u'disk_format': u'aki',
  u'file': u'/v2/images/c002c82e-2cfa-4952-8461-2095b69c18a6/file',
  u'id': u'c002c82e-2cfa-4952-8461-2095b69c18a6',
  u'min_disk': 0,
  u'min_ram': 0,
  u'name': u'cirros-0.3.2-x86_64-uec-kernel',
  u'protected': False,
  u'schema': u'/v2/schemas/image',
  u'size': 4955792,
  u'status': u'active',
  u'tags': [],
  u'updated_at': u'2013-10-20T14:28:09Z',
  u'visibility': u'public'}]
```

5.3.2 Get image by ID

To retrieve an image object from its ID, call the <u>`glanceclient.v2.images.Controller.get`</u> method:

```
import glanceclient.v2.client as glclient
image_id = 'c002c82e-2cfa-4952-8461-2095b69c18a6'
glance = glclient.Client(...)
image = glance.images.get(image_id)
```

5.3.3 Get image by name

The Image service Python bindings do not support the retrieval of an image object by name. However, the Compute Python bindings enable you to get an image object by name. To get an image object by name, call the <u>`novaclient.v1_1.images.ImageManager.find`</u> method:

```
import novaclient.v1_1.client as nvclient
name = "cirros"
nova = nvclient.Client(...)
image = nova.images.find(name=name)
```

5.3.4 Upload an image

To upload an image, call the <u>`glanceclient.v2.images.ImageManager.create`</u> method:

```
import glanceclient.v2.client as glclient
imagefile = "/tmp/myimage.img"
glance = glclient.Client(...)
with open(imagefile) as fimage:
  glance.images.create(name="myimage", is_public=False, disk_format="qcow2",
                       container_format="bare", data=fimage)
```

5.4 Assign CORS headers to requests

Cross-Origin Resource Sharing (CORS) is a specification that defines how browsers and servers communicate across origins by using HTTP headers, such as those assigned by Object Storage API requests. The Object Storage API supports the following headers:

- Access-Control-Allow-Credentials

- Access-Control-Allow-Methods

- Access-Control-Allow-Origin

- Access-Control-Expose-Headers

- Access-Control-Max-Age

- Access-Control-Request-Headers

- Access-Control-Request-Method

- Origin

You can only assign these headers to objects. For more information, see www.w3.org/TR/access-control/ (http://www.w3.org/TR/access-control/) ↗ .

This example assigns the file origin to the `Origin` header, which ensures that the file originated from a reputable source.

```
$ curl -i -X POST -H "Origin: example.com" -H "X-Auth-Token:
48e17715dfce47bb90dc2a336f63493a"
https://storage.example.com/v1/MossoCloudFS_c31366f1-9f1c-40dc-a
b92-6b3f0b5a8c45/ephotos
HTTP/1.1 204 No Content
Content-Length: 0
Content-Type: text/html; charset=UTF-8
Access-Control-Allow-Origin: example.com
Access-Control-Expose-Headers: cache-control, content-language,
content-type, expires, last-modified, pragma, etag, x-timestamp, x-trans-id
X-Trans-Id: tx979bfe26be6649c489ada-0054cba1d9ord1
Date: Fri, 30 Jan 2015 15:23:05 GMT
```

5.5 Schedule objects for deletion

To determine whether your Object Storage system supports this feature, see . Alternatively, check with your service provider.

Scheduling an object for deletion is helpful for managing objects that you do not want to permanently store, such as log files, recurring full backups of a dataset, or documents or images that become outdated at a specified time.

To schedule an object for deletion, include one of these headers with the `PUT` or `POST` request on the object:

X-Delete-At

A UNIX epoch timestamp, in integer form. For example, `1348691905` represents `Wed, 26 Sept 2012 20:38:25 GMT`. It specifies the time you want the object to expire, no longer be served, and be deleted completely from the object store.

X-Delete-After

An integer value which specifies the number of seconds from the time of the request to when you want to delete the object. This header is converted to a `X-Delete-At` header that is set to the sum of the `X-Delete-After` value plus the current time, in seconds.

 Note

Use http://www.epochconverter.com/ ↗ to convert dates to and from epoch timestamps and for batch conversions.

Use the POST method to assign expiration headers to existing objects that you want to expire.

In this example, the `X-Delete-At` header is assigned a UNIX epoch timestamp in integer form for `Mon, 11 Jun 2012 15:38:25 GMT`.

```
$ curl -i publicURL/marktwain/goodbye -X PUT -H "X-Auth-Token: token" \
  -H "X-Delete-At: 1390581073" -H "Content-Length: 14" -H \
  "Content-Type: application/octet-stream"
```

In this example, the `X-Delete-After` header is set to 864000 seconds. The object expires after this time.

```
PUT /<api version>/<account>/<container>/<object> HTTP/1.1
Host: storage.example.com
```

```
X-Auth-Token: eaaafd18-0fed-4b3a-81b4-663c99ec1cbb
Content-Type: image/jpeg
X-Delete-After: 864000
```

5.6 Configure access and security for instances

When working with images in the SDK, you will call `novaclient` methods.

5.6.1 Add a keypair

To generate a keypair, call the novaclient.v1_1.keypairs.KeypairManager.create (http://docs.openstack.org/developer/python-novaclient/api/novaclient.v1_1.keypairs.html#novaclient.v1_1.keypairs.KeypairManager.create)↗ **method:**

```
import novaclient.v1_1.client as nvclient
nova = nvclient.Client(...)
keypair_name = "staging"
keypair = nova.keypairs.create(name=keypair_name)
print keypair.private_key
```

The Python script output looks something like this:

```
-----BEGIN RSA PRIVATE KEY-----
MIIEowIBAAKCAQEA8XkaMqInSPfy0hMfWO+OZRtIgrQAbQkNcaNHmv2GN2G6xZlb\nuBRux5Xk/6SZ
ABaNPm1nRWm/ZDHnxCsFTcAl2LYOQXx3Cl2qKNY4r2di4G48GAkd\n7k5lDP2RgQatUM8npO0CD9PU
...
mmrceYYK08/lQ7JKLmVkdzdQKt77+vloBBuHiykLfI6h1m77NRDw9r8cV\nzczYeoALifpjTPMkKS8
ECfDCuDn/vc9K1He8CRaJHf8AMLQLM3MN
-----END RSA PRIVATE KEY-----
```

You typically write the private key to a file to use it later. The file must be readable and writeable by only the file owner; otherwise, the SSH client will refuse to read the private key file. The safest way is to create the file with the appropriate permissions, as shown in the following example:

```
import novaclient.v1_1.client as nvclient
import os
```

```
nova = nvclient.Client(...)
keypair_name = "staging"
private_key_filename = "/home/alice/id-staging"
keypair = nova.keypairs.create(name=keypair_name)


# Create a file for writing that can only be read and written by
owner
fp = os.open(private_key_filename, os.O_WRONLY | os.O_CREAT, 0o600)
with os.fdopen(fp, 'w') as f:
    f.write(keypair.private_key)
```

5.6.2 Import a keypair

If you have already generated a keypair with the public key located at `~/.ssh/id_rsa.pub`, pass the contents of the file to the novaclient.v1_1.keypairs.KeypairManager.create (http://docs.openstack.org/developer/python-novaclient/api/novaclient.v1_1.keypairs.html#novaclient.v1_1.keypairs.KeypairManager.create) ↗ method to import the public key to Compute:

```
import novaclient.v1_1.client as nvclient
import os.path
with open(os.path.expanduser('~/.ssh/id_rsa.pub')) as f:
    public_key = f.read()
nova = nvclient.Client(...)
nova.keypairs.create('mykey', public_key)
```

5.6.3 List keypairs

To list keypairs, call the novaclient.v1_1.keypairs.KeypairManager.list (http://docs.openstack.org/developer/python-novaclient/api/novaclient.v1_1.keypairs.html#novaclient.v1_1.keypairs.KeypairManager.list) ↗ method:

```
import novaclient.v1_1.client as nvclient
nova = nvclient.Client(...)
keypairs = nova.keypairs.list()
```

5.6.4   Create and manage security groups

To   list   security   groups   for   the   current   project,   call   the
novaclient.v_1.security_groups.SecurityGroupManager.list   (http://docs.openstack.org/develop-
er/python-novaclient/api/

novaclient.v1_1.security_groups.html#novaclient.v1_1.security_groups.SecurityGroupManager.list) ↗
method:

```
import novaclient.v1_1.client as nvclient
nova = nvclient.Client(...)
security_groups = nova.security_groups.list()
```

To   create   a   security   group   with   a   specified   name   and   description,   call   the
novaclient.v_1.security_groups.SecurityGroupManager.create   (http://docs.openstack.org/develop-
er/python-novaclient/api/

novaclient.v1_1.security_groups.html#novaclient.v1_1.security_groups.SecurityGroupManager.create) ↗
method:

```
import novaclient.v1_1.client as nvclient
nova = nvclient.Client(...)
nova.security_groups.create(name="web", description="Web servers")
```

To delete a security group, call the novaclient.v_1.security_groups.SecurityGroupManager.delete
(http://docs.openstack.org/developer/python-novaclient/api/

novaclient.v1_1.security_groups.html#novaclient.v1_1.security_groups.SecurityGroupManager.delete) ↗

method,   passing   either   a   novaclient.v1_1.security_groups.SecurityGroup   (http://
docs.openstack.org/developer/python-novaclient/api/

novaclient.v1_1.security_groups.html#novaclient.v1_1.security_groups.SecurityGroup) ↗ **object or**
group ID as an argument:

```
import novaclient.v1_1.client as nvclient
nova = nvclient.Client(...)
group = nova.security_groups.find(name="web")
nova.security_groups.delete(group)
# The following lines would also delete the group:
# nova.security_groups.delete(group.id)
# group.delete()
```

5.6.5 Create and manage security group rules

Access the security group rules from the `rules` attribute of a novaclient.v1_1.security_groups.SecurityGroup (http://docs.openstack.org/developer/python-nova-client/api/novaclient.v1_1.security_groups.html#novaclient.v1_1.security_groups.SecurityGroup) ↗ object:

```
import novaclient.v1_1.client as nvclient
nova = nvclient.Client(...)
group = nova.security_groups.find(name="web")
print group.rules
```

To add a rule to a security group, call the novaclient.v1_1.security_group_rules.SecurityGroupRuleManager.create (http://docs.openstack.org/developer/python-novaclient/api/novaclient.v1_1.security_group_rules.html#novaclient.v1_1.security_group_rules.SecurityGroupRuleManager.cr method:

```
import novaclient.v1_1.client as nvclient
nova = nvclient.Client(...)
group = nova.security_groups.find(name="web")
# Add rules for ICMP, tcp/80 and tcp/443
nova.security_group_rules.create(group.id, ip_protocol="icmp",
                                 from_port=-1, to_port=-1)
nova.security_group_rules.create(group.id, ip_protocol="tcp",
                                 from_port=80, to_port=80)
nova.security_group_rules.create(group.id, ip_protocol="tcp",
                                 from_port=443, to_port=443)
```

5.7 Networking

To use the information in this section, you should have a general understanding of OpenStack Networking, OpenStack Compute, and the integration between the two. You should also have access to a plug-in that implements the Networking API v2.0.

5.7.1 Set environment variables

Make sure that you set the relevant environment variables.

As an example, see the sample shell file that sets these variables to get credentials:

```
export OS_USERNAME="admin"
export OS_PASSWORD="password"
export OS_TENANT_NAME="admin"
export OS_AUTH_URL="http://IPADDRESS/v2.0"
```

5.7.2 Get credentials

The examples in this section use the `get_credentials` method:

```
def get_credentials():
    d = {}
    d['username'] = os.environ['OS_USERNAME']
    d['password'] = os.environ['OS_PASSWORD']
    d['auth_url'] = os.environ['OS_AUTH_URL']
    d['tenant_name'] = os.environ['OS_TENANT_NAME']
    return d
```

This code resides in the `credentials.py` file, which all samples import.

Use the `get_credentials()` method to populate and get a dictionary:

```
credentials = get_credentials()
```

5.7.3 Get Nova credentials

The examples in this section use the `get_nova_credentials` method:

```
def get_nova_credentials():
    d = {}
    d['username'] = os.environ['OS_USERNAME']
    d['api_key'] = os.environ['OS_PASSWORD']
```

```
    d['auth_url'] = os.environ['OS_AUTH_URL']
    d['project_id'] = os.environ['OS_TENANT_NAME']
    return d
```

This code resides in the `credentials.py` file, which all samples import.

Use the `get_nova_credentials()` method to populate and get a dictionary:

```
nova_credentials = get_nova_credentials()
```

5.7.4   Print values

The examples in this section use the `print_values` and `print_values_server` methods:

```
def print_values(val, type):
    if type == 'ports':
        val_list = val['ports']
    if type == 'networks':
        val_list = val['networks']
    if type == 'routers':
        val_list = val['routers']
    for p in val_list:
        for k, v in p.items():
            print("%s : %s" % (k, v))
        print('\n')


def print_values_server(val, server_id, type):
    if type == 'ports':
        val_list = val['ports']

    if type == 'networks':
        val_list = val['networks']
    for p in val_list:
        bool = False
        for k, v in p.items():
            if k == 'device_id' and v == server_id:
```

```
        bool = True
    if bool:
        for k, v in p.items():
            print("%s : %s" % (k, v))
        print('\n')
```

This code resides in the `utils.py` file, which all samples import.

5.7.5   Create network

The following program creates a network:

```
#!/usr/bin/env python
from neutronclient.v2_0 import client
from credentials import get_credentials


network_name = 'sample_network'
credentials = get_credentials()
neutron = client.Client(**credentials)
try:
    body_sample = {'network': {'name': network_name,
                   'admin_state_up': True}}

    netw = neutron.create_network(body=body_sample)
    net_dict = netw['network']
    network_id = net_dict['id']
    print('Network %s created' % network_id)

    body_create_subnet = {'subnets': [{'cidr': '192.168.199.0/24',
                          'ip_version': 4, 'network_id': network_id}]}

    subnet = neutron.create_subnet(body=body_create_subnet)
    print('Created subnet %s' % subnet)
finally:
    print("Execution completed")
```

5.7.6   List networks

The following program lists networks:

```
#!/usr/bin/env python
from neutronclient.v2_0 import client
from credentials import get_credentials
from utils import print_values

credentials = get_credentials()
neutron = client.Client(**credentials)
netw = neutron.list_networks()

print_values(netw, 'networks')
```

For `print_values`, see *Section 5.7.4, "Print values"*.

5.7.7   Create ports

The following program creates a port:

```
#!/usr/bin/env python
from neutronclient.v2_0 import client
import novaclient.v1_1.client as nvclient
from credentials import get_credentials
from credentials import get_nova_credentials

credentials = get_nova_credentials()
nova_client = nvclient.Client(**credentials)

# Replace with server_id and network_id from your environment

server_id = '9a52795a-a70d-49a8-a5d0-5b38d78bd12d'
network_id = 'ce5d204a-93f5-43ef-bd89-3ab99ad09a9a'
server_detail = nova_client.servers.get(server_id)
print(server_detail.id)
```

```
if server_detail != None:

    credentials = get_credentials()

    neutron = client.Client(**credentials)


    body_value = {
                  "port": {
                           "admin_state_up": True,
                           "device_id": server_id,
                           "name": "port1",
                           "network_id": network_id
                  }
            }
    response = neutron.create_port(body=body_value)

    print(response)
```

For `get_nova_credentials`, see *Section 5.7.3, "Get Nova credentials".*

For `get_credentials`, see *Section 5.7.2, "Get credentials".*

5.7.8   List ports

The following program lists ports:

```
#!/usr/bin/env python
from neutronclient.v2_0 import client
from credentials import get_credentials
from utils import print_values


credentials = get_credentials()
neutron = client.Client(**credentials)
ports = neutron.list_ports()
print_values(ports, 'ports')
```

For `get_credentials` see *Section 5.7.2, "Get credentials".*

For `print_values`, see *Section 5.7.4, "Print values".*

5.7.9   List server ports

The following program lists the ports for a server:

```python
#!/usr/bin/env python
from neutronclient.v2_0 import client
import novaclient.v1_1.client as nvclient
from credentials import get_credentials
from credentials import get_nova_credentials
from utils import print_values_server

credentials = get_nova_credentials()
nova_client = nvclient.Client(**credentials)


# change these values according to your environment

server_id = '9a52795a-a70d-49a8-a5d0-5b38d78bd12d'
network_id = 'ce5d204a-93f5-43ef-bd89-3ab99ad09a9a'
server_detail = nova_client.servers.get(server_id)
print(server_detail.id)

if server_detail is not None:
    credentials = get_credentials()
    neutron = client.Client(**credentials)
    ports = neutron.list_ports()

    print_values_server(ports, server_id, 'ports')
    body_value = {'port': {
        'admin_state_up': True,
        'device_id': server_id,
        'name': 'port1',
        'network_id': network_id,
        }}

    response = neutron.create_port(body=body_value)
    print(response)
```

5.7.10   Create router and add port to subnet

This example queries OpenStack Networking to create a router and add a port to a subnet.

1. Import the following modules:

```
from neutronclient.v2_0 import client
import novaclient.v1_1.client as nvclient
from credentials import get_credentials
from credentials import get_nova_credentials
from utils import print_values_server
```

2. Get Nova Credentials. See :ref:'Get Nova credentials <get-nova-credentials>'.

3. Instantiate the nova_client client object by using the credentials dictionary object:

```
nova_client = nvclient.Client(**credentials)
```

4. Create a router and add a port to the subnet:

```
# Replace with network_id from your environment

network_id = '81bf592a-9e3f-4f84-a839-ae87df188dc1'

credentials = get_credentials()
neutron = client.Client(**credentials)
neutron.format = json
request = {'router': {'name': 'router name',
                      'admin_state_up': True}}

router = neutron.create_router(request)
router_id = router['router']['id']
# for example: '72cf1682-60a8-4890-b0ed-6bad7d9f5466'
router = neutron.show_router(router_id)
print(router)
body_value = {'port': {
    'admin_state_up': True,
    'device_id': router_id,
```

```
        'name': 'port1',
        'network_id': network_id,
        }}

    response = neutron.create_port(body=body_value)
    print(response)
    print("Execution Completed")
```

5.7.10.1   Create router: complete code listing example

```
#!/usr/bin/env python
from neutronclient.v2_0 import client
import novaclient.v1_1.client as nvclient
from credentials import get_credentials
from credentials import get_nova_credentials
from utils import print_values_server


credentials = get_nova_credentials()
nova_client = nvclient.Client(**credentials)


# Replace with network_id from your environment

network_id = '81bf592a-9e3f-4f84-a839-ae87df188dc1'
try:
    credentials = get_credentials()
    neutron = client.Client(**credentials)
    neutron.format = 'json'
    request = {'router': {'name': 'router name',
                          'admin_state_up': True}}
    router = neutron.create_router(request)
    router_id = router['router']['id']
    # for example: '72cf1682-60a8-4890-b0ed-6bad7d9f5466'
    router = neutron.show_router(router_id)
    print(router)
    body_value = {'port': {
```

```
        'admin_state_up': True,
        'device_id': router_id,
        'name': 'port1',
        'network_id': network_id,
        }}

    response = neutron.create_port(body=body_value)
    print(response)
finally:
    print("Execution completed")
```

5.7.11   Delete a network

This example queries OpenStack Networking to delete a network.

To delete a network:

1. Import the following modules:

   ```
   from neutronclient.v2_0 import client
   from credentials import get_credentials
   ```

2. Get credentials. See *Section 5.7.3, "Get Nova credentials"*.

3. Instantiate the `neutron` client object by using the `credentials` dictionary object:

   ```
   neutron = client.Client(**credentials)
   ```

4. Delete the network:

   ```
   body_sample = {'network': {'name': network_name,
                    'admin_state_up': True}}

   netw = neutron.create_network(body=body_sample)
   net_dict = netw['network']
   network_id = net_dict['id']
   print('Network %s created' % network_id)
   ```

```
        body_create_subnet = {'subnets': [{'cidr': '192.168.199.0/24',
                              'ip_version': 4, 'network_id': network_id}]}


        subnet = neutron.create_subnet(body=body_create_subnet)
        print('Created subnet %s' % subnet)


        neutron.delete_network(network_id)
        print('Deleted Network %s' % network_id)


        print("Execution completed")
```

5.7.11.1   Delete network: complete code listing example

```
#!/usr/bin/env python
from neutronclient.v2_0 import client
from credentials import get_credentials


network_name = 'temp_network'
credentials = get_credentials()
neutron = client.Client(**credentials)
try:
    body_sample = {'network': {'name': network_name,
                   'admin_state_up': True}}


    netw = neutron.create_network(body=body_sample)
    net_dict = netw['network']
    network_id = net_dict['id']
    print('Network %s created' % network_id)


    body_create_subnet = {'subnets': [{'cidr': '192.168.199.0/24',
                          'ip_version': 4, 'network_id': network_id}]}


    subnet = neutron.create_subnet(body=body_create_subnet)
    print('Created subnet %s' % subnet)
```

```
    neutron.delete_network(network_id)
    print('Deleted Network %s' % network_id)
finally:
    print("Execution Completed")
```

5.7.12 List routers

This example queries OpenStack Networking to list all routers.

1. Import the following modules:

   ```
   from neutronclient.v2_0 import client
   from credentials import get_credentials
   from utils import print_values
   ```

2. Get credentials. See *Section 5.7.3, "Get Nova credentials"*.

3. Instantiate the neutron client object by using the credentials dictionary object:

   ```
   neutron = client.Client(**credentials)
   ```

4. List the routers:

   ```
   routers_list = neutron.list_routers(retrieve_all=True)
   print_values(routers_list, 'routers')
   print("Execution completed")
   ```

   For print_values, see *Section 5.7.4, "Print values"*.

5.7.12.1 List routers: complete code listing example

```
#!/usr/bin/env python
from neutronclient.v2_0 import client
from credentials import get_credentials
from utils import print_values
```

```
try:
    credentials = get_credentials()
    neutron = client.Client(**credentials)
    routers_list = neutron.list_routers(retrieve_all=True)
    print_values(routers_list, 'routers')
finally:
    print("Execution completed")
```

5.7.13   List security groups

This example queries OpenStack Networking to list security groups.

1. Import the following modules:

   ```
   from neutronclient.v2_0 import client
   from credentials import get_credentials
   from utils import print_values
   ```

2. Get credentials. See *Section 5.7.2, "Get credentials"*.

3. Instantiate the `neutron` client object by using the `credentials` dictionary object:

   ```
   neutron = client.Client(**credentials)
   ```

4. List Security groups

   ```
   sg = neutron.list_security_groups()
   print(sg)
   ```

5.7.13.1   List security groups: complete code listing example

```
#!/usr/bin/env python
from neutronclient.v2_0 import client
from credentials import get_credentials
from utils import print_values
```

```
credentials = get_credentials()
neutron = client.Client(**credentials)
sg = neutron.list_security_groups()
print(sg)


.. note::


  OpenStack Networking security groups are case-sensitive while the
  nova-network security groups are case-insensitive.
```

5.7.14 List subnets

This example queries OpenStack Networking to list subnets.

1. Import the following modules:

   ```
   from neutronclient.v2_0 import client
   from credentials import get_credentials
   from utils import print_values
   ```

2. Get credentials. See :ref:'Get credentials < get-credentials >'.

3. Instantiate the neutron client object by using the credentials dictionary object:

   ```
   neutron = client.Client(**credentials)
   ```

4. List subnets:

   ```
   subnets = neutron.list_subnets()
   print(subnets)
   ```

5.7.14.1 List subnets: complete code listing example

```
#!/usr/bin/env python
from neutronclient.v2_0 import client
```

```
from credentials import get_credentials
from utils import print_values


credentials = get_credentials()
neutron = client.Client(**credentials)
subnets = neutron.list_subnets()
print(subnets)
```

5.8 Compute

To use the information in this section, you must be familiar with OpenStack Compute.

5.8.1 Set environment variables

To set up environmental variables and authenticate against Compute API endpoints, see *Section 5.2, "Authenticate"*.

5.8.2 Get OpenStack credentials (API v2)

This example uses the get_nova_credentials_v2 method:

```
def get_nova_credentials_v2():
    d = {}
    d['version'] = '2'
    d['username'] = os.environ['OS_USERNAME']
    d['api_key'] = os.environ['OS_PASSWORD']
    d['auth_url'] = os.environ['OS_AUTH_URL']
    d['project_id'] = os.environ['OS_TENANT_NAME']
    return d
```

This code resides in the credentials.py file, which all samples import.

Use the get_nova_credentials_v2() method to populate and get a dictionary:

```
credentials = get_nova_credentials_v2()
```

5.8.3　List servers (API v2)

The following program lists servers by using the Compute API v2.

1. Import the following modules:

```
from credentials import get_nova_credentials_v2
from novaclient.client import Client
```

2. Get Nova credentials. See *Section 5.8.2, "Get OpenStack credentials (API v2)"*.

3. Instantiate the `nova_client` client object by using the `credentials` dictionary object:

```
nova_client = Client(**credentials)
```

4. List servers by calling `servers.list` on `nova_client` object:

```
print(nova_client.servers.list())
```

5.8.3.1　List server code listing example

```
#!/usr/bin/env python
from credentials import get_nova_credentials_v2
from novaclient.client import Client

credentials = get_nova_credentials_v2()
nova_client = Client(**credentials)

print(nova_client.servers.list())
```

5.8.4　Create server (API v2)

The following program creates a server (VM) by using the Compute API v2.

1. Import the following modules:

```
import time
```

```
from credentials import get_nova_credentials_v2
from novaclient.client import Client
```

2. Get OpenStack credentials. See *Section 5.8.2, "Get OpenStack credentials (API v2)"*.

3. Instantiate the nova_client client object by using the credentials dictionary object:

```
nova_client = Client(**credentials)
```

4. Get the flavor and image to use to create a server. This code uses the cirros image, the m1.tiny flavor, and the private network:

```
image = nova_client.images.find(name="cirros")
flavor = nova_client.flavors.find(name="m1.tiny")
net = nova_client.networks.find(label="private")
```

5. To create the server, use the network, image, and flavor:

```
nics = [{'net-id': net.id}]
instance = nova_client.servers.create(name="vm2", image=image,
flavor=flavor, key_name="keypair-1", nics=nics)
```

6. Run the "Sleep for five seconds" command, and determine whether the server/vm was created by calling nova_client.servers.list():

```
print("Sleeping for 5s after create command")
time.sleep(5)
print("List of VMs")
print(nova_client.servers.list())
```

5.8.4.1   Create server code listing example

```
#!/usr/bin/env python
import time
from credentials import get_nova_credentials_v2
from novaclient.client import Client


try:
```

```
    credentials = get_nova_credentials_v2()
    nova_client = Client(**credentials)


    image = nova_client.images.find(name="cirros")

    flavor = nova_client.flavors.find(name="m1.tiny")

    net = nova_client.networks.find(label="private")

    nics = [{'net-id': net.id}]

    instance = nova_client.servers.create(name="vm2", image=image,
                                          flavor=flavor, key_name="keypair-1", nics=nics)
    print("Sleeping for 5s after create command")

    time.sleep(5)

    print("List of VMs")

    print(nova_client.servers.list())
finally:
    print("Execution Completed")
```

5.8.5 Delete server (API v2)

The following program deletes a server (VM) by using the Compute API v2.

1. Import the following modules:

   ```
   import time
   from credentials import get_nova_credentials_v2
   from novaclient.client import Client
   ```

2. Get Nova credentials. See *Section 5.8.2, "Get OpenStack credentials (API v2)"*.

3. Instantiate the `nova_client` client object by using the `credentials` dictionary object:

   ```
   nova_client = Client(**credentials)
   ```

4. Determine whether the `vm1` server exists:

   1. List servers: `servers_list`.

   2. Iterate over `servers_list` and compare name with `vm1`.

3. If true, set the variable name `server_exists` to `True` and break from the for loop:

```
servers_list = nova_client.servers.list()
server_del = "vm1"
server_exists = False

for s in servers_list:
    if s.name == server_del:
        print("This server %s exists" % server_del)
        server_exists = True
        break
```

5. If the server exists, run the `delete` method of the `nova_client.servers` object:

```
nova_client.servers.delete(s)
```

5.8.5.1   Delete server code example

```
#!/usr/bin/env python
from credentials import get_nova_credentials_v2
from novaclient.client import Client

credentials = get_nova_credentials_v2()
nova_client = Client(**credentials)

servers_list = nova_client.servers.list()
server_del = "vm1"
server_exists = False

for s in servers_list:
    if s.name == server_del:
        print("This server %s exists" % server_del)
        server_exists = True
        break
if not server_exists:
```

```
    print("server %s does not exist" % server_del)
else:
    print("deleting server.........")
    nova_client.servers.delete(s)
    print("server %s deleted" % server_del)
```

5.8.6 Update server (API v2)

The following program updates the name of a server (VM) by using the Compute API v2.

1. Import the following modules:

```
from credentials import get_nova_credentials_v2
from novaclient.client import Client
from utils import print_server
```

print_server is a method defined in utils.py and prints the server details as shown in the code listing below:

```
def print_server(server):
    print("-"*35)
    print("server id: %s" % server.id)
    print("server name: %s" % server.name)
    print("server image: %s" % server.image)
    print("server flavor: %s" % server.flavor)
    print("server key name: %s" % server.key_name)
    print("user_id: %s" % server.user_id)
    print("-"*35)
```

2. Get OpenStack Credentials. See *Section 5.8.2, "Get OpenStack credentials (API v2)"*.

3. Instantiate the nova_client client object by using the credentials dictionary object:

```
nova_client = Client(**credentials)
```

4. Get the server instance using `server_id` and print the details by calling `print_server` method:

```
server_id = '99889c8d-113f-4a7e-970c-77f1916bfe14'
server = nova_client.servers.get(server_id)
n = server.name
print_server(server)
```

5. Call `server.update` on the server object with the new value for `name` variable:

```
server.update(name = n + '1')
```

6. Get the updated instance of the server:

```
server_updated = nova_client.servers.get(server_id)
```

7. Call `print_server` again to check the update server details:

```
print_server(server_updated)
```

5.8.6.1 Update server code listing example

```
#!/usr/bin/env python


from credentials import get_nova_credentials_v2
from novaclient.client import Client
from utils import print_server


credentials = get_nova_credentials_v2()
nova_client = Client(**credentials)


# Change the server_id specific to your environment


server_id = '99889c8d-113f-4a7e-970c-77f1916bfe14'
server = nova_client.servers.get(server_id)
n = server.name
print_server(server)
```

```
server.update(name=n +'1')
server_updated = nova_client.servers.get(server_id)
print_server(server_updated)
```

5.8.7   List flavors (API v2)

The following program lists flavors and their details by using the Compute API v2.

1. Import the following modules:

   ```
   from credentials import get_nova_credentials_v2
   from novaclient.client import Client
   from utils import print_flavors
   ```

   The `print_flavors` method is defined in `utils.py` and prints the flavor details:

   ```
   def print_flavors(flavor_list):
       for flavor in flavor_list:
           print("-"*35)
           print("flavor id : %s" % flavor.id)
           print("flavor name : %s" % flavor.name)
           print("-"*35)
   ```

2. Get OpenStack credentials. *Section 5.8.2, "Get OpenStack credentials (API v2)".*

3. Instantiate the `nova_client` client object by using the `credentials` dictionary object:

   ```
   nova_client = Client(**credentials)
   ```

4. List flavors by calling `list()` on `nova_client.flavors` object:

   ```
   flavors_list =  nova_client.flavors.list()
   ```

5. Print the flavor details, id and name by calling `print_flavors`:

   ```
   print_flavors(flavors_list)
   ```

5.8.7.1 List flavors code listing example

```python
#!/usr/bin/env python


from credentials import get_nova_credentials_v2
from novaclient.client import Client
from utils import print_flavors


credentials = get_nova_credentials_v2()
nova_client = Client(**credentials)


flavors_list = nova_client.flavors.list()
print_flavors(flavors_list)
```

5.8.8 List floating IPs (API v2)

The following program lists the floating IPs and their details by using the Compute API v2.

1. Import the following modules:

```python
from credentials import get_nova_credentials_v2
from novaclient.client import Client
from utils import print_values_ip
```

The `print_values_ip` method is defined in `utils.py` and prints the floating_ip object details:

```python
def print_values_ip(ip_list):
    ip_dict_lisl = []
    for ip in ip_list:
        print("-"*35)
        print("fixed_ip : %s" % ip.fixed_ip)
        print("id : %s" % ip.id)
        print("instance_id : %s" % ip.instance_id)
        print("ip : %s" % ip.ip)
        print("pool : %s" % ip.pool)
```

2. Get OpenStack credentials. See *Section 5.8.2, "Get OpenStack credentials (API v2)"*.

3. Instantiate the `nova_client` client object by using the `credentials` dictionary object:

```
nova_client = Client(**credentials)
```

4. List floating IPs by calling `list()` on `nova_client.floating_ips` object:

```
ip_list = nova_client.floating_ips.list()
```

5. Print the floating IP object details by calling `print_values_ip`:

```
print_values_ip(ip_list)
```

5.8.8.1   List floating IPs code listing example

```
#!/usr/bin/env python


from credentials import get_nova_credentials_v2
from novaclient.client import Client
from utils import print_values_ip


credentials = get_nova_credentials_v2()
nova_client = Client(**credentials)
ip_list = nova_client.floating_ips.list()
print_values_ip(ip_list)
```

5.8.9   List hosts (API v2)

The following program lists the hosts by using the Compute API v2.

1. Import the following modules:

```
from credentials import get_nova_credentials_v2
from novaclient.client import Client
```

```
from utils import print_hosts
```

The `print_hosts` method is defined in `utils.py` and prints the host object details:

```python
def print_hosts(host_list):
    for host in host_list:
        print("-"*35)
        print("host_name : %s" % host.host_name)
        print("service : %s" % host.service)
        print("zone : %s" % host.zone)
        print("-"*35)
```

2. Get OpenStack credentials. See *Section 5.8.2, "Get OpenStack credentials (API v2)"*.

3. Instantiate the `nova_client` client object by using the `credentials` dictionary object:

```python
nova_client = Client(**credentials)
```

4. List hosts by calling `list()` on `nova_client.hosts` object:

```python
host_list = nova_client.hosts.list()
```

5. Print the host object details by calling `print_hosts(host_list)`:

```python
print_hosts(host_list)
```

5.8.9.1 List hosts code listing example

```python
#!/usr/bin/env python

from credentials import get_nova_credentials_v2
from novaclient.client import Client
from utils import print_hosts

credentials = get_nova_credentials_v2()
nova_client = Client(**credentials)
host_list = nova_client.hosts.list()
```

```
print_hosts(host_list)
```

6 HOT Guide

The HOT Guide is now maintained as part of the Heat repository and is available on the OpenStack developer documentation website: Heat Template Guide (http://docs.openstack.org/developer/heat/template_guide/index.html) ↗

7 OpenStack command-line interface cheat sheet

Here is a list of common commands for reference.

7.1 Identity (keystone)

List all users

```
$ keystone user-list
```

List Identity service catalog

```
$ keystone catalog
```

7.2 Images (glance)

List images you can access

```
$ glance image-list
```

Delete specified image

```
$ glance image-delete IMAGE
```

Describe a specific image

```
$ glance image-show IMAGE
```

Update image

```
$ glance image-update IMAGE
```

Upload kernel image

```
$ glance image-create --name "cirros-threepart-kernel" \
```

```
--disk-format aki --container-format aki --is-public False \
--file ~/images/cirros-0.3.1~pre4-x86_64-vmlinuz
```

Upload RAM image

```
$ glance image-create --name "cirros-threepart-ramdisk" \
  --disk-format ari --container-format ari --is-public False \
  --file ~/images/cirros-0.3.1~pre4-x86_64-initrd
```

Upload three-part image

```
$ glance image-create --name "cirros-threepart" --disk-format ami \
  --container-format ami --is-public False \
  --property kernel_id=$KID-property ramdisk_id=$RID \
  --file ~/images/cirros-0.3.1~pre4-x86_64-blank.img
```

Register raw image

```
$ glance image-create --name "cirros-qcow2" --disk-format qcow2 \
  --container-format bare --is-public False \
  --file ~/images/cirros-0.3.1~pre4-x86_64-disk.img
```

7.3 Compute (nova)

List instances, check status of instance

```
$ nova list
```

List images

```
$ nova image-list
```

List flavors

```
$ nova flavor-list
```

Boot an instance using flavor and image names (if names are unique)

```
$ nova boot --image IMAGE --flavor FLAVOR INSTANCE_NAME
$ nova boot --image cirros-0.3.1-x86_64-uec --flavor m1.tiny \
  MyFirstInstance
```

Login to instance

```
# ip netns
# ip netns exec NETNS_NAME ssh USER@SERVER
# ip netns exec qdhcp-6021a3b4-8587-4f9c-8064-0103885dfba2 \
  ssh cirros@10.0.0.2
```

 Note

In CirrOS the password for user `cirros` is "cubswin:)" without the quotes.

Show details of instance

```
$ nova show NAME
$ nova show MyFirstInstance
```

View console log of instance

```
$ nova console-log MyFirstInstance
```

Set metadata on an instance

```
$ nova meta volumeTwoImage set newmeta='my meta data'
```

Create an instance snapshot

```
$ nova image-create volumeTwoImage snapshotOfVolumeImage
$ nova image-show snapshotOfVolumeImage
```

7.3.1   Pause, suspend, stop, rescue, resize, rebuild, reboot an instance

Pause

```
$ nova pause NAME
$ nova pause volumeTwoImage
```

Unpause

```
$ nova unpause NAME
```

Suspend

```
$ nova suspend NAME
```

Unsuspend

```
$ nova resume NAME
```

Stop

```
$ nova stop NAME
```

Start

```
$ nova start NAME
```

Rescue

```
$ nova rescue NAME
$ nova rescue NAME --rescue_image_ref RESCUE_IMAGE
```

Resize

```
$ nova resize NAME FLAVOR
$ nova resize my-pem-server m1.small
$ nova resize-confirm my-pem-server1
```

Rebuild

```
$ nova rebuild NAME IMAGE
$ nova rebuild newtinny cirros-qcow2
```

Reboot

```
$ nova reboot NAME
$ nova reboot newtinny
```

Inject user data and files into an instance

```
$ nova boot --user-data FILE INSTANCE
$ nova boot --user-data userdata.txt --image cirros-qcow2 \
  --flavor m1.tiny MyUserdataInstance2
```

To validate that the file was injected, use ssh to connect to the instance, and look in /var/lib/cloud for the file.

Inject a keypair into an instance and access the instance with that keypair

Create keypair

```
$ nova keypair-add test > test.pem
$ chmod 600 test.pem
```

Start an instance (boot)

```
$ nova boot --image cirros-0.3.0-x86_64 --flavor m1.small \
  --key_name test MyFirstServer
```

Use ssh to connect to the instance

```
# ip netns exec qdhcp-98f09f1e-64c4-4301-a897-5067ee6d544f \
  ssh -i test.pem cirros@10.0.0.4
```

Manage security groups

Add rules to default security group allowing ping and SSH between instances in the default security group

```
$ nova secgroup-add-group-rule default default icmp -1 -1
$ nova secgroup-add-group-rule default default tcp 22 22
```

7.4 Networking (neutron)

Create network

```
$ neutron net-create NAME
```

Create a subnet

```
$ neutron subnet-create NETWORK_NAME CIDR
$ neutron subnet-create my-network 10.0.0.0/29
```

7.5 Block Storage (cinder)

Used to manage volumes and volume snapshots that attach to instances.

Create a new volume

```
$ cinder create SIZE_IN_GB --display-name NAME
$ cinder create 1 --display-name MyFirstVolume
```

Boot an instance and attach to volume

```
$ nova boot --image cirros-qcow2 --flavor m1.tiny MyVolumeInstance
```

List volumes, notice status of volume

```
$ cinder list
```

Attach volume to instance after instance is active, and volume is available

```
$ nova volume-attach INSTANCE_ID VOLUME_ID auto
$ nova volume-attach MyVolumeInstance /dev/vdb auto
```

Manage volumes after login into the instance

List storage devices

```
# fdisk -l
```

Make filesystem on volume

```
# mkfs.ext3 /dev/vdb
```

Create a mountpoint

```
# mkdir /myspace
```

Mount the volume at the mountpoint

```
# mount /dev/vdb /myspace
```

Create a file on the volume

```
# touch /myspace/helloworld.txt
# ls /myspace
```

Unmount the volume

```
# umount /myspace
```

7.6 Object Storage (swift)

Display information for the account, container, or object

```
$ swift stat
$ swift stat ACCOUNT
$ swift stat CONTAINER
$ swift stat OBJECT
```

List containers

```
$ swift list
```

8 Community support

The following resources are available to help you run and use OpenStack. The OpenStack community constantly improves and adds to the main features of OpenStack, but if you have any questions, do not hesitate to ask. Use the following resources to get OpenStack support, and troubleshoot your installations.

8.1 Documentation

For the available OpenStack documentation, see docs.openstack.org (http://docs.openstack.org) ↗.

To provide feedback on documentation, join and use the openstack-docs@lists.openstack.org (mailto:openstack-docs@lists.openstack.org) ↗ mailing list at OpenStack Documentation Mailing List (http://lists.openstack.org/cgi-bin/mailman/listinfo/openstack-docs) ↗, or report a bug (https://bugs.launchpad.net/openstack-manuals/+filebug) ↗.

The following books explain how to install an OpenStack cloud and its associated components:

- Installation Guide for openSUSE 13.2 and SUSE Linux Enterprise Server 12 (http://docs.openstack.org/liberty/install-guide-obs/) ↗

- Installation Guide for Red Hat Enterprise Linux 7 and CentOS 7 (http://docs.openstack.org/liberty/install-guide-rdo/) ↗

- Installation Guide for Ubuntu 14.04 (http://docs.openstack.org/liberty/install-guide-ubuntu/) ↗

The following books explain how to configure and run an OpenStack cloud:

- Architecture Design Guide (http://docs.openstack.org/arch-design/) ↗

- Cloud Administrator Guide (http://docs.openstack.org/admin-guide-cloud/) ↗

- Configuration Reference (http://docs.openstack.org/liberty/config-reference/content/) ↗

- Operations Guide (http://docs.openstack.org/ops/) ↗

- Networking Guide (http://docs.openstack.org/liberty/networking-guide) ↗

- High Availability Guide (http://docs.openstack.org/ha-guide/) ↗

- Security Guide (http://docs.openstack.org/sec/)↗

- Virtual Machine Image Guide (http://docs.openstack.org/image-guide/)↗

The following books explain how to use the OpenStack dashboard and command-line clients:

- API Guide (http://developer.openstack.org/api-guide/quick-start/)↗

- End User Guide (http://docs.openstack.org/user-guide/)↗

- Admin User Guide (http://docs.openstack.org/user-guide-admin/)↗

- Command-Line Interface Reference (http://docs.openstack.org/cli-reference/)↗

The following documentation provides reference and guidance information for the OpenStack APIs:

- OpenStack API Complete Reference (HTML) (http://developer.openstack.org/api-ref.html)↗

- API Complete Reference (PDF) (http://developer.openstack.org/api-ref-guides/bk-api-ref.pdf)↗

The following guide provides how to contribute to OpenStack documentation:

- Documentation contributor guide (http://docs.openstack.org/contributor-guide/)↗

8.2 ask.openstack.org

During the set up or testing of OpenStack, you might have questions about how a specific task is completed or be in a situation where a feature does not work correctly. Use the ask.openstack.org (https://ask.openstack.org)↗ site to ask questions and get answers. When you visit the https://ask.openstack.org↗ site, scan the recently asked questions to see whether your question has already been answered. If not, ask a new question. Be sure to give a clear, concise summary in the title and provide as much detail as possible in the description. Paste in your command output or stack traces, links to screen shots, and any other information which might be useful.

8.3 OpenStack mailing lists

A great way to get answers and insights is to post your question or problematic scenario to the OpenStack mailing list. You can learn from and help others who might have similar issues. To subscribe or view the archives, go to http://lists.openstack.org/cgi-bin/mailman/listinfo/openstack ↗. You might be interested in the other mailing lists for specific projects or development, which you can find on the wiki (https://wiki.openstack.org/wiki/MailingLists) ↗. A description of all mailing lists is available at https://wiki.openstack.org/wiki/MailingLists ↗.

8.4   The OpenStack wiki

The OpenStack wiki (https://wiki.openstack.org/) ↗ contains a broad range of topics but some of the information can be difficult to find or is a few pages deep. Fortunately, the wiki search feature enables you to search by title or content. If you search for specific information, such as about networking or OpenStack Compute, you can find a large amount of relevant material. More is being added all the time, so be sure to check back often. You can find the search box in the upper-right corner of any OpenStack wiki page.

8.5   The Launchpad Bugs area

The OpenStack community values your set up and testing efforts and wants your feedback. To log a bug, you must sign up for a Launchpad account at https://launchpad.net/+login ↗. You can view existing bugs and report bugs in the Launchpad Bugs area. Use the search feature to determine whether the bug has already been reported or already been fixed. If it still seems like your bug is unreported, fill out a bug report.

Some tips:

- Give a clear, concise summary.

- Provide as much detail as possible in the description. Paste in your command output or stack traces, links to screen shots, and any other information which might be useful.

- Be sure to include the software and package versions that you are using, especially if you are using a development branch, such as, `"Kilo release" vs git commit bc79c3ecc55929bac585d04a03475b72e06a3208`.

- Any deployment-specific information is helpful, such as whether you are using Ubuntu 14.04 or are performing a multi-node installation.

The following Launchpad Bugs areas are available:

- Bugs: OpenStack Block Storage (cinder) (https://bugs.launchpad.net/cinder) ↗

- Bugs: OpenStack Compute (nova) (https://bugs.launchpad.net/nova) ↗

- Bugs: OpenStack Dashboard (horizon) (https://bugs.launchpad.net/horizon) ↗

- Bugs: OpenStack Identity (keystone) (https://bugs.launchpad.net/keystone) ↗

- Bugs: OpenStack Image service (glance) (https://bugs.launchpad.net/glance) ↗

- Bugs: OpenStack Networking (neutron) (https://bugs.launchpad.net/neutron) ↗

- Bugs: OpenStack Object Storage (swift) (https://bugs.launchpad.net/swift) ↗

- Bugs: Application catalog (murano) (https://bugs.launchpad.net/murano) ↗

- Bugs: Bare metal service (ironic) (https://bugs.launchpad.net/ironic) ↗

- Bugs: Clustering service (senlin) (https://bugs.launchpad.net/senlin) ↗

- Bugs: Containers service (magnum) (https://bugs.launchpad.net/magnum) ↗

- Bugs: Data processing service (sahara) (https://bugs.launchpad.net/sahara) ↗

- Bugs: Database service (trove) (https://bugs.launchpad.net/trove) ↗

- Bugs: Deployment service (fuel) (https://bugs.launchpad.net/fuel) ↗

- Bugs: DNS service (designate) (https://bugs.launchpad.net/designate) ↗

- Bugs: Key Manager Service (barbican) (https://bugs.launchpad.net/barbican) ↗

- Bugs: Monitoring (monasca) (https://bugs.launchpad.net/monasca) ↗

- Bugs: Orchestration (heat) (https://bugs.launchpad.net/heat) ↗

- Bugs: Rating (cloudkitty) (https://bugs.launchpad.net/cloudkitty) ↗

- Bugs: Shared file systems (manila) (https://bugs.launchpad.net/manila) ↗

- Bugs: Telemetry (ceilometer) (https://bugs.launchpad.net/ceilometer) ↗

- Bugs: Telemetry v3 (gnocchi) (https://bugs.launchpad.net/gnocchi) ↗

- Bugs: Workflow service (mistral) (https://bugs.launchpad.net/mistral) ↗

- Bugs: Messaging service (zaqar) (https://bugs.launchpad.net/zaqar) ↗

- Bugs: OpenStack API Documentation (developer.openstack.org) (https://bugs.launchpad.net/openstack-api-site) ↗

- Bugs: OpenStack Documentation (docs.openstack.org) (https://bugs.launchpad.net/open-stack-manuals) ↗

8.6 The OpenStack IRC channel

The OpenStack community lives in the #openstack IRC channel on the Freenode network. You can hang out, ask questions, or get immediate feedback for urgent and pressing issues. To install an IRC client or use a browser-based client, go to https://webchat.freenode.net/ (https://webchat.freenode.net) ↗. You can also use Colloquy (Mac OS X, http://colloquy.info/ ↗), mIRC (Windows, http://www.mirc.com/ ↗), or XChat (Linux). When you are in the IRC channel and want to share code or command output, the generally accepted method is to use a Paste Bin. The OpenStack project has one at http://paste.openstack.org ↗. Just paste your longer amounts of text or logs in the web form and you get a URL that you can paste into the channel. The OpenStack IRC channel is `#openstack` on `irc.freenode.net`. You can find a list of all OpenStack IRC channels at https://wiki.openstack.org/wiki/IRC ↗.

8.7 Documentation feedback

To provide feedback on documentation, join and use the openstack-docs@lists.openstack.org (mailto:openstack-docs@lists.openstack.org) ↗ mailing list at OpenStack Documentation Mailing List (http://lists.openstack.org/cgi-bin/mailman/listinfo/openstack-docs) ↗, or report a bug (https://bugs.launchpad.net/openstack-manuals/+filebug) ↗.

8.8 OpenStack distribution packages

The following Linux distributions provide community-supported packages for OpenStack:

- **Debian:** https://wiki.debian.org/OpenStack ↗

- **CentOS, Fedora, and Red Hat Enterprise Linux:** https://www.rdoproject.org/ ↗

- **openSUSE and SUSE Linux Enterprise Server:** https://en.opensuse.org/ Portal:OpenStack ↗

- **Ubuntu:** https://wiki.ubuntu.com/ServerTeam/CloudArchive ↗

Glossary

This glossary offers a list of terms and definitions to define a vocabulary for OpenStack-related concepts.

To add to OpenStack glossary, clone the openstack/openstack-manuals repository (https://git.openstack.org/cgit/openstack/openstack-manuals) ↗ and update the source file `doc/glossary/glossary-terms.xml` through the OpenStack contribution process.

6to4

A mechanism that allows IPv6 packets to be transmitted over an IPv4 network, providing a strategy for migrating to IPv6.

absolute limit

Impassable limits for guest VMs. Settings include total RAM size, maximum number of vCPUs, and maximum disk size.

access control list

A list of permissions attached to an object. An ACL specifies which users or system processes have access to objects. It also defines which operations can be performed on specified objects. Each entry in a typical ACL specifies a subject and an operation. For instance, the ACL entry `(Alice, delete)` for a file gives Alice permission to delete the file.

access key

Alternative term for an Amazon EC2 access key. See EC2 access key.

account

The Object Storage context of an account. Do not confuse with a user account from an authentication service, such as Active Directory, /etc/passwd, OpenLDAP, OpenStack Identity, and so on.

account auditor

Checks for missing replicas and incorrect or corrupted objects in a specified Object Storage account by running queries against the back-end SQLite database.

account database

A SQLite database that contains Object Storage accounts and related metadata and that the accounts server accesses.

account reaper

An Object Storage worker that scans for and deletes account databases and that the account server has marked for deletion.

account server

Lists containers in Object Storage and stores container information in the account database.

account service

An Object Storage component that provides account services such as list, create, modify, and audit. Do not confuse with OpenStack Identity service, OpenLDAP, or similar user-account services.

accounting

The Compute service provides accounting information through the event notification and system usage data facilities.

ACL

See access control list.

active/active configuration

In a high-availability setup with an active/active configuration, several systems share the load together and if one fails, the load is distributed to the remaining systems.

Active Directory

Authentication and identity service by Microsoft, based on LDAP. Supported in OpenStack.

active/passive configuration

In a high-availability setup with an active/passive configuration, systems are set up to bring additional resources online to replace those that have failed.

address pool

A group of fixed and/or floating IP addresses that are assigned to a project and can be used by or assigned to the VM instances in a project.

admin API

A subset of API calls that are accessible to authorized administrators and are generally not accessible to end users or the public Internet. They can exist as a separate service (keystone) or can be a subset of another API (nova).

admin server

In the context of the Identity service, the worker process that provides access to the admin API.

Advanced Message Queuing Protocol (AMQP)

The open standard messaging protocol used by OpenStack components for intra-service communications, provided by RabbitMQ, Qpid, or ZeroMQ.

Advanced RISC Machine (ARM)

Lower power consumption CPU often found in mobile and embedded devices. Supported by OpenStack.

alert

The Compute service can send alerts through its notification system, which includes a facility to create custom notification drivers. Alerts can be sent to and displayed on the horizon dashboard.

allocate

The process of taking a floating IP address from the address pool so it can be associated with a fixed IP on a guest VM instance.

Amazon Kernel Image (AKI)

Both a VM container format and disk format. Supported by Image service.

Amazon Machine Image (AMI)

Both a VM container format and disk format. Supported by Image service.

Amazon Ramdisk Image (ARI)

Both a VM container format and disk format. Supported by Image service.

Anvil

A project that ports the shell script-based project named DevStack to Python.

Apache

The Apache Software Foundation supports the Apache community of open-source software projects. These projects provide software products for the public good.

Apache License 2.0

All OpenStack core projects are provided under the terms of the Apache License 2.0 license.

Apache Web Server

The most common web server software currently used on the Internet.

API endpoint

The daemon, worker, or service that a client communicates with to access an API. API endpoints can provide any number of services, such as authentication, sales data, performance meters, Compute VM commands, census data, and so on.

API extension

Custom modules that extend some OpenStack core APIs.

API extension plug-in

Alternative term for a Networking plug-in or Networking API extension.

API key

Alternative term for an API token.

API server

Any node running a daemon or worker that provides an API endpoint.

API token

Passed to API requests and used by OpenStack to verify that the client is authorized to run the requested operation.

API version

In OpenStack, the API version for a project is part of the URL. For example, `example.com/nova/v1/foobar`.

applet

A Java program that can be embedded into a web page.

Application Programming Interface (API)

A collection of specifications used to access a service, application, or program. Includes service calls, required parameters for each call, and the expected return values.

Application catalog

OpenStack project that provides an application catalog service so that users can compose and deploy composite environments on an application abstraction level while managing the application lifecycle. The code name of the project is murano.

application server

A piece of software that makes available another piece of software over a network.

Application Service Provider (ASP)

Companies that rent specialized applications that help businesses and organizations provide additional services with lower cost.

Address Resolution Protocol (ARP)

The protocol by which layer-3 IP addresses are resolved into layer-2 link local addresses.

arptables

Tool used for maintaining Address Resolution Protocol packet filter rules in the Linux kernel firewall modules. Used along with iptables, ebtables, and ip6tables in Compute to provide firewall services for VMs.

associate

The process associating a Compute floating IP address with a fixed IP address.

Asynchronous JavaScript and XML (AJAX)

A group of interrelated web development techniques used on the client-side to create asynchronous web applications. Used extensively in horizon.

ATA over Ethernet (AoE)

A disk storage protocol tunneled within Ethernet.

attach

The process of connecting a VIF or vNIC to a L2 network in Networking. In the context of Compute, this process connects a storage volume to an instance.

attachment (network)

Association of an interface ID to a logical port. Plugs an interface into a port.

auditing

Provided in Compute through the system usage data facility.

auditor

A worker process that verifies the integrity of Object Storage objects, containers, and accounts. Auditors is the collective term for the Object Storage account auditor, container auditor, and object auditor.

Austin

The code name for the initial release of OpenStack. The first design summit took place in Austin, Texas, US.

auth node

Alternative term for an Object Storage authorization node.

authentication

The process that confirms that the user, process, or client is really who they say they are through private key, secret token, password, fingerprint, or similar method.

authentication token

A string of text provided to the client after authentication. Must be provided by the user or process in subsequent requests to the API endpoint.

AuthN

The Identity service component that provides authentication services.

authorization

The act of verifying that a user, process, or client is authorized to perform an action.

authorization node

An Object Storage node that provides authorization services.

AuthZ

The Identity component that provides high-level authorization services.

Auto ACK

Configuration setting within RabbitMQ that enables or disables message acknowledgment. Enabled by default.

auto declare

A Compute RabbitMQ setting that determines whether a message exchange is automatically created when the program starts.

availability zone

An Amazon EC2 concept of an isolated area that is used for fault tolerance. Do not confuse with an OpenStack Compute zone or cell.

AWS

Amazon Web Services.

AWS CloudFormation template

AWS CloudFormation allows AWS users to create and manage a collection of related resources. The Orchestration service supports a CloudFormation-compatible format (CFN).

back end

Interactions and processes that are obfuscated from the user, such as Compute volume mount, data transmission to an iSCSI target by a daemon, or Object Storage object integrity checks.

back-end catalog

The storage method used by the Identity service catalog service to store and retrieve information about API endpoints that are available to the client. Examples include a SQL database, LDAP database, or KVS back end.

back-end store

The persistent data store used to save and retrieve information for a service, such as lists of Object Storage objects, current state of guest VMs, lists of user names, and so on. Also, the method that the Image service uses to get and store VM images. Options include Object Storage, local file system, S3, and HTTP.

backup restore and disaster recovery as a service

The OpenStack project that provides integrated tooling for backing up, restoring, and recovering file systems, instances, or database backups. The project name is freezer.

bandwidth

The amount of available data used by communication resources, such as the Internet. Represents the amount of data that is used to download things or the amount of data available to download.

barbican

Code name of the key management service for OpenStack.

bare

An Image service container format that indicates that no container exists for the VM image.

Bare metal service

OpenStack project that provisions bare metal, as opposed to virtual, machines. The code name for the project is ironic.

base image

An OpenStack-provided image.

Bell-LaPadula model

A security model that focuses on data confidentiality and controlled access to classified information. This model divide the entities into subjects and objects. The clearance of a subject is compared to the classification of the object to determine if the subject is authorized for the specific access mode. The clearance or classification scheme is expressed in terms of a lattice.

Benchmark service

OpenStack project that provides a framework for performance analysis and benchmarking of individual OpenStack components as well as full production OpenStack cloud deployments. The code name of the project is rally.

Bexar

A grouped release of projects related to OpenStack that came out in February of 2011. It included only Compute (nova) and Object Storage (swift). Bexar is the code name for the second release of OpenStack. The design summit took place in San Antonio, Texas, US, which is the county seat for Bexar county.

binary

Information that consists solely of ones and zeroes, which is the language of computers.

bit

A bit is a single digit number that is in base of 2 (either a zero or one). Bandwidth usage is measured in bits per second.

bits per second (BPS)

The universal measurement of how quickly data is transferred from place to place.

block device

A device that moves data in the form of blocks. These device nodes interface the devices, such as hard disks, CD-ROM drives, flash drives, and other addressable regions of memory.

block migration

A method of VM live migration used by KVM to evacuate instances from one host to another with very little downtime during a user-initiated switchover. Does not require shared storage. Supported by Compute.

Block Storage

The OpenStack core project that enables management of volumes, volume snapshots, and volume types. The project name of Block Storage is cinder.

Block Storage API

An API on a separate endpoint for attaching, detaching, and creating block storage for compute VMs.

BMC

Baseboard Management Controller. The intelligence in the IPMI architecture, which is a specialized micro-controller that is embedded on the motherboard of a computer and acts as a server. Manages the interface between system management software and platform hardware.

bootable disk image

A type of VM image that exists as a single, bootable file.

Bootstrap Protocol (BOOTP)

A network protocol used by a network client to obtain an IP address from a configuration server. Provided in Compute through the dnsmasq daemon when using either the FlatDHCP manager or VLAN manager network manager.

Border Gateway Protocol (BGP)

The Border Gateway Protocol is a dynamic routing protocol that connects autonomous systems. Considered the backbone of the Internet, this protocol connects disparate networks to form a larger network.

browser

Any client software that enables a computer or device to access the Internet.

builder file

Contains configuration information that Object Storage uses to reconfigure a ring or to re-create it from scratch after a serious failure.

bursting

The practice of utilizing a secondary environment to elastically build instances on-demand when the primary environment is resource constrained.

button class

A group of related button types within horizon. Buttons to start, stop, and suspend VMs are in one class. Buttons to associate and disassociate floating IP addresses are in another class, and so on.

byte

Set of bits that make up a single character; there are usually 8 bits to a byte.

CA

Certificate Authority or Certification Authority. In cryptography, an entity that issues digital certificates. The digital certificate certifies the ownership of a public key by the named subject of the certificate. This enables others (relying parties) to rely upon signatures or assertions made by the private key that corresponds to the certified public key. In this model of trust relationships, a CA is a trusted third party for both the subject (owner) of the certificate and the party relying upon the certificate. CAs are characteristic of many public key infrastructure (PKI) schemes.

cache pruner

A program that keeps the Image service VM image cache at or below its configured maximum size.

Cactus

An OpenStack grouped release of projects that came out in the spring of 2011. It included Compute (nova), Object Storage (swift), and the Image service (glance). Cactus is a city in Texas, US and is the code name for the third release of OpenStack. When OpenStack releases went from three to six months long, the code name of the release changed to match a geography nearest the previous summit.

CADF

Cloud Auditing Data Federation (CADF) is a specification for audit event data. CADF is supported by OpenStack Identity.

CALL

One of the RPC primitives used by the OpenStack message queue software. Sends a message and waits for a response.

capability

Defines resources for a cell, including CPU, storage, and networking. Can apply to the specific services within a cell or a whole cell.

capacity cache

A Compute back-end database table that contains the current workload, amount of free RAM, and number of VMs running on each host. Used to determine on which host a VM starts.

capacity updater

A notification driver that monitors VM instances and updates the capacity cache as needed.

CAST

One of the RPC primitives used by the OpenStack message queue software. Sends a message and does not wait for a response.

catalog

A list of API endpoints that are available to a user after authentication with the Identity service.

catalog service

An Identity service that lists API endpoints that are available to a user after authentication with the Identity service.

ceilometer

The project name for the Telemetry service, which is an integrated project that provides metering and measuring facilities for OpenStack.

cell

Provides logical partitioning of Compute resources in a child and parent relationship. Requests are passed from parent cells to child cells if the parent cannot provide the requested resource.

cell forwarding

A Compute option that enables parent cells to pass resource requests to child cells if the parent cannot provide the requested resource.

cell manager

The Compute component that contains a list of the current capabilities of each host within the cell and routes requests as appropriate.

CentOS

A Linux distribution that is compatible with OpenStack.

Ceph

Massively scalable distributed storage system that consists of an object store, block store, and POSIX-compatible distributed file system. Compatible with OpenStack.

CephFS

The POSIX-compliant file system provided by Ceph.

certificate authority

A simple certificate authority provided by Compute for cloudpipe VPNs and VM image decryption.

Challenge-Handshake Authentication Protocol (CHAP)

An iSCSI authentication method supported by Compute.

chance scheduler

A scheduling method used by Compute that randomly chooses an available host from the pool.

changes since

A Compute API parameter that downloads changes to the requested item since your last request, instead of downloading a new, fresh set of data and comparing it against the old data.

Chef

An operating system configuration management tool supporting OpenStack deployments.

child cell

If a requested resource such as CPU time, disk storage, or memory is not available in the parent cell, the request is forwarded to its associated child cells. If the child cell can fulfill the request, it does. Otherwise, it attempts to pass the request to any of its children.

cinder

A core OpenStack project that provides block storage services for VMs.

CirrOS

A minimal Linux distribution designed for use as a test image on clouds such as OpenStack.

Cisco neutron plug-in

A Networking plug-in for Cisco devices and technologies, including UCS and Nexus.

cloud architect

A person who plans, designs, and oversees the creation of clouds.

cloud computing

A model that enables access to a shared pool of configurable computing resources, such as networks, servers, storage, applications, and services, that can be rapidly provisioned and released with minimal management effort or service provider interaction.

cloud controller

Collection of Compute components that represent the global state of the cloud; talks to services, such as Identity authentication, Object Storage, and node/storage workers through a queue.

cloud controller node

A node that runs network, volume, API, scheduler, and image services. Each service may be broken out into separate nodes for scalability or availability.

Cloud Data Management Interface (CDMI)

SINA standard that defines a RESTful API for managing objects in the cloud, currently unsupported in OpenStack.

Cloud Infrastructure Management Interface (CIMI)

An in-progress specification for cloud management. Currently unsupported in OpenStack.

cloud-init

A package commonly installed in VM images that performs initialization of an instance after boot using information that it retrieves from the metadata service, such as the SSH public key and user data.

cloudadmin

One of the default roles in the Compute RBAC system. Grants complete system access.

Cloudbase-Init

A Windows project providing guest initialization features, similar to cloud-init.

cloudpipe

A compute service that creates VPNs on a per-project basis.

cloudpipe image

A pre-made VM image that serves as a cloudpipe server. Essentially, OpenVPN running on Linux.

Clustering

The OpenStack project that OpenStack project that implements clustering services and libraries for the management of groups of homogeneous objects exposed by other OpenStack services. The project name of Clustering service is senlin.

CMDB

Configuration Management Database.

congress

OpenStack project that provides the Governance service.

command filter

Lists allowed commands within the Compute rootwrap facility.

Common Internet File System (CIFS)

A file sharing protocol. It is a public or open variation of the original Server Message Block (SMB) protocol developed and used by Microsoft. Like the SMB protocol, CIFS runs at a higher level and uses the TCP/IP protocol.

community project

A project that is not officially endorsed by the OpenStack Foundation. If the project is successful enough, it might be elevated to an incubated project and then to a core project, or it might be merged with the main code trunk.

compression

Reducing the size of files by special encoding, the file can be decompressed again to its original content. OpenStack supports compression at the Linux file system level but does not support compression for things such as Object Storage objects or Image service VM images.

Compute

The OpenStack core project that provides compute services. The project name of Compute service is nova.

Compute API

The nova-api daemon provides access to nova services. Can communicate with other APIs, such as the Amazon EC2 API.

compute controller

The Compute component that chooses suitable hosts on which to start VM instances.

compute host

Physical host dedicated to running compute nodes.

compute node

A node that runs the nova-compute daemon that manages VM instances that provide a wide range of services, such as web applications and analytics.

Compute service

Name for the Compute component that manages VMs.

compute worker

The Compute component that runs on each compute node and manages the VM instance life cycle, including run, reboot, terminate, attach/detach volumes, and so on. Provided by the nova-compute daemon.

concatenated object

A set of segment objects that Object Storage combines and sends to the client.

conductor

In Compute, conductor is the process that proxies database requests from the compute process. Using conductor improves security because compute nodes do not need direct access to the database.

consistency window

The amount of time it takes for a new Object Storage object to become accessible to all clients.

console log

Contains the output from a Linux VM console in Compute.

container

Organizes and stores objects in Object Storage. Similar to the concept of a Linux directory but cannot be nested. Alternative term for an Image service container format.

container auditor

Checks for missing replicas or incorrect objects in specified Object Storage containers through queries to the SQLite back-end database.

container database

A SQLite database that stores Object Storage containers and container metadata. The container server accesses this database.

container format

A wrapper used by the Image service that contains a VM image and its associated metadata, such as machine state, OS disk size, and so on.

container server

An Object Storage server that manages containers.

Containers service

OpenStack project that provides a set of services for management of application containers in a multi-tenant cloud environment. The code name of the project name is magnum.

container service

The Object Storage component that provides container services, such as create, delete, list, and so on.

content delivery network (CDN)

A content delivery network is a specialized network that is used to distribute content to clients, typically located close to the client for increased performance.

controller node

Alternative term for a cloud controller node.

core API

Depending on context, the core API is either the OpenStack API or the main API of a specific core project, such as Compute, Networking, Image service, and so on.

core project

An official OpenStack project. Currently consists of Compute (nova), Object Storage (swift), Image service (glance), Identity (keystone), Dashboard (horizon), Networking (neutron), and Block Storage (cinder), Telemetry (ceilometer), Orchestration (heat), Database service (trove), Bare Metal service (ironic), Data processing service (sahara). However, this definition is changing based on community discussions about the "Big Tent".

cost

Under the Compute distributed scheduler, this is calculated by looking at the capabilities of each host relative to the flavor of the VM instance being requested.

credentials

Data that is only known to or accessible by a user and used to verify that the user is who he says he is. Credentials are presented to the server during authentication. Examples include a password, secret key, digital certificate, and fingerprint.

Cross-Origin Resource Sharing (CORS)

A mechanism that allows many resources (for example, fonts, JavaScript) on a web page to be requested from another domain outside the domain from which the resource originated. In particular, JavaScript's AJAX calls can use the XMLHttpRequest mechanism.

Crowbar

An open source community project by Dell that aims to provide all necessary services to quickly deploy clouds.

current workload

An element of the Compute capacity cache that is calculated based on the number of build, snapshot, migrate, and resize operations currently in progress on a given host.

customer

Alternative term for tenant.

customization module

A user-created Python module that is loaded by horizon to change the look and feel of the dashboard.

daemon

A process that runs in the background and waits for requests. May or may not listen on a TCP or UDP port. Do not confuse with a worker.

DAC

Discretionary access control. Governs the ability of subjects to access objects, while enabling users to make policy decisions and assign security attributes. The traditional UNIX system of users, groups, and read-write-execute permissions is an example of DAC.

dashboard

The web-based management interface for OpenStack. An alternative name for horizon.

data encryption

Both Image service and Compute support encrypted virtual machine (VM) images (but not instances). In-transit data encryption is supported in OpenStack using technologies such as HTTPS, SSL, TLS, and SSH. Object Storage does not support object encryption at the application level but may support storage that uses disk encryption.

database ID

A unique ID given to each replica of an Object Storage database.

database replicator

An Object Storage component that copies changes in the account, container, and object databases to other nodes.

Database service

An integrated project that provide scalable and reliable Cloud Database-as-a-Service functionality for both relational and non-relational database engines. The project name of Database service is trove.

Data processing service

OpenStack project that provides a scalable data-processing stack and associated management interfaces. The code name for the project is sahara.

data store

A database engine supported by the Database service.

deallocate

The process of removing the association between a floating IP address and a fixed IP address. Once this association is removed, the floating IP returns to the address pool.

Debian

A Linux distribution that is compatible with OpenStack.

deduplication

The process of finding duplicate data at the disk block, file, and/or object level to minimize storage use—currently unsupported within OpenStack.

default panel

The default panel that is displayed when a user accesses the horizon dashboard.

default tenant

New users are assigned to this tenant if no tenant is specified when a user is created.

default token

An Identity service token that is not associated with a specific tenant and is exchanged for a scoped token.

delayed delete

An option within Image service so that an image is deleted after a predefined number of seconds instead of immediately.

delivery mode

Setting for the Compute RabbitMQ message delivery mode; can be set to either transient or persistent.

denial of service (DoS)

Denial of service (DoS) is a short form for denial-of-service attack. This is a malicious attempt to prevent legitimate users from using a service.

deprecated auth

An option within Compute that enables administrators to create and manage users through the `nova-manage` command as opposed to using the Identity service.

Designate

Code name for the DNS service project for OpenStack.

Desktop-as-a-Service

A platform that provides a suite of desktop environments that users access to receive a desktop experience from any location. This may provide general use, development, or even homogeneous testing environments.

developer

One of the default roles in the Compute RBAC system and the default role assigned to a new user.

device ID

Maps Object Storage partitions to physical storage devices.

device weight

Distributes partitions proportionately across Object Storage devices based on the storage capacity of each device.

DevStack

Community project that uses shell scripts to quickly build complete OpenStack development environments.

DHCP

Dynamic Host Configuration Protocol. A network protocol that configures devices that are connected to a network so that they can communicate on that network by using the Internet Protocol (IP). The protocol is implemented in a client-server model where DHCP clients request configuration data, such as an IP address, a default route, and one or more DNS server addresses from a DHCP server.

DHCP agent

OpenStack Networking agent that provides DHCP services for virtual networks.

Diablo

A grouped release of projects related to OpenStack that came out in the fall of 2011, the fourth release of OpenStack. It included Compute (nova 2011.3), Object Storage (swift 1.4.3), and the Image service (glance). Diablo is the code name for the fourth release of OpenStack. The design summit took place in in the Bay Area near Santa Clara, California, US and Diablo is a nearby city.

direct consumer

An element of the Compute RabbitMQ that comes to life when a RPC call is executed. It connects to a direct exchange through a unique exclusive queue, sends the message, and terminates.

direct exchange

A routing table that is created within the Compute RabbitMQ during RPC calls; one is created for each RPC call that is invoked.

direct publisher

Element of RabbitMQ that provides a response to an incoming MQ message.

disassociate

The process of removing the association between a floating IP address and fixed IP and thus returning the floating IP address to the address pool.

disk encryption

The ability to encrypt data at the file system, disk partition, or whole-disk level. Supported within Compute VMs.

disk format

The underlying format that a disk image for a VM is stored as within the Image service back-end store. For example, AMI, ISO, QCOW2, VMDK, and so on.

dispersion

In Object Storage, tools to test and ensure dispersion of objects and containers to ensure fault tolerance.

distributed virtual router (DVR)

Mechanism for highly-available multi-host routing when using OpenStack Networking (neutron).

Django

A web framework used extensively in horizon.

DNS

Domain Name System. A hierarchical and distributed naming system for computers, services, and resources connected to the Internet or a private network. Associates a human-friendly names to IP addresses.

DNS record

A record that specifies information about a particular domain and belongs to the domain.

DNS service

OpenStack project that provides scalable, on demand, self service access to authoritative DNS services, in a technology-agnostic manner. The code name for the project is designate.

dnsmasq

Daemon that provides DNS, DHCP, BOOTP, and TFTP services for virtual networks.

domain

An Identity API v3 entity. Represents a collection of projects, groups and users that defines administrative boundaries for managing OpenStack Identity entities. On the Internet, separates a website from other sites. Often, the domain name has two or more parts that are separated by dots. For example, yahoo.com, usa.gov, harvard.edu, or mail.yahoo.com. Also, a domain is an entity or container of all DNS-related information containing one or more records.

Domain Name System (DNS)

A system by which Internet domain name-to-address and address-to-name resolutions are determined. DNS helps navigate the Internet by translating the IP address into an address that is easier to remember. For example, translating 111.111.111.1 into www.yahoo.com. All domains and their components, such as mail servers, utilize DNS to resolve to the appropriate locations. DNS servers are usually set up in a master-slave relationship such that failure of the master invokes the slave. DNS servers might also be clustered or replicated such that changes made to one DNS server are automatically propagated to other active servers. In Compute, the support that enables associating DNS entries with floating IP addresses, nodes, or cells so that hostnames are consistent across reboots.

download

The transfer of data, usually in the form of files, from one computer to another.

DRTM

Dynamic root of trust measurement.

durable exchange

The Compute RabbitMQ message exchange that remains active when the server restarts.

durable queue

A Compute RabbitMQ message queue that remains active when the server restarts.

Dynamic Host Configuration Protocol (DHCP)

A method to automatically configure networking for a host at boot time. Provided by both Networking and Compute.

Dynamic HyperText Markup Language (DHTML)

Pages that use HTML, JavaScript, and Cascading Style Sheets to enable users to interact with a web page or show simple animation.

east-west traffic

Network traffic between servers in the same cloud or data center. See also north-south traffic.

EBS boot volume

An Amazon EBS storage volume that contains a bootable VM image, currently unsupported in OpenStack.

ebtables

Filtering tool for a Linux bridging firewall, enabling filtering of network traffic passing through a Linux bridge. Used in Compute along with arptables, iptables, and ip6tables to ensure isolation of network communications.

EC2

The Amazon commercial compute product, similar to Compute.

EC2 access key

Used along with an EC2 secret key to access the Compute EC2 API.

EC2 API

OpenStack supports accessing the Amazon EC2 API through Compute.

EC2 Compatibility API

A Compute component that enables OpenStack to communicate with Amazon EC2.

EC2 secret key

Used along with an EC2 access key when communicating with the Compute EC2 API; used to digitally sign each request.

Elastic Block Storage (EBS)

The Amazon commercial block storage product.

encryption

OpenStack supports encryption technologies such as HTTPS, SSH, SSL, TLS, digital certificates, and data encryption.

endpoint

See API endpoint.

endpoint registry

Alternative term for an Identity service catalog.

encapsulation

The practice of placing one packet type within another for the purposes of abstracting or securing data. Examples include GRE, MPLS, or IPsec.

endpoint template

A list of URL and port number endpoints that indicate where a service, such as Object Storage, Compute, Identity, and so on, can be accessed.

entity

Any piece of hardware or software that wants to connect to the network services provided by Networking, the network connectivity service. An entity can make use of Networking by implementing a VIF.

ephemeral image

A VM image that does not save changes made to its volumes and reverts them to their original state after the instance is terminated.

ephemeral volume

Volume that does not save the changes made to it and reverts to its original state when the current user relinquishes control.

Essex

A grouped release of projects related to OpenStack that came out in April 2012, the fifth release of OpenStack. It included Compute (nova 2012.1), Object Storage (swift 1.4.8), Image (glance), Identity (keystone), and Dashboard (horizon). Essex is the code name for the fifth release of OpenStack. The design summit took place in Boston, Massachusetts, US and Essex is a nearby city.

ESXi

An OpenStack-supported hypervisor.

ETag

MD5 hash of an object within Object Storage, used to ensure data integrity.

euca2ools

A collection of command-line tools for administering VMs; most are compatible with OpenStack.

Eucalyptus Kernel Image (EKI)

Used along with an ERI to create an EMI.

Eucalyptus Machine Image (EMI)

VM image container format supported by Image service.

Eucalyptus Ramdisk Image (ERI)

Used along with an EKI to create an EMI.

evacuate

The process of migrating one or all virtual machine (VM) instances from one host to another, compatible with both shared storage live migration and block migration.

exchange

Alternative term for a RabbitMQ message exchange.

exchange type

A routing algorithm in the Compute RabbitMQ.

exclusive queue

Connected to by a direct consumer in RabbitMQ—Compute, the message can be consumed only by the current connection.

extended attributes (xattr)

File system option that enables storage of additional information beyond owner, group, permissions, modification time, and so on. The underlying Object Storage file system must support extended attributes.

extension

Alternative term for an API extension or plug-in. In the context of Identity service, this is a call that is specific to the implementation, such as adding support for OpenID.

external network

A network segment typically used for instance Internet access.

extra specs

Specifies additional requirements when Compute determines where to start a new instance. Examples include a minimum amount of network bandwidth or a GPU.

FakeLDAP

An easy method to create a local LDAP directory for testing Identity and Compute. Requires Redis.

fan-out exchange

Within RabbitMQ and Compute, it is the messaging interface that is used by the scheduler service to receive capability messages from the compute, volume, and network nodes.

federated identity

A method to establish trusts between identity providers and the OpenStack cloud.

Fedora

A Linux distribution compatible with OpenStack.

Fibre Channel

Storage protocol similar in concept to TCP/IP; encapsulates SCSI commands and data.

Fibre Channel over Ethernet (FCoE)

The fibre channel protocol tunneled within Ethernet.

fill-first scheduler

The Compute scheduling method that attempts to fill a host with VMs rather than starting new VMs on a variety of hosts.

filter

The step in the Compute scheduling process when hosts that cannot run VMs are eliminated and not chosen.

firewall

Used to restrict communications between hosts and/or nodes, implemented in Compute using iptables, arptables, ip6tables, and ebtables.

FWaaS

A Networking extension that provides perimeter firewall functionality.

fixed IP address

An IP address that is associated with the same instance each time that instance boots, is generally not accessible to end users or the public Internet, and is used for management of the instance.

Flat Manager

The Compute component that gives IP addresses to authorized nodes and assumes DHCP, DNS, and routing configuration and services are provided by something else.

flat mode injection

A Compute networking method where the OS network configuration information is injected into the VM image before the instance starts.

flat network

Virtual network type that uses neither VLANs nor tunnels to segregate tenant traffic. Each flat network typically requires a separate underlying physical interface defined by bridge mappings. However, a flat network can contain multiple subnets.

FlatDHCP Manager

The Compute component that provides dnsmasq (DHCP, DNS, BOOTP, TFTP) and radvd (routing) services.

flavor

Alternative term for a VM instance type.

flavor ID

UUID for each Compute or Image service VM flavor or instance type.

floating IP address

An IP address that a project can associate with a VM so that the instance has the same public IP address each time that it boots. You create a pool of floating IP addresses and assign them to instances as they are launched to maintain a consistent IP address for maintaining DNS assignment.

Folsom

A grouped release of projects related to OpenStack that came out in the fall of 2012, the sixth release of OpenStack. It includes Compute (nova), Object Storage (swift), Identity (keystone), Networking (neutron), Image service (glance), and Volumes or Block Storage (cinder). Folsom is the code name for the sixth release of OpenStack. The design summit took place in San Francisco, California, US and Folsom is a nearby city.

FormPost

Object Storage middleware that uploads (posts) an image through a form on a web page.

freezer

OpenStack project that provides backup restore and disaster recovery as a service.

front end

The point where a user interacts with a service; can be an API endpoint, the horizon dashboard, or a command-line tool.

gateway

An IP address, typically assigned to a router, that passes network traffic between different networks.

generic receive offload (GRO)

Feature of certain network interface drivers that combines many smaller received packets into a large packet before delivery to the kernel IP stack.

generic routing encapsulation (GRE)

Protocol that encapsulates a wide variety of network layer protocols inside virtual point-to-point links.

glance

A core project that provides the OpenStack Image service.

glance API server

Processes client requests for VMs, updates Image service metadata on the registry server, and communicates with the store adapter to upload VM images from the back-end store.

glance registry

Alternative term for the Image service image registry.

global endpoint template

The Identity service endpoint template that contains services available to all tenants.

GlusterFS

A file system designed to aggregate NAS hosts, compatible with OpenStack.

golden image

A method of operating system installation where a finalized disk image is created and then used by all nodes without modification.

Governance service

OpenStack project to provide Governance-as-a-Service across any collection of cloud services in order to monitor, enforce, and audit policy over dynamic infrastructure. The code name for the project is congress.

Graphic Interchange Format (GIF)

A type of image file that is commonly used for animated images on web pages.

Graphics Processing Unit (GPU)

Choosing a host based on the existence of a GPU is currently unsupported in OpenStack.

Green Threads

The cooperative threading model used by Python; reduces race conditions and only context switches when specific library calls are made. Each OpenStack service is its own thread.

Grizzly

The code name for the seventh release of OpenStack. The design summit took place in San Diego, California, US and Grizzly is an element of the state flag of California.

Group

An Identity v3 API entity. Represents a collection of users that is owned by a specific domain.

guest OS

An operating system instance running under the control of a hypervisor.

Hadoop

Apache Hadoop is an open source software framework that supports data-intensive distributed applications.

Hadoop Distributed File System (HDFS)

A distributed, highly fault-tolerant file system designed to run on low-cost commodity hardware.

handover

An object state in Object Storage where a new replica of the object is automatically created due to a drive failure.

hard reboot

A type of reboot where a physical or virtual power button is pressed as opposed to a graceful, proper shutdown of the operating system.

Havana

The code name for the eighth release of OpenStack. The design summit took place in Portland, Oregon, US and Havana is an unincorporated community in Oregon.

heat

An integrated project that aims to orchestrate multiple cloud applications for OpenStack.

Heat Orchestration Template (HOT)

Heat input in the format native to OpenStack.

health monitor

Determines whether back-end members of a VIP pool can process a request. A pool can have several health monitors associated with it. When a pool has several monitors associated with it, all monitors check each member of the pool. All monitors must declare a member to be healthy for it to stay active.

high availability (HA)

A high availability system design approach and associated service implementation ensures that a prearranged level of operational performance will be met during a contractual measurement period. High availability systems seeks to minimize system downtime and data loss.

horizon

OpenStack project that provides a dashboard, which is a web interface.

horizon plug-in

A plug-in for the OpenStack dashboard (horizon).

host

A physical computer, not a VM instance (node).

host aggregate

A method to further subdivide availability zones into hypervisor pools, a collection of common hosts.

Host Bus Adapter (HBA)

Device plugged into a PCI slot, such as a fibre channel or network card.

hybrid cloud

A hybrid cloud is a composition of two or more clouds (private, community or public) that remain distinct entities but are bound together, offering the benefits of multiple deployment models. Hybrid cloud can also mean the ability to connect colocation, managed and/or dedicated services with cloud resources.

Hyper-V

One of the hypervisors supported by OpenStack.

hyperlink

Any kind of text that contains a link to some other site, commonly found in documents where clicking on a word or words opens up a different website.

Hypertext Transfer Protocol (HTTP)

An application protocol for distributed, collaborative, hypermedia information systems. It is the foundation of data communication for the World Wide Web. Hypertext is structured text that uses logical links (hyperlinks) between nodes containing text. HTTP is the protocol to exchange or transfer hypertext.

Hypertext Transfer Protocol Secure (HTTPS)

An encrypted communications protocol for secure communication over a computer network, with especially wide deployment on the Internet. Technically, it is not a protocol in and of itself; rather, it is the result of simply layering the Hypertext Transfer Protocol (HTTP) on top of the TLS or SSL protocol, thus adding the security capabilities of TLS or SSL to standard HTTP communications. most OpenStack API endpoints and many inter-component communications support HTTPS communication.

hypervisor

Software that arbitrates and controls VM access to the actual underlying hardware.

hypervisor pool

A collection of hypervisors grouped together through host aggregates.

IaaS

Infrastructure-as-a-Service. IaaS is a provisioning model in which an organization outsources physical components of a data center, such as storage, hardware, servers, and networking components. A service provider owns the equipment and is responsible for housing, operating and maintaining it. The client typically pays on a per-use basis. IaaS is a model for providing cloud services.

Icehouse

The code name for the ninth release of OpenStack. The design summit took place in Hong Kong and Ice House is a street in that city.

ICMP

Internet Control Message Protocol, used by network devices for control messages. For example, `ping` uses ICMP to test connectivity.

ID number

Unique numeric ID associated with each user in Identity, conceptually similar to a Linux or LDAP UID.

Identity API

Alternative term for the Identity service API.

Identity back end

The source used by Identity service to retrieve user information; an OpenLDAP server, for example.

identity provider

A directory service, which allows users to login with a user name and password. It is a typical source of authentication tokens.

Identity

The OpenStack core project that provides a central directory of users mapped to the OpenStack services they can access. It also registers endpoints for OpenStack services. It acts as a common authentication system. The project name of Identity is keystone.

Identity service API

The API used to access the OpenStack Identity service provided through keystone.

IDS

Intrusion Detection System.

image

A collection of files for a specific operating system (OS) that you use to create or rebuild a server. OpenStack provides pre-built images. You can also create custom images, or snapshots, from servers that you have launched. Custom images can be used for data backups or as "gold" images for additional servers.

Image API

The Image service API endpoint for management of VM images.

image cache

Used by Image service to obtain images on the local host rather than re-downloading them from the image server each time one is requested.

image ID

Combination of a URI and UUID used to access Image service VM images through the image API.

image membership

A list of tenants that can access a given VM image within Image service.

image owner

The tenant who owns an Image service virtual machine image.

image registry

A list of VM images that are available through Image service.

Image service

An OpenStack core project that provides discovery, registration, and delivery services for disk and server images. The project name of the Image service is glance.

Image service API

Alternative name for the glance image API.

image status

The current status of a VM image in Image service, not to be confused with the status of a running instance.

image store

The back-end store used by Image service to store VM images, options include Object Storage, local file system, S3, or HTTP.

image UUID

UUID used by Image service to uniquely identify each VM image.

incubated project

A community project may be elevated to this status and is then promoted to a core project.

ingress filtering

The process of filtering incoming network traffic. Supported by Compute.

INI

The OpenStack configuration files use an INI format to describe options and their values. It consists of sections and key value pairs.

injection

The process of putting a file into a virtual machine image before the instance is started.

instance

A running VM, or a VM in a known state such as suspended, that can be used like a hardware server.

instance ID

Alternative term for instance UUID.

instance state

The current state of a guest VM image.

instance tunnels network

A network segment used for instance traffic tunnels between compute nodes and the network node.

instance type

Describes the parameters of the various virtual machine images that are available to users; includes parameters such as CPU, storage, and memory. Alternative term for flavor.

instance type ID

Alternative term for a flavor ID.

instance UUID

Unique ID assigned to each guest VM instance.

interface

A physical or virtual device that provides connectivity to another device or medium.

interface ID

Unique ID for a Networking VIF or vNIC in the form of a UUID.

Internet protocol (IP)

Principal communications protocol in the internet protocol suite for relaying datagrams across network boundaries.

Internet Service Provider (ISP)

Any business that provides Internet access to individuals or businesses.

Internet Small Computer System Interface (iSCSI)

Storage protocol that encapsulates SCSI frames for transport over IP networks.

ironic

OpenStack project that provisions bare metal, as opposed to virtual, machines.

IOPS

IOPS (Input/Output Operations Per Second) are a common performance measurement used to benchmark computer storage devices like hard disk drives, solid state drives, and storage area networks.

IP address

Number that is unique to every computer system on the Internet. Two versions of the Internet Protocol (IP) are in use for addresses: IPv4 and IPv6.

IP Address Management (IPAM)

The process of automating IP address allocation, deallocation, and management. Currently provided by Compute, melange, and Networking.

IPL

Initial Program Loader.

IPMI

Intelligent Platform Management Interface. IPMI is a standardized computer system interface used by system administrators for out-of-band management of computer systems and monitoring of their operation. In layman's terms, it is a way to manage a computer using a direct network connection, whether it is turned on or not; connecting to the hardware rather than an operating system or login shell.

ip6tables

Tool used to set up, maintain, and inspect the tables of IPv6 packet filter rules in the Linux kernel. In OpenStack Compute, ip6tables is used along with arptables, ebtables, and iptables to create firewalls for both nodes and VMs.

ipset

Extension to iptables that allows creation of firewall rules that match entire "sets" of IP addresses simultaneously. These sets reside in indexed data structures to increase efficiency, particularly on systems with a large quantity of rules.

iptables

Used along with arptables and ebtables, iptables create firewalls in Compute. iptables are the tables provided by the Linux kernel firewall (implemented as different Netfilter modules) and the chains and rules it stores. Different kernel modules and programs are currently used for different protocols: iptables applies to IPv4, ip6tables to IPv6, arptables to ARP, and ebtables to Ethernet frames. Requires root privilege to manipulate.

IQN

iSCSI Qualified Name (IQN) is the format most commonly used for iSCSI names, which uniquely identify nodes in an iSCSI network. All IQNs follow the pattern iqn.yyyy-mm.domain:identifier, where 'yyyy-mm' is the year and month in which the domain was registered, 'domain' is the reversed domain name of the issuing organization, and 'identifier' is an optional string which makes each IQN under the same domain unique. For example, 'iqn.2015-10.org.openstack.408ae959bce1'.

iSCSI

The SCSI disk protocol tunneled within Ethernet, supported by Compute, Object Storage, and Image service.

ISO9660

One of the VM image disk formats supported by Image service.

itsec

A default role in the Compute RBAC system that can quarantine an instance in any project.

Java

A programming language that is used to create systems that involve more than one computer by way of a network.

JavaScript

A scripting language that is used to build web pages.

JavaScript Object Notation (JSON)

One of the supported response formats in OpenStack.

Jenkins

Tool used to run jobs automatically for OpenStack development.

jumbo frame

Feature in modern Ethernet networks that supports frames up to approximately 9000 bytes.

Juno

The code name for the tenth release of OpenStack. The design summit took place in Atlanta, Georgia, US and Juno is an unincorporated community in Georgia.

Kerberos

A network authentication protocol which works on the basis of tickets. Kerberos allows nodes communication over a non-secure network, and allows nodes to prove their identity to one another in a secure manner.

kernel-based VM (KVM)

An OpenStack-supported hypervisor. KVM is a full virtualization solution for Linux on x86 hardware containing virtualization extensions (Intel VT or AMD-V), ARM, IBM Power, and IBM zSeries. It consists of a loadable kernel module, that provides the core virtualization infrastructure and a processor specific module.

Key management service

OpenStack project that produces a secret storage and generation system capable of providing key management for services wishing to enable encryption features. The code name of the project is barbican.

keystone

The project that provides OpenStack Identity services.

Kickstart

A tool to automate system configuration and installation on Red Hat, Fedora, and CentOS-based Linux distributions.

Kilo

The code name for the eleventh release of OpenStack. The design summit took place in Paris, France. Due to delays in the name selection, the release was known only as K. Because k is the unit symbol for kilo and the reference artifact is stored near Paris in the Pavillon de Breteuil in Sèvres, the community chose Kilo as the release name.

large object

An object within Object Storage that is larger than 5 GB.

Launchpad

The collaboration site for OpenStack.

Layer-2 network

Term used in the OSI network architecture for the data link layer. The data link layer is responsible for media access control, flow control and detecting and possibly correcting errors that may occur in the physical layer.

Layer-3 network

Term used in the OSI network architecture for the network layer. The network layer is responsible for packet forwarding including routing from one node to another.

Layer-2 (L2) agent

OpenStack Networking agent that provides layer-2 connectivity for virtual networks.

Layer-3 (L3) agent

OpenStack Networking agent that provides layer-3 (routing) services for virtual networks.

Liberty

The code name for the twelfth release of OpenStack. The design summit took place in Vancouver, Canada and Liberty is the name of a village in the Canadian province of Saskatchewan.

libvirt

Virtualization API library used by OpenStack to interact with many of its supported hypervisors.

Lightweight Directory Access Protocol (LDAP)

An application protocol for accessing and maintaining distributed directory information services over an IP network.

Linux bridge

Software that enables multiple VMs to share a single physical NIC within Compute.

Linux Bridge neutron plug-in

Enables a Linux bridge to understand a Networking port, interface attachment, and other abstractions.

Linux containers (LXC)

An OpenStack-supported hypervisor.

live migration

The ability within Compute to move running virtual machine instances from one host to another with only a small service interruption during switchover.

load balancer

A load balancer is a logical device that belongs to a cloud account. It is used to distribute workloads between multiple back-end systems or services, based on the criteria defined as part of its configuration.

load balancing

The process of spreading client requests between two or more nodes to improve performance and availability.

LBaaS

Enables Networking to distribute incoming requests evenly between designated instances.

Logical Volume Manager (LVM)

Provides a method of allocating space on mass-storage devices that is more flexible than conventional partitioning schemes.

magnum

Code name for the OpenStack project that provides the Containers Service.

management API

Alternative term for an admin API.

management network

A network segment used for administration, not accessible to the public Internet.

manager

Logical groupings of related code, such as the Block Storage volume manager or network manager.

manifest

Used to track segments of a large object within Object Storage.

manifest object

A special Object Storage object that contains the manifest for a large object.

manila

OpenStack project that provides shared file systems as service to applications.

maximum transmission unit (MTU)

Maximum frame or packet size for a particular network medium. Typically 1500 bytes for Ethernet networks.

mechanism driver

A driver for the Modular Layer 2 (ML2) neutron plug-in that provides layer-2 connectivity for virtual instances. A single OpenStack installation can use multiple mechanism drivers.

melange

Project name for OpenStack Network Information Service. To be merged with Networking.

membership

The association between an Image service VM image and a tenant. Enables images to be shared with specified tenants.

membership list

A list of tenants that can access a given VM image within Image service.

memcached

A distributed memory object caching system that is used by Object Storage for caching.

memory overcommit

The ability to start new VM instances based on the actual memory usage of a host, as opposed to basing the decision on the amount of RAM each running instance thinks it has available. Also known as RAM overcommit.

message broker

The software package used to provide AMQP messaging capabilities within Compute. Default package is RabbitMQ.

message bus

The main virtual communication line used by all AMQP messages for inter-cloud communications within Compute.

message queue

Passes requests from clients to the appropriate workers and returns the output to the client after the job completes.

Message service

OpenStack project that aims to produce an OpenStack messaging service that affords a variety of distributed application patterns in an efficient, scalable and highly-available manner, and to create and maintain associated Python libraries and documentation. The code name for the project is zaqar.

Metadata agent

OpenStack Networking agent that provides metadata services for instances.

Meta-Data Server (MDS)

Stores CephFS metadata.

migration

The process of moving a VM instance from one host to another.

mistral

OpenStack project that provides the Workflow service.

Mitaka

The code name for the thirteenth release of OpenStack. The design summit took place in Tokyo, Japan. Mitaka is a city in Tokyo.

monasca

OpenStack project that provides a Monitoring service.

multi-host

High-availability mode for legacy (nova) networking. Each compute node handles NAT and DHCP and acts as a gateway for all of the VMs on it. A networking failure on one compute node doesn't affect VMs on other compute nodes.

multinic

Facility in Compute that allows each virtual machine instance to have more than one VIF connected to it.

murano

OpenStack project that provides an Application catalog.

Modular Layer 2 (ML2) neutron plug-in

Can concurrently use multiple layer-2 networking technologies, such as 802.1Q and VXLAN, in Networking.

Monitor (LBaaS)

LBaaS feature that provides availability monitoring using the `ping` command, TCP, and HTTP/HTTPS GET.

Monitor (Mon)

A Ceph component that communicates with external clients, checks data state and consistency, and performs quorum functions.

Monitoring

The OpenStack project that provides a multi-tenant, highly scalable, performant, fault-tolerant Monitoring-as-a-Service solution for metrics, complex event processing, and logging. It builds an extensible platform for advanced monitoring services that can be used by both operators and tenants to gain operational insight and visibility, ensuring availability and stability. The project name is monasca.

multi-factor authentication

Authentication method that uses two or more credentials, such as a password and a private key. Currently not supported in Identity.

MultiNic

Facility in Compute that enables a virtual machine instance to have more than one VIF connected to it.

network namespace

Linux kernel feature that provides independent virtual networking instances on a single host with separate routing tables and interfaces. Similar to virtual routing and forwarding (VRF) services on physical network equipment.

Nebula

Released as open source by NASA in 2010 and is the basis for Compute.

netadmin

One of the default roles in the Compute RBAC system. Enables the user to allocate publicly accessible IP addresses to instances and change firewall rules.

NetApp volume driver

Enables Compute to communicate with NetApp storage devices through the NetApp On-Command Provisioning Manager.

network

A virtual network that provides connectivity between entities. For example, a collection of virtual ports that share network connectivity. In Networking terminology, a network is always a layer-2 network.

NAT

Network Address Translation; Process of modifying IP address information while in transit. Supported by Compute and Networking.

network controller

A Compute daemon that orchestrates the network configuration of nodes, including IP addresses, VLANs, and bridging. Also manages routing for both public and private networks.

Network File System (NFS)

A method for making file systems available over the network. Supported by OpenStack.

network ID

Unique ID assigned to each network segment within Networking. Same as network UUID.

network manager

The Compute component that manages various network components, such as firewall rules, IP address allocation, and so on.

network node

Any compute node that runs the network worker daemon.

network segment

Represents a virtual, isolated OSI layer-2 subnet in Networking.

NTP

Network Time Protocol; Method of keeping a clock for a host or node correct via communication with a trusted, accurate time source.

network UUID

Unique ID for a Networking network segment.

network worker

The `nova-network` worker daemon; provides services such as giving an IP address to a booting nova instance.

Networking

A core OpenStack project that provides a network connectivity abstraction layer to OpenStack Compute. The project name of Networking is neutron.

Networking API

API used to access OpenStack Networking. Provides an extensible architecture to enable custom plug-in creation.

neutron

A core OpenStack project that provides a network connectivity abstraction layer to OpenStack Compute.

neutron API

An alternative name for Networking API.

neutron manager

Enables Compute and Networking integration, which enables Networking to perform network management for guest VMs.

neutron plug-in

Interface within Networking that enables organizations to create custom plug-ins for advanced features, such as QoS, ACLs, or IDS.

Nexenta volume driver

Provides support for NexentaStor devices in Compute.

No ACK

Disables server-side message acknowledgment in the Compute RabbitMQ. Increases performance but decreases reliability.

node

A VM instance that runs on a host.

non-durable exchange

Message exchange that is cleared when the service restarts. Its data is not written to persistent storage.

non-durable queue

Message queue that is cleared when the service restarts. Its data is not written to persistent storage.

non-persistent volume

Alternative term for an ephemeral volume.

north-south traffic

Network traffic between a user or client (north) and a server (south), or traffic into the cloud (south) and out of the cloud (north). See also east-west traffic.

nova

OpenStack project that provides compute services.

Nova API

Alternative term for the Compute API.

nova-network

A Compute component that manages IP address allocation, firewalls, and other network-related tasks. This is the legacy networking option and an alternative to Networking.

object

A BLOB of data held by Object Storage; can be in any format.

object auditor

Opens all objects for an object server and verifies the MD5 hash, size, and metadata for each object.

object expiration

A configurable option within Object Storage to automatically delete objects after a specified amount of time has passed or a certain date is reached.

object hash

Uniquely ID for an Object Storage object.

object path hash

Used by Object Storage to determine the location of an object in the ring. Maps objects to partitions.

object replicator

An Object Storage component that copies an object to remote partitions for fault tolerance.

object server

An Object Storage component that is responsible for managing objects.

Object Storage

The OpenStack core project that provides eventually consistent and redundant storage and retrieval of fixed digital content. The project name of OpenStack Object Storage is swift.

Object Storage API

API used to access OpenStack Object Storage.

Object Storage Device (OSD)

The Ceph storage daemon.

object versioning

Allows a user to set a flag on an Object Storage container so that all objects within the container are versioned.

Oldie

Term for an Object Storage process that runs for a long time. Can indicate a hung process.

Open Cloud Computing Interface (OCCI)

A standardized interface for managing compute, data, and network resources, currently unsupported in OpenStack.

Open Virtualization Format (OVF)

Standard for packaging VM images. Supported in OpenStack.

Open vSwitch

Open vSwitch is a production quality, multilayer virtual switch licensed under the open source Apache 2.0 license. It is designed to enable massive network automation through programmatic extension, while still supporting standard management interfaces and protocols (for example NetFlow, sFlow, SPAN, RSPAN, CLI, LACP, 802.1ag).

Open vSwitch (OVS) agent

Provides an interface to the underlying Open vSwitch service for the Networking plug-in.

Open vSwitch neutron plug-in

Provides support for Open vSwitch in Networking.

OpenLDAP

An open source LDAP server. Supported by both Compute and Identity.

OpenStack

OpenStack is a cloud operating system that controls large pools of compute, storage, and networking resources throughout a data center, all managed through a dashboard that gives administrators control while empowering their users to provision resources through a web interface. OpenStack is an open source project licensed under the Apache License 2.0.

OpenStack code name

Each OpenStack release has a code name. Code names ascend in alphabetical order: Austin, Bexar, Cactus, Diablo, Essex, Folsom, Grizzly, Havana, Icehouse, Juno, Kilo, Liberty, and Mitaka. Code names are cities or counties near where the corresponding OpenStack design summit took place. An exception, called the Waldon exception, is granted to elements of the state flag that sound especially cool. Code names are chosen by popular vote.

openSUSE

A Linux distribution that is compatible with OpenStack.

operator

The person responsible for planning and maintaining an OpenStack installation.

Orchestration

An integrated project that orchestrates multiple cloud applications for OpenStack. The project name of Orchestration is heat.

orphan

In the context of Object Storage, this is a process that is not terminated after an upgrade, restart, or reload of the service.

Oslo

OpenStack project that produces a set of Python libraries containing code shared by OpenStack projects.

parent cell

If a requested resource, such as CPU time, disk storage, or memory, is not available in the parent cell, the request is forwarded to associated child cells.

partition

A unit of storage within Object Storage used to store objects. It exists on top of devices and is replicated for fault tolerance.

partition index

Contains the locations of all Object Storage partitions within the ring.

partition shift value

Used by Object Storage to determine which partition data should reside on.

path MTU discovery (PMTUD)

Mechanism in IP networks to detect end-to-end MTU and adjust packet size accordingly.

pause

A VM state where no changes occur (no changes in memory, network communications stop, etc); the VM is frozen but not shut down.

PCI passthrough

Gives guest VMs exclusive access to a PCI device. Currently supported in OpenStack Havana and later releases.

persistent message

A message that is stored both in memory and on disk. The message is not lost after a failure or restart.

persistent volume

Changes to these types of disk volumes are saved.

personality file

A file used to customize a Compute instance. It can be used to inject SSH keys or a specific network configuration.

Platform-as-a-Service (PaaS)

Provides to the consumer the ability to deploy applications through a programming language or tools supported by the cloud platform provider. An example of Platform-as-a-Service is an Eclipse/Java programming platform provided with no downloads required.

plug-in

Software component providing the actual implementation for Networking APIs, or for Compute APIs, depending on the context.

policy service

Component of Identity that provides a rule-management interface and a rule-based authorization engine.

pool

A logical set of devices, such as web servers, that you group together to receive and process traffic. The load balancing function chooses which member of the pool handles the new requests or connections received on the VIP address. Each VIP has one pool.

pool member

An application that runs on the back-end server in a load-balancing system.

port

A virtual network port within Networking; VIFs / vNICs are connected to a port.

port UUID

Unique ID for a Networking port.

preseed

A tool to automate system configuration and installation on Debian-based Linux distributions.

private image

An Image service VM image that is only available to specified tenants.

private IP address

An IP address used for management and administration, not available to the public Internet.

private network

The Network Controller provides virtual networks to enable compute servers to interact with each other and with the public network. All machines must have a public and private network interface. A private network interface can be a flat or VLAN network interface. A flat network interface is controlled by the flat_interface with flat managers. A VLAN network interface is controlled by the `vlan_interface` option with VLAN managers.

project

Projects represent the base unit of "ownership" in OpenStack, in that all resources in OpenStack should be owned by a specific project. In OpenStack Identity, a project must be owned by a specific domain.

project ID

User-defined alphanumeric string in Compute; the name of a project.

project VPN

Alternative term for a cloudpipe.

promiscuous mode

Causes the network interface to pass all traffic it receives to the host rather than passing only the frames addressed to it.

protected property

Generally, extra properties on an Image service image to which only cloud administrators have access. Limits which user roles can perform CRUD operations on that property. The cloud administrator can configure any image property as protected.

provider

An administrator who has access to all hosts and instances.

proxy node

A node that provides the Object Storage proxy service.

proxy server

Users of Object Storage interact with the service through the proxy server, which in turn looks up the location of the requested data within the ring and returns the results to the user.

public API

An API endpoint used for both service-to-service communication and end-user interactions.

public image

An Image service VM image that is available to all tenants.

public IP address

An IP address that is accessible to end-users.

public key authentication

Authentication method that uses keys rather than passwords.

public network

The Network Controller provides virtual networks to enable compute servers to interact with each other and with the public network. All machines must have a public and private network interface. The public network interface is controlled by the `public_interface` option.

Puppet

An operating system configuration-management tool supported by OpenStack.

Python

Programming language used extensively in OpenStack.

QEMU Copy On Write 2 (QCOW2)

One of the VM image disk formats supported by Image service.

Qpid

Message queue software supported by OpenStack; an alternative to RabbitMQ.

quarantine

If Object Storage finds objects, containers, or accounts that are corrupt, they are placed in this state, are not replicated, cannot be read by clients, and a correct copy is re-replicated.

Quick EMUlator (QEMU)

QEMU is a generic and open source machine emulator and virtualizer. One of the hypervisors supported by OpenStack, generally used for development purposes.

quota

In Compute and Block Storage, the ability to set resource limits on a per-project basis.

RabbitMQ

The default message queue software used by OpenStack.

Rackspace Cloud Files

Released as open source by Rackspace in 2010; the basis for Object Storage.

RADOS Block Device (RBD)

Ceph component that enables a Linux block device to be striped over multiple distributed data stores.

radvd

The router advertisement daemon, used by the Compute VLAN manager and FlatDHCP manager to provide routing services for VM instances.

rally

OpenStack project that provides the Benchmark service.

RAM filter

The Compute setting that enables or disables RAM overcommitment.

RAM overcommit

The ability to start new VM instances based on the actual memory usage of a host, as opposed to basing the decision on the amount of RAM each running instance thinks it has available. Also known as memory overcommit.

rate limit

Configurable option within Object Storage to limit database writes on a per-account and/ or per-container basis.

raw

One of the VM image disk formats supported by Image service; an unstructured disk image.

rebalance

The process of distributing Object Storage partitions across all drives in the ring; used during initial ring creation and after ring reconfiguration.

reboot

Either a soft or hard reboot of a server. With a soft reboot, the operating system is signaled to restart, which enables a graceful shutdown of all processes. A hard reboot is the equivalent of power cycling the server. The virtualization platform should ensure that the reboot action has completed successfully, even in cases in which the underlying domain/VM is paused or halted/stopped.

rebuild

Removes all data on the server and replaces it with the specified image. Server ID and IP addresses remain the same.

Recon

An Object Storage component that collects meters.

record

Belongs to a particular domain and is used to specify information about the domain. There are several types of DNS records. Each record type contains particular information used to describe the purpose of that record. Examples include mail exchange (MX) records, which specify the mail server for a particular domain; and name server (NS) records, which specify the authoritative name servers for a domain.

record ID

A number within a database that is incremented each time a change is made. Used by Object Storage when replicating.

Red Hat Enterprise Linux (RHEL)

A Linux distribution that is compatible with OpenStack.

reference architecture

A recommended architecture for an OpenStack cloud.

region

A discrete OpenStack environment with dedicated API endpoints that typically shares only the Identity (keystone) with other regions.

registry

Alternative term for the Image service registry.

registry server

An Image service that provides VM image metadata information to clients.

Reliable, Autonomic Distributed Object Store

(RADOS)

A collection of components that provides object storage within Ceph. Similar to OpenStack Object Storage.

Remote Procedure Call (RPC)

The method used by the Compute RabbitMQ for intra-service communications.

replica

Provides data redundancy and fault tolerance by creating copies of Object Storage objects, accounts, and containers so that they are not lost when the underlying storage fails.

replica count

The number of replicas of the data in an Object Storage ring.

replication

The process of copying data to a separate physical device for fault tolerance and performance.

replicator

The Object Storage back-end process that creates and manages object replicas.

request ID

Unique ID assigned to each request sent to Compute.

rescue image

A special type of VM image that is booted when an instance is placed into rescue mode. Allows an administrator to mount the file systems for an instance to correct the problem.

resize

Converts an existing server to a different flavor, which scales the server up or down. The original server is saved to enable rollback if a problem occurs. All resizes must be tested and explicitly confirmed, at which time the original server is removed.

RESTful

A kind of web service API that uses REST, or Representational State Transfer. REST is the style of architecture for hypermedia systems that is used for the World Wide Web.

ring

An entity that maps Object Storage data to partitions. A separate ring exists for each service, such as account, object, and container.

ring builder

Builds and manages rings within Object Storage, assigns partitions to devices, and pushes the configuration to other storage nodes.

Role Based Access Control (RBAC)

Provides a predefined list of actions that the user can perform, such as start or stop VMs, reset passwords, and so on. Supported in both Identity and Compute and can be configured using the horizon dashboard.

role

A personality that a user assumes to perform a specific set of operations. A role includes a set of rights and privileges. A user assuming that role inherits those rights and privileges.

role ID

Alphanumeric ID assigned to each Identity service role.

rootwrap

A feature of Compute that allows the unprivileged "nova" user to run a specified list of commands as the Linux root user.

round-robin scheduler

Type of Compute scheduler that evenly distributes instances among available hosts.

router

A physical or virtual network device that passes network traffic between different networks.

routing key

The Compute direct exchanges, fanout exchanges, and topic exchanges use this key to determine how to process a message; processing varies depending on exchange type.

RPC driver

Modular system that allows the underlying message queue software of Compute to be changed. For example, from RabbitMQ to ZeroMQ or Qpid.

rsync

Used by Object Storage to push object replicas.

RXTX cap

Absolute limit on the amount of network traffic a Compute VM instance can send and receive.

RXTX quota

Soft limit on the amount of network traffic a Compute VM instance can send and receive.

S3

Object storage service by Amazon; similar in function to Object Storage, it can act as a back-end store for Image service VM images.

sahara

OpenStack project that provides a scalable data-processing stack and associated management interfaces.

SAML assertion

Contains information about a user as provided by the identity provider. It is an indication that a user has been authenticated.

scheduler manager

A Compute component that determines where VM instances should start. Uses modular design to support a variety of scheduler types.

scoped token

An Identity service API access token that is associated with a specific tenant.

scrubber

Checks for and deletes unused VMs; the component of Image service that implements delayed delete.

secret key

String of text known only by the user; used along with an access key to make requests to the Compute API.

secure shell (SSH)

Open source tool used to access remote hosts through an encrypted communications channel, SSH key injection is supported by Compute.

security group

A set of network traffic filtering rules that are applied to a Compute instance.

segmented object

An Object Storage large object that has been broken up into pieces. The re-assembled object is called a concatenated object.

self-service

For IaaS, ability for a regular (non-privileged) account to manage a virtual infrastructure component such as networks without involving an administrator.

SELinux

Linux kernel security module that provides the mechanism for supporting access control policies.

senlin

OpenStack project that provides a Clustering service.

server

Computer that provides explicit services to the client software running on that system, often managing a variety of computer operations. A server is a VM instance in the Compute system. Flavor and image are requisite elements when creating a server.

server image

Alternative term for a VM image.

server UUID

Unique ID assigned to each guest VM instance.

service

An OpenStack service, such as Compute, Object Storage, or Image service. Provides one or more endpoints through which users can access resources and perform operations.

service catalog

Alternative term for the Identity service catalog.

service ID

Unique ID assigned to each service that is available in the Identity service catalog.

service provider

A system that provides services to other system entities. In case of federated identity, OpenStack Identity is the service provider.

service registration

An Identity service feature that enables services, such as Compute, to automatically register with the catalog.

service tenant

Special tenant that contains all services that are listed in the catalog.

service token

An administrator-defined token used by Compute to communicate securely with the Identity service.

session back end

The method of storage used by horizon to track client sessions, such as local memory, cookies, a database, or memcached.

session persistence

A feature of the load-balancing service. It attempts to force subsequent connections to a service to be redirected to the same node as long as it is online.

session storage

A horizon component that stores and tracks client session information. Implemented through the Django sessions framework.

share

A remote, mountable file system in the context of the Shared File Systems. You can mount a share to, and access a share from, several hosts by several users at a time.

share network

An entity in the context of the Shared File Systems that encapsulates interaction with the Networking service. If the driver you selected runs in the mode requiring such kind of interaction, you need to specify the share network to create a share.

Shared File Systems API

A Shared File Systems service that provides a stable RESTful API. The service authenticates and routes requests throughout the Shared File Systems service. There is python-manilaclient to interact with the API.

Shared File Systems service

An OpenStack service that provides a set of services for management of shared file systems in a multi-tenant cloud environment. The service is similar to how OpenStack provides block-based storage management through the OpenStack Block Storage service project. With the Shared File Systems service, you can create a remote file system and mount the file system on your instances. You can also read and write data from your instances to and from your file system. The project name of the Shared File Systems service is manila.

shared IP address

An IP address that can be assigned to a VM instance within the shared IP group. Public IP addresses can be shared across multiple servers for use in various high-availability scenarios. When an IP address is shared to another server, the cloud network restrictions are modified to enable each server to listen to and respond on that IP address. You can optionally specify that the target server network configuration be modified. Shared IP addresses can be used with many standard heartbeat facilities, such as keepalive, that monitor for failure and manage IP failover.

shared IP group

A collection of servers that can share IPs with other members of the group. Any server in a group can share one or more public IPs with any other server in the group. With the exception of the first server in a shared IP group, servers must be launched into shared IP groups. A server may be a member of only one shared IP group.

shared storage

Block storage that is simultaneously accessible by multiple clients, for example, NFS.

Sheepdog

Distributed block storage system for QEMU, supported by OpenStack.

Simple Cloud Identity Management (SCIM)

Specification for managing identity in the cloud, currently unsupported by OpenStack.

Single-root I/O Virtualization (SR-IOV)

A specification that, when implemented by a physical PCIe device, enables it to appear as multiple separate PCIe devices. This enables multiple virtualized guests to share direct access to the physical device, offering improved performance over an equivalent virtual device. Currently supported in OpenStack Havana and later releases.

Service Level Agreement (SLA)

Contractual obligations that ensure the availability of a service.

SmokeStack

Runs automated tests against the core OpenStack API; written in Rails.

snapshot

A point-in-time copy of an OpenStack storage volume or image. Use storage volume snapshots to back up volumes. Use image snapshots to back up data, or as "gold" images for additional servers.

soft reboot

A controlled reboot where a VM instance is properly restarted through operating system commands.

Software Development Lifecycle Automation service

OpenStack project that aims to make cloud services easier to consume and integrate with application development process by automating the source-to-image process, and simplifying app-centric deployment. The project name is solum.

SolidFire Volume Driver

The Block Storage driver for the SolidFire iSCSI storage appliance.

solum

OpenStack project that provides a Software Development Lifecycle Automation service.

SPICE

The Simple Protocol for Independent Computing Environments (SPICE) provides remote desktop access to guest virtual machines. It is an alternative to VNC. SPICE is supported by OpenStack.

spread-first scheduler

The Compute VM scheduling algorithm that attempts to start a new VM on the host with the least amount of load.

SQL-Alchemy

An open source SQL toolkit for Python, used in OpenStack.

SQLite

A lightweight SQL database, used as the default persistent storage method in many OpenStack services.

stack

A set of OpenStack resources created and managed by the Orchestration service according to a given template (either an AWS CloudFormation template or a Heat Orchestration Template (HOT)).

StackTach

Community project that captures Compute AMQP communications; useful for debugging.

static IP address

Alternative term for a fixed IP address.

StaticWeb

WSGI middleware component of Object Storage that serves container data as a static web page.

storage back end

The method that a service uses for persistent storage, such as iSCSI, NFS, or local disk.

storage node

An Object Storage node that provides container services, account services, and object services; controls the account databases, container databases, and object storage.

storage manager

A XenAPI component that provides a pluggable interface to support a wide variety of persistent storage back ends.

storage manager back end

A persistent storage method supported by XenAPI, such as iSCSI or NFS.

storage services

Collective name for the Object Storage object services, container services, and account services.

strategy

Specifies the authentication source used by Image service or Identity. In the Database service, it refers to the extensions implemented for a data store.

subdomain

A domain within a parent domain. Subdomains cannot be registered. Subdomains enable you to delegate domains. Subdomains can themselves have subdomains, so third-level, fourth-level, fifth-level, and deeper levels of nesting are possible.

subnet

Logical subdivision of an IP network.

SUSE Linux Enterprise Server (SLES)

A Linux distribution that is compatible with OpenStack.

suspend

Alternative term for a paused VM instance.

swap

Disk-based virtual memory used by operating systems to provide more memory than is actually available on the system.

swawth

An authentication and authorization service for Object Storage, implemented through WSGI middleware; uses Object Storage itself as the persistent backing store.

swift

An OpenStack core project that provides object storage services.

swift All in One (SAIO)

Creates a full Object Storage development environment within a single VM.

swift middleware

Collective term for Object Storage components that provide additional functionality.

swift proxy server

Acts as the gatekeeper to Object Storage and is responsible for authenticating the user.

swift storage node

A node that runs Object Storage account, container, and object services.

sync point

Point in time since the last container and accounts database sync among nodes within Object Storage.

sysadmin

One of the default roles in the Compute RBAC system. Enables a user to add other users to a project, interact with VM images that are associated with the project, and start and stop VM instances.

system usage

A Compute component that, along with the notification system, collects meters and usage information. This information can be used for billing.

Telemetry

An integrated project that provides metering and measuring facilities for OpenStack. The project name of Telemetry is ceilometer.

TempAuth

An authentication facility within Object Storage that enables Object Storage itself to perform authentication and authorization. Frequently used in testing and development.

Tempest

Automated software test suite designed to run against the trunk of the OpenStack core project.

TempURL

An Object Storage middleware component that enables creation of URLs for temporary object access.

tenant

A group of users; used to isolate access to Compute resources. An alternative term for a project.

Tenant API

An API that is accessible to tenants.

tenant endpoint

An Identity service API endpoint that is associated with one or more tenants.

tenant ID

Unique ID assigned to each tenant within the Identity service. The project IDs map to the tenant IDs.

token

An alpha-numeric string of text used to access OpenStack APIs and resources.

token services

An Identity service component that manages and validates tokens after a user or tenant has been authenticated.

tombstone

Used to mark Object Storage objects that have been deleted; ensures that the object is not updated on another node after it has been deleted.

topic publisher

A process that is created when a RPC call is executed; used to push the message to the topic exchange.

Torpedo

Community project used to run automated tests against the OpenStack API.

transaction ID

Unique ID assigned to each Object Storage request; used for debugging and tracing.

transient

Alternative term for non-durable.

transient exchange

Alternative term for a non-durable exchange.

transient message

A message that is stored in memory and is lost after the server is restarted.

transient queue

Alternative term for a non-durable queue.

TripleO

OpenStack-on-OpenStack program. The code name for the OpenStack Deployment program.

trove

OpenStack project that provides database services to applications.

Ubuntu

A Debian-based Linux distribution.

unscoped token

Alternative term for an Identity service default token.

updater

Collective term for a group of Object Storage components that processes queued and failed updates for containers and objects.

user

In OpenStack Identity, entities represent individual API consumers and are owned by a specific domain. In OpenStack Compute, a user can be associated with roles, projects, or both.

user data

A blob of data that the user can specify when they launch an instance. The instance can access this data through the metadata service or config drive. Commonly used to pass a shell script that the instance runs on boot.

User Mode Linux (UML)

An OpenStack-supported hypervisor.

VIF UUID

Unique ID assigned to each Networking VIF.

VIP

The primary load balancing configuration object. Specifies the virtual IP address and port where client traffic is received. Also defines other details such as the load balancing method to be used, protocol, and so on. This entity is sometimes known in load-balancing products as a virtual server, vserver, or listener.

Virtual Central Processing Unit (vCPU)

Subdivides physical CPUs. Instances can then use those divisions.

Virtual Disk Image (VDI)

One of the VM image disk formats supported by Image service.

VXLAN

A network virtualization technology that attempts to reduce the scalability problems associated with large cloud computing deployments. It uses a VLAN-like encapsulation technique to encapsulate Ethernet frames within UDP packets.

Virtual Hard Disk (VHD)

One of the VM image disk formats supported by Image service.

virtual IP

An Internet Protocol (IP) address configured on the load balancer for use by clients connecting to a service that is load balanced. Incoming connections are distributed to back-end nodes based on the configuration of the load balancer.

virtual machine (VM)

An operating system instance that runs on top of a hypervisor. Multiple VMs can run at the same time on the same physical host.

virtual network

An L2 network segment within Networking.

virtual networking

A generic term for virtualization of network functions such as switching, routing, load balancing, and security using a combination of VMs and overlays on physical network infrastructure.

Virtual Network Computing (VNC)

Open source GUI and CLI tools used for remote console access to VMs. Supported by Compute.

Virtual Network InterFace (VIF)

An interface that is plugged into a port in a Networking network. Typically a virtual network interface belonging to a VM.

virtual port

Attachment point where a virtual interface connects to a virtual network.

virtual private network (VPN)

Provided by Compute in the form of cloudpipes, specialized instances that are used to create VPNs on a per-project basis.

virtual server

Alternative term for a VM or guest.

virtual switch (vSwitch)

Software that runs on a host or node and provides the features and functions of a hardware-based network switch.

virtual VLAN

Alternative term for a virtual network.

VirtualBox

An OpenStack-supported hypervisor.

VLAN manager

A Compute component that provides dnsmasq and radvd and sets up forwarding to and from cloudpipe instances.

VLAN network

The Network Controller provides virtual networks to enable compute servers to interact with each other and with the public network. All machines must have a public and private network interface. A VLAN network is a private network interface, which is controlled by the `vlan_interface` option with VLAN managers.

VM disk (VMDK)

One of the VM image disk formats supported by Image service.

VM image

Alternative term for an image.

VM Remote Control (VMRC)

Method to access VM instance consoles using a web browser. Supported by Compute.

VMware API

Supports interaction with VMware products in Compute.

VMware NSX Neutron plug-in

Provides support for VMware NSX in Neutron.

VNC proxy

A Compute component that provides users access to the consoles of their VM instances through VNC or VMRC.

volume

Disk-based data storage generally represented as an iSCSI target with a file system that supports extended attributes; can be persistent or ephemeral.

Volume API

Alternative name for the Block Storage API.

volume controller

A Block Storage component that oversees and coordinates storage volume actions.

volume driver

Alternative term for a volume plug-in.

volume ID

Unique ID applied to each storage volume under the Block Storage control.

volume manager

A Block Storage component that creates, attaches, and detaches persistent storage volumes.

volume node

A Block Storage node that runs the cinder-volume daemon.

volume plug-in

Provides support for new and specialized types of back-end storage for the Block Storage volume manager.

volume worker

A cinder component that interacts with back-end storage to manage the creation and deletion of volumes and the creation of compute volumes, provided by the cinder-volume daemon.

vSphere

An OpenStack-supported hypervisor.

weighting

A Compute process that determines the suitability of the VM instances for a job for a particular host. For example, not enough RAM on the host, too many CPUs on the host, and so on.

weight

Used by Object Storage devices to determine which storage devices are suitable for the job. Devices are weighted by size.

weighted cost

The sum of each cost used when deciding where to start a new VM instance in Compute.

worker

A daemon that listens to a queue and carries out tasks in response to messages. For example, the cinder-volume worker manages volume creation and deletion on storage arrays.

Workflow service

OpenStack project that provides a simple YAML-based language to write workflows, tasks and transition rules, and a service that allows to upload them, modify, run them at scale and in a highly available manner, manage and monitor workflow execution state and state of individual tasks. The code name of the project is mistral.

Xen

Xen is a hypervisor using a microkernel design, providing services that allow multiple computer operating systems to execute on the same computer hardware concurrently.

Xen API

The Xen administrative API, which is supported by Compute.

Xen Cloud Platform (XCP)

An OpenStack-supported hypervisor.

Xen Storage Manager Volume Driver

A Block Storage volume plug-in that enables communication with the Xen Storage Manager API.

XenServer

An OpenStack-supported hypervisor.

XFS

High-performance 64-bit file system created by Silicon Graphics. Excels in parallel I/O operations and data consistency.

zaqar

OpenStack project that provides a message service to applications.

ZeroMQ

Message queue software supported by OpenStack. An alternative to RabbitMQ. Also spelled 0MQ.

Zuul

Tool used in OpenStack development to ensure correctly ordered testing of changes in parallel.